CROWDED OUT

CROWDED OUT

THE TRUE COSTS OF CROWDFUNDING HEALTHCARE

NORA KENWORTHY

THE MIT PRESS CAMBRIDGE, MASSACHUSETTS LONDON, ENGLAND

The MIT Press would like to thank the anonymous peer reviewers who provided comments on drafts of this book. The generous work of academic experts is essential for establishing the authority and quality of our publications. We acknowledge with gratitude the contributions of these otherwise uncredited readers.

This book was set in ITC Stone and Avenir by New Best-set Typesetters Ltd. Printed and bound in the United States of America.

Library of Congress Cataloging-in-Publication Data

Names: Kenworthy, Nora J., author.
Title: Crowded out : the true costs of crowdfunding healthcare / Nora Kenworthy.
Description: Cambridge, Massachusetts : The MIT Press, [2024] | Includes bibliographical references and index.
Identifiers: LCCN 2023030415 (print) | LCCN 2023030416 (ebook) | ISBN 9780262548038 (paperback) | ISBN 9780262378604 (epub) | ISBN 9780262378611 (pdf)
Subjects: MESH: Healthcare Financing | Crowdsourcing | Fund Raising | Health Care Costs | Social Determinants of Health | Bioethical Issues | United States
Classification: LCC RA971.3 (print) | LCC RA971.3 (ebook) | NLM W 74 AA1 | DDC 362.1068/1—dc23/eng/20231101
LC record available at https://lccn.loc.gov/2023030415
LC ebook record available at https://lccn.loc.gov/2023030416

10 9 8 7 6 5 4 3 2 1

For Josie,
and dedicated to all those
who need justice more than charity.

CONTENTS

INTRODUCTION

"You should start a GoFundMe."

More and more, in our current world, this is our answer to crisis. Charitable crowdfunding sites like GoFundMe have proliferated in dozens of countries, attracting millions of users who leverage these sites to seek help with their own and others' needs. The charitable crowdfunding site GoFundMe.com has become so popular that it's an eponym for these new ways of providing or seeking help. On GoFundMe, as on many other platforms, crowdfunders are most often seeking help with medical or health-related needs.

For many people, crowdfunding appeals seem to be everywhere—on social media feeds, in the news and on TV shows, and in conversations with friends and family. Every new disaster elicits a wave of crowdfunding efforts to help those affected. So, too, do most cancer diagnoses, car accidents, or personal misfortunes. All around the world, people are increasingly expressing care by donating money via digital platforms.[1]

When Emily[2] was diagnosed with leukemia at twenty-two, she joined the millions of Americans who have started crowdfunding campaigns for health needs. With an alcoholic father and a mother who was already going through leukemia treatment, Emily would have been homeless if a distant family friend had not offered her a place to live. Even still, her financial and medical situation was dire: when Emily was first diagnosed, she had no health insurance and a physically demanding seasonal job. She was initially told she had a week to live. Though Emily's medical luck improved, her financial situation did not. With extended stays at an urban hospital far from home, and treatment that left her unable to work, Emily found it nearly impossible to get by, even after she qualified for Medicare. She recalled going hungry during hospital visits because she couldn't afford the cafeteria food: "They won't let you work but they charge you for your medications. . . . I understand hospitals need money but how can they expect you to come up with the money for meds and parking and food and everything else when you can't work?"

Emily was experiencing firsthand what cancer researchers have labeled the "financial toxicities" of the disease—the many uncovered (and often unbearable) costs of surviving cancer that lead to poorer health outcomes and a great deal of struggle for patients, especially those who are already marginalized.[3] Social workers at the hospital suggested Emily raise money by making and selling T-shirts, but as a savvy social media user, she decided to start a crowdfunding campaign instead. "I hate asking for money," she wrote, "but i've gotten to the point i don't have a choice anymore. . . . We are trying our hardest but it seams like we always fall short. Thank you." She placed a beaming picture of herself at the top of the page, using a Snapchat filter to add sparkly cat ears atop her bald head.

For Emily, crowdfunding offered a lifeline to financial help and a way to share the twists and turns of her illness journey, especially as treatment left her isolated and far from home. "I think GoFundMe is amazing," she said frankly. She posted her campaign to Instagram and Facebook and wrote regular updates on her treatments, knowing these could help her campaign to spread. But her expectations were low, in part because of how she thought she might be perceived. She said, frankly, "especially because with the weight fluctuations [associated with chemotherapy] and stuff, I didn't think a lot of people were gonna donate to me." As a person who grew up alongside social media, Emily was not immune to the powerful norms of what is often seen as successful, attractive, and successful on such platforms. She was not particularly hopeful about her chances: "When I first started, I didn't think I was gonna get very much. I thought it was a good idea to try to share my story and get it out there. When I started getting money it kind of hit me, like, people actually care. . . . It was like, whoa, people might not actually show that they care, but they care."

To me, Emily's campaign seemed like a textbook example of what it takes to be successful on GoFundMe: she had a dramatic, appealing story and obvious needs; she was tech and social media savvy and was willing to put in extra effort to get out her story. Her page came across as direct, honest, and, yes, attractive. She neatly fit the cynical description another crowdfunder offered of what seems to be "popular" on GoFundMe: "blond-haired, blue-eyed girls with rare cancer."

Emily's campaign ultimately raised a bit more than $1,000. It was enough to pay for some of the hospital's exorbitant food and parking but not nearly enough to get her out of debt and more securely housed. It's hard to say whether Emily considered her campaign a win or a loss. "I was hoping to get enough money to be able to scrape by," she reflected. She appreciated the unexpected attention and expressions of care, particularly as she was estranged from her parents. But crowdfunding only slightly lessened the financial toxicities of her disease.

Many would point to Emily's case, and many others, as signs of a broken health system. "[Crowdfunding's] a nice thing to do and generally people will contribute what they can," Tracey, a health-care worker, told me, "but there's also a sense of, like, *man*, we shouldn't have to do this to get healthcare." Increasingly, in public conversations I hear crowdfunding referred to as an informal or ad hoc "safety net."[4] But Emily's story shows how poorly this perceived safety net actually functions—even though her campaign did better than most. Crowdfunding for personal needs means entering a highly competitive marketplace where some succeed and many more lose.[5] Profound social and economic inequalities shape those wins and losses. The realities of this new marketplace raise important questions: Why has crowdfunding become so popular? How is it reshaping the ways we seek and provide care and influencing health-care systems? What does a future shaped by crowdfunding mean for people like Emily—and, by extension, for all of us?

GIG CHARITY GOES BIG

The first time I saw a medical crowdfunding campaign, it was in the form of a flyer posted to a telephone pole in Seattle (figure 0.1). At the time, in 2014, people who started a GoFundMe were provided with a printable flyer they could circulate since the site had little name recognition. Much like dog walking or babysitting flyers, the tear-off tabs at the bottom

Figure 0.1 Early crowdfunding campaigns from GoFundMe relied on paper flyers to direct attention to campaigns. Photo by author.

directed passerby to a campaign's web address. At the time, it reminded me of an electronic version of the donation jars I often saw in grocery and convenience stores for a neighbor's surgery or cancer treatment. Though the Affordable Care Act (ACA), or Obamacare, had been passed several years earlier, many Americans still went uninsured or struggled with the costs of care that insurance would not cover. Getting sick or injured in America, as many know all too well, is a very expensive business. Crowdfunding offered a way out: an easy digital way to ask friends, family, and strangers for small donations. If enough of them gave donations, you could raise money to pay off bills, afford a much-needed surgery, or have time to recover without going into debt.

Crowdfunding refers to a practice of appealing for donations or investments from large groups of people, typically using online digital platforms.[6] These digital platforms can be grouped into two general categories: entrepreneurial crowdfunding supports business or creative projects, and charitable crowdfunding collects donations that go to individual or collective causes.[7] There are crowdfunding platforms for supporting artists, helping pay for animals' vet bills, contributing to classroom supplies for teachers, or even helping underwrite breast enhancement surgeries. But the largest proportion of charitable crowdfunding in the United States seeks donations for health needs.[8] Most commonly, people seek medical crowdfunding to pay off medical bills and debts; to help minimize some of the harms of health emergencies, accidents, and disasters; and to cover the many additional costs that come with illness, such as taking time off work.

Digital crowdfunding sites mostly emerged in the years following the 2008 financial crisis, which marked the beginning of an increasingly precarious economy for citizens in many countries, including Americans.[9] As governments implemented austerity measures to cut back public programs, digital platforms helped usher in new "gig economies." While pop culture embraced the "hustle and grind" ethos of these new markets, gig economies also limit rights and organizing, make worker struggles ever more invisible, and leave workers less safe, healthy, and protected.[10] Crowdfunding, while organized for the charitable economy, adopts the same ethos as the gig economy: users have freedom and autonomy, and their success seemingly depends on their ability to hustle, work hard, and outcompete others. But beneath this ethos is a harsher reality: success is rare even for those who work very hard, platforms often exacerbate inequalities, and many are left more precarious than they started out.

Despite these realities, the feel-good veneer of charitable crowdfunding is powerful and has ushered in a meteoric rise for platforms like GoFundMe. Started in 2010, GoFundMe initially grew slowly. But by 2015, founders Brad Damphousse and Andrew Ballester sold their majority stake in the company to investors; at the time the deal was valued at $600 million, and the site had amassed an estimated $1 billion in donations.[11] Two years later, GoFundMe had reached more than $3 billion in donations, generating an estimated $100 million in annual revenue for the company.[12] By 2019, CEO Rob Solomon disclosed the platform had raised more than $7 billion in donations,[13] and a year later, GoFundMe said it had processed more than $9 billion in donations,[14] from more than fifty million donors.[15] And by 2022, the company reported it had raised more than $17 billion from more than two hundred million donations.[16]

Throughout this period of astronomical growth, the company aggressively acquired competitors, edging out nearly all other platforms in marketplaces such as the United States. And it made these acquisitions without publicly announcing further venture capital investment, indicating that it is generating enormous revenue to sustain this expansion.[17]

Along the way, GoFundMe has garnered widespread public recognition, positioning itself at the helm of a dramatic cultural shift in how Americans think about, and practice, charity and help seeking.[18] "We've become part of the social fabric in many countries," Solomon said in 2017. "We're a part of the zeitgeist. When news events happen in the world, GoFundMe is a big part of the story."[19] A year prior he had claimed, "if we were a non-profit or a foundation we'd be the fourth or fifth largest nonprofit in the world, and the second largest foundation after the Bill and Melinda Gates Foundation."[20]

It is undeniable that crowdfunding has become a major cultural phenomenon. GoFundMe sees charity—what it often calls "the giving space"—as an enormous market for potential profit-making.[21] But as this book will explore, it also seeks to alter how people engage in help seeking and caregiving. Nor does GoFundMe plan to stop there: in 2019, Solomon told a journalist that the company's "grand ambition" was to ensure that all online charitable donations—whether to individuals or nonprofit organizations—eventually go through the site.[22]

Crowdfunding's rise to prominence can also be tracked by the exponential growth in money raised by its most successful campaigns. One of the earliest crowdfunding success stories was the "Saving Eliza" campaign, started by parents of a young girl with Sanfilippo syndrome, a rare genetic condition, who were seeking donations to fund research that they hoped would save her life.[23] With the help of compellingly produced videos and ample media coverage, their original campaign raised more than $2 million.[24] In 2016, Equality Florida started a fund for victims of the Pulse Nightclub shooting, which became GoFundMe's largest campaign to date, raising more than $4 million in a matter of days.[25] By 2018, Brian Kolfage's highly controversial "We Build the Wall" campaign to fundraise for President Trump's proposed wall on the Mexico-US border raised $20 million before becoming embroiled in legal troubles.[26] In the summer of 2020, as Black Lives Matter demonstrations spread across the United

States, campaigns for victims of police violence became some of the highest-earning personal campaigns on the site: the George Floyd Memorial campaign raised more than $14 million.[27] As COVID-19 wracked the United States that year, GoFundMe's most successful campaign to date raised $44 million: its purpose was to address food insecurity arising from the pandemic.[28]

It sometimes feels that we can trace America's moments of crisis, trauma, hate, and, sometimes, hope by hopscotching from one viral campaign to the next. But the stories these campaigns tell is only one facet of the realities of crowdfunding. Most of us experience crowdfunding when friends, family, or we ourselves have to turn to it for help. Few of those campaigns go viral. Some do very well, and most earn a modest few thousand dollars.[29] As this book will show, crowdfunding can powerfully reproduce the status quo rather than change the fates of those who are most in need.

Finally, there is a facet of crowdfunding that most of us will never see or experience: many campaigns are started only to get a few, if any, shares or donations. These campaigns aren't likely to show up on social media feeds or on the landing pages of GoFundMe's website. They are a remarkably common, if nearly invisible, phenomenon. During the early months of COVID-19 when a surge of people turned to GoFundMe to seek and give help, nearly half of campaigns got no donations at all.[30] This is the hidden side of the new crowdfunding marketplace, and in this book I try to shine a light onto the full range of experiences and outcomes that people find there.

GRINDING STONES AND MORAL TOXICITIES

Despite the grim odds of viral success, many people do find that crowdfunding has distinct benefits. For some, it can offer a lifeline to cash that tides them over during moments of serious crisis; for others, the benefits are more emotional than financial. It can offer connection to friends and family, particularly when isolated by illness or its treatment, as Emily experienced. It can provide an easy way to communicate during health crises, even helping people feel validated or empowered. Some people also told me that it strengthened their relationships with family and friends, deepening ties to social support. Others found that navigating crowdfunding platforms was far easier than traversing the complicated bureaucracies of the US social safety net. But these experiences sit alongside, and even coexist with, feelings of shame, humiliation, stigma, judgment, and failure when it comes to asking for help online.[31]

Many Americans will say, at first glance, that they think sites like GoFundMe are great—in Emily's words, "amazing." Yet these same people will also express sadness at seeing the many campaigns that go unfulfilled, fears about scammers and fraudulent campaigns, and feelings of ambivalence about who to help and why. My purpose in this book is not to portray digital crowdfunding as simply good or bad but to explore the complexities of how it has embedded itself in our contemporary lives and social support systems, and examine the impacts of its ubiquity, both for individual users and for society at large. Nor am I solely interested in the experiences of influencers or highly visible campaigners. Rather, my focus is on why everyday people turn to crowdfunding and what they find when they do.

Trevor, a single father from Arkansas, reflects some of the ambivalent feelings and lesser-told stories of crowdfunding. We were texting one night while I was rushing to make dinner for my daughter, when Trevor revealed that he worried I might not want to interview him because of how badly his campaign had gone. "I certainly have data for you, but it isn't a pretty picture," he told me. Indeed, Trevor's campaign was a wrenching archive of bad breaks and financial woes. He had type 1 diabetes and was recovering from a severe accident while navigating a flatlined labor market and single parenthood. He worried about whether he could provide Christmas for his son and about having to choose between buying insulin and keeping their house from foreclosure. Trevor's page seemed bracingly honest to me, but his campaign had been unsuccessful by almost any measure. He found himself among that large but unseen group of crowdfunders whose campaigns had never gotten donations. He hadn't even, he later confided, gotten any page views beyond my own voyeuristic visits.

As we texted, Trevor seemed to waver between blaming himself and shrugging off his campaign's lack of success: "It's nobody's fault, and certainly not yours. . . . Life is a grinding stone, it either grinds you down, or polishes you up depending on what kind of metal you're made of. Those of us who fight to survive will always cast a wide net. That or I'm a failure as an individual and I have to beg strangers for extra money while I work 40+ hours a week as a full-time single dad. That's the struggle in my head anyways. Regardless no one has donated a red cent lol so it doesn't cut too deeply." Trevor used the metaphor of a "grinding stone" to invoke the dominant American myth of meritocracy. But his experience speaks to the precarity and stress of crowdfunding, how it leaves some people's prospects more polished while many others' turn to dust. Much like the broader myth of meritocracy, crowdfunding seems like something where hard work and deservingness will beget success, but this is rarely the case. For whom, exactly, is crowdfunding an opportunity, and for whom is it a dismantling?

When we later got a chance to speak over the phone, Trevor repeatedly insisted that his campaign had been "just another line that could be cast into the water"—yet another way of trying to get help. Trevor lived in a state where it was hard to get Medicaid, and he admitted to feeling great shame about using those benefits when he qualified for them. For him, GoFundMe appealed to his sense of independence and his skills as a part-time web developer. But as Trevor looked deeper into the GoFundMe economy, he felt less and less deserving of help:

> I understand the dynamic to run a successful GoFundMe . . . to just get it out on Facebook, make it a huge social media scene . . . and I did research to look at other people's GoFundMe pages and I was just like, holy shit. I have no right to be asking for money on this page with some of the [other] stories that I read and what they're going through. So, my fucking story of just being a poor single dad with just bills he can't afford, you know medical bills, that's . . . a lot for me to ask. I certainly couldn't go on Facebook and make it some big social media thing where I'm begging for money to pay for insulin. I mean, my pride's worth more than that to me.

Trevor revealed that he posted his campaign online but never told anyone about it. He hoped someone would just come across it and decide to donate. Trevor was an astute observer of the moral hierarchies of the crowdfunding system, internalizing that he was not as deserving as others—so much so that he felt asking for help was shameful, an affront to his "pride." How many campaigns are like Trevor's—created but not shared? It's hard to say without access to industry data, but industry experts have told me that this phenomenon is more common than we might think. It's also hard to say whether Trevor gave an accurate account of his campaigning. Maybe he had shared his campaign with his social network, gotten no donations, and his aforementioned "pride" prompted him to tell me a different story.

It is clear that for many crowdfunders, asking for help online is not, as Emily put it, "amazing." It is an experience filled with discomfort, shame, and loss of pride. In fact, Emily felt some of that herself when she first started her campaign. "I was really down and depressed, because I felt like I was asking for charity," she reflected. "I felt like I didn't really deserve [donations] because I'm not doing anything." Emily and Trevor's experiences raise questions about how crowdfunding is affected by social taboos about asking for help and how it reinforces long-standing ideas about who is and is not deserving of assistance. When people turn to the crowd for charity, they often do it with very low expectations and concerns about how they will be perceived; when Emily experienced that "people actually do care," it was with a sense of pleasant surprise. But is $1,000 of support for two years of cancer care really "amazing"? And does it distract us from more systematic ways we could care for people and think in terms of what everyone deserves regardless of how they are perceived by the crowd? As I will argue throughout this book, crowdfunding powerfully *lowers* the expectations of vulnerable people as to what they deserve while enabling those in positions of privilege to assume they are *more* deserving of assistance because their campaigns are often more successful.

These dynamics are typically invisible to donors, broader publics, and even, at times, crowdfunders themselves. They arise from implicit moral values that crowdfunding feeds on and reinforces. In this book I call these "moral toxicities"—harmful ideas, rooted in widely shared social values, about whether and under what conditions, people deserve help, healthcare, and social protection. I call these moral *toxicities*, because, like toxins, they suffuse our environments and can harm our health in numerous ways.[32] Like environmental toxins, these harms are much more likely to accumulate in, and impact, already vulnerable and marginalized populations. Because of crowdfunding's tremendous visibility, and because it asks users to engage in complex moral questions about whose needs should be supported, it becomes a powerful amplifier and normalizer of certain moral toxicities.

The chapters of this book explore how crowdfunding spreads and reinforces several key moral toxicities and examine the broader impacts this has for how we think about health and social care in our contemporary world. The first of these toxicities is free market ethics—the widespread idea that unfettered, competitive marketplaces should extend to things like health-care systems or, in the case of crowdfunding, deciding who gets financial help for life-threatening conditions. The second moral toxicity is selective deservingness—the idea that not everyone is equally deserving of help, assistance, or access to healthcare. It is fueled by long histories of social policies in the United States that punish, surveil, and dehumanize poor people, immigrants, people of color, and those most in need of assistance.[33] The third toxicity combines rugged individualism with false meritocracy—promoting the idea that every person is solely responsible for their own fates rather than the social or economic inequalities that broadly shape our life chances in the United States. Finally, there is the toxic belief in downstream solutions: the idea that clever, often technological fixes can be used to patch over gaping, systemic problems in our social safety nets. Of course, crowdfunding can also amplify powerfully beneficial moral norms as well—such as mutual solidarity, communal caregiving, and collective transformation. In the final chapter of the book I explore the possibilities and limits of these as crowdfunding becomes more and more ubiquitous.

We can see how moral toxicities shaped Trevor's crowdfunding experience. He felt uniquely responsible for his survival and less deserving than others, so much so that he hesitated to share his story or even use Medicaid when he had it. He blamed himself for his failure to succeed in either the crowdfunding marketplace or the broader US economy. And as he kept his page up for more than a year, he hoped, even still, that crowdfunding might provide a fix for the complex problems he faced. Trevor is hardly alone in these perspectives—these values are so common that it sometimes feels like they are in the air we breathe. They are particularly central to American political and social discourses. But Trevor's story shows how crowdfunding can further reinforce the power of these moral toxicities, particularly as he turned to this economy and deemed himself unworthy of its help. Trevor's experience reminds us that "appealing to the crowd" can be a profoundly isolating, and even damaging, experience.[34]

In the crowdfunding economy, moral toxicities are joined by the financial toxicities that are all too common in market-based health systems. From Emily's burdensome cancer treatment costs to Trevor's worries over the cost of his insulin, experiences of illness and injury in the United States are made much harder and more harmful by the costs that accompany them. As this book argues, the financial and moral toxicities of our health and political systems create ideal conditions for crowdfunding to become an attractive—and in some cases the only—option for help.

Even people I speak to who are enthusiastic about crowdfunding often say that it is a good option for support *given how bad things are*. As Akhil, a tech worker from near Seattle told me, "[crowdfunding] is very important because systems created by government . . . there will always be people who fall through [them] . . . crowdfunding used to happen in local communities earlier, and now it is more spread out [due to the technology]." Akhil is right that many communities have had systems of mutual support for decades, and even centuries, before the appearance of crowdfunding sites. But the appeal of these sites now, in this contemporary moment, has to do with the sheer volume of need created by market-based health systems and how technology is being leveraged to bandage over these gaping needs. As Lillian, a woman from New York explained, "mostly, people in America . . . they have financial problems . . . paying off medical debts. So, for our society [crowdfunding is] a very good opportunity which has helped a lot of people."

Lillian and Akhil are not alone in these opinions. A University of Chicago survey estimated that nearly *a quarter* of all Americans had started or donated to crowdfunding campaigns raising money for medical expenses by 2020.[35] At the same time, 85 percent of respondents to the survey said that the government should have a great deal, a lot, or some responsibility "for providing help when medical care is unaffordable."[36] Crowdfunding is appealing precisely because there are so few other options for affording care when crisis hits. Lisa, a nurse from Tennessee, said she completely understood why people would crowdfund when medical bills were so unaffordable: "[I'll] be caring for patients, for, you know, a couple months, and then their insurance isn't willing to cover [them] anymore, and so either I have to discharge them or they can appeal it and choose to stay if they're paying out of pocket, but obviously it's not like people have thousands and thousands of dollars like on the side ready at will to just drop to pay for whatever they need." Camilla, from Kentucky, agreed: "My family is not from America, so I'm first generation here. And I personally think it's *insane* that [parents of a] type one diabetic . . . would have to be worried about affording insulin and even have to do GoFundMe [to get it]. . . . I haven't seen GoFundMes for, like, plastic surgery, because you hate that your nose is not perfect. You know, the things that I've seen medical expenses for . . . on GoFundMe are necessities."

Even casual observers of crowdfunding can recognize that the financial toxicities of the American health-care system make it a necessary option for many people. In 2022, more than half of Americans couldn't cover the cost of a $1,000 emergency expense.[37] In half of the states in the US, the median out-of-pocket spending on medical care among people who had employer-provided health insurance was more than $1,000 each year.[38] While costs of hospitalization can vary significantly, researchers found that by 2013, the average out-of-pocket cost of hospitalization for adults with insurance was more than $1,000.[39] Left with few other choices for paying hefty medical bills, crowdfunding is often embraced as a last resort. There, but for the grace of GoFundMe, go we all.

Rather than equalizing access to healthcare, however, crowdfunding exacerbates inequities by reinforcing these toxicities. As chapter 3 will show, it provides the most help to those who already have *more*, not less, access to income, education, health benefits, media literacy, social capital, and other kinds of privilege. Troublingly, in states where medical debt and uninsurance is highest, medical crowdfunding campaigns tend to earn the least.[40] As a result, crowdfunding is an inescapable cultural phenomenon that reinforces both the financial and moral toxicities of marketized health systems. In doing so, it is reshaping how we value, access, and practice healthcare and public health. Understanding crowdfunding's role in our health system—and understanding how it is changing that system—is crucial for anyone who cares about health equity, the future of health technologies, and building fairer health systems for all. This book offers a view behind crowdfunding websites—to the stories, statistics, and hidden values that tell a more complex, and more honest, story about crowdfunding and health in the United States.

APPROACH AND METHODS

What does it mean to go "behind the website?" I find it helpful to think of crowdfunding campaigns—from those flyers I first saw posted around my neighborhood in 2014 to the more complex digital stories on web platforms today—like a performance on a stage. Crowdfunding stories are created for an anticipated audience, with careful attention to the words, tone, images, and feeling of what is conveyed. An array of stagehands and technical tools—friends, digital apps, other social media accounts—can help this message reach broader audiences. And crowdfunding platforms, much like theaters, have their own rules, customs, and profit interests in hosting these performances. This doesn't mean that crowdfunding stories aren't real but rather that they are versions of real stories crafted with this particular audience, stage, and theater in mind. So to really understand these stories, we need to better understand how crowdfunders decide to crowdfund in the first place and how they craft their campaigns; how they understand and appeal to their audiences; how they move about, negotiate with, and become impacted by the platforms they use; how those who interact with their campaigns see them and make choices to help or donate; and how companies themselves design their platforms, promote their content, and handle users and their data.

To explore this complex web of questions, I have used a variety of data sources ranging from interviews with crowdfunders, their families and friends, and industry experts, to popular discourses and news stories, to large quantitative datasets my research team has gathered over the years. While I am trained as an ethnographer—someone who traditionally spends long periods of time in community with other people, studying their behavior, beliefs, and the forces shaping their lives—this project pushed me to adopt multiple approaches to collecting data. While my initial research began by looking at data directly from crowdfunding sites and narratives, it quickly expanded into to larger efforts. The first was a qualitative effort, undertaken with my colleague Lauren Berliner, to understand people's experiences with crowdfunding outside of what was represented on the sites themselves. This involved in-depth interviews with crowdfunders and those being crowdfunded for as well as with experts in the crowdfunding industry. The purpose of these interviews was to delve deep into people's experiences with, and feelings about, crowdfunding, illness, and finances. I complemented these perspectives with a series of discussions with diverse groups of people from all across the United States who had donated to medical crowdfunding campaigns. These focus group discussions helped me better understand the ways donors read, evaluate, and make decisions about others' campaigns; how donating makes them feel; and what values they use to engage with this new digital technology.

To make better sense of this specific qualitative data, I also observed trends in medical crowdfunding more broadly, both as a cultural phenomenon and as an industry. Over an eight-year period, I read and analyzed thousands and thousands of medical campaign pages, studying them as they moved across spaces both on the internet and in "real life" and attempting to find commonalities and differences in those texts. My dual aim was to understand large patterns among the unique stories of diverse crowdfunders and to absorb, as much as possible, the cultures and moral worlds of crowdfunding as a shared platform and phenomenon in our society. My research increasingly focused on GoFundMe as it came to dominate the market, but I also studied YouCaring, FundRazr, Watsi, and several platforms popular in marketplaces outside the US. In addition, with the help of people who understand this technology better than I do, I studied the "back end" of sites' web architectures and observed how their site operations, such as search engines, changed over time.

Along with a team of researchers, I also branched out into more quantitative inquiries, recognizing that without access to reliable industry data, I needed a better understanding of the broad terrain of crowdfunding in the United States: Who crowdfunds and where? Why do they crowdfund? What successes do they find? And what sorts of factors shape those crowdfunding outcomes? This involved the collection and analysis of several large datasets, including a study of the largest-to-date collection of US medical crowdfunding campaigns from 2016 to 2020[41] and a slightly smaller study of COVID-related campaigns from the first seven months of the pandemic in the United States.[42] The appendix details these methods and collaborators in far greater detail.

These research efforts did not just move between qualitative and quantitative approaches but rather attempted to build toward a more complex digital ethnography—one that would help me understand not just individual and collective experiences of crowdfunding but also how cultures, discourses, norms, and practices emerge in and around digital crowdfunding platforms.[43] In this book, I pay close attention to the ways crowdfunding moves through our collective social lives and the kinds of stories that become common as crowdfunding becomes more ubiquitous. How is it changing the way we think, relate to one another, and imagine our collective futures?

To this end, this book relies on a diverse bricolage of data—from stories of popular campaigns to debates and discourses about crowdfunding to explorations of lesser-known crowdfunding platforms. Finally, at times, I also rely on more creative methods of parsing crowdfunding data, as with the found poems that are interspersed between chapters throughout the book. These poems are composed from anonymized snippets of text from campaign narratives and organized around common narrative themes that are seen across many different campaigns. The purpose is to convey some of the thematic and affective similarities between campaigns while attending to the haunting idiosyncrasies of such deeply human stories.

These efforts, particularly the larger quantitative studies, involved collaborations across disciplines and methodologies. Over nearly a decade, colleagues contributed their expertise, questions, and perspectives to important parts of the research, and some ultimately took up parts of this research and carried it in other fruitful directions. While this book largely focuses on my own core interests in how crowdfunding is impacting and influencing health in the United States, it could not have come into existence without these many collaborations, in particular with Lauren Berliner, Mark Igra, and Jin-Kyu Jung. Throughout these chapters, I summarize parts of what we learned through those collaborative projects alongside extended stories from crowdfunders about their experiences and perspectives. In the appendix, I provide a fuller description of these collaborations and their contributions to this research project.

It would be impossible to fully capture every dimension of the complex and evolving world of medical crowdfunding and, further still, to distill it into a single book. Instead, this book focuses on broad contours and intersperses these with the unique and divergent details of individual experiences. Because I wanted to capture a broad array of experiences with crowdfunding and set these against the backdrop of a fairly comprehensive set of quantitative data about crowdfunding across the United States, I have been particularly careful about how I sample data, whether it be large-scale quantitative data or detailed qualitative stories. In particular with qualitative data, I have emphasized the diversity and depth of stories and perspectives over the quantity of such perspectives. My goal throughout this book is not to force these perspectives to tell a single story of crowdfunding; in fact, it's quite the opposite. I am interested in how people's stories diverge and why, and I attempt to explore the complex, often ambivalent experiences they have when they use crowdfunding to pay for health needs.

Finally, as is the norm in qualitative research, I use pseudonyms throughout the book to protect the privacy of those who have spoken with me, with the exception of a few crowdfunding industry experts who asked that I use their real names. I also try, as much as possible, to conceal details from participants' stories that might lead readers to find their crowdfunding pages or identifying information. In cases where campaigns have been particularly popular, this sometimes means withholding more detailed information about crowdfunders' circumstances. I discuss the ways I approach handling and protecting data in far greater detail in the appendix.

OUTLINE OF THE BOOK

Crowded Out brings the experiences and logics of crowdfunding to light and contemplates the ways it may be changing how we access and provide care, how we decide who is entitled to it, and how we work toward more equitable health futures. The first three chapters of the book aim to provide answers to some of the most common questions I get about medical crowdfunding and reveal central moral toxicities that anchor the story of why crowdfunding is so popular and what impacts it is having on our society. These questions are ones that I have heard many times in conversations with people as they express concerns about crowdfunding and the role it is playing in our lives. They have gone largely unanswered for too long, and they have real public urgency as we try to build fairer health futures.

The first chapter asks, *Why is this happening?* It looks at how the uniquely market-based and exclusionary US health and social safety systems have fueled financial toxicities that drive people to rely on crowdfunding and shows how crowdfunding reinforces the free market ethics of these systems. The second chapter answers the question, *What kinds of campaigns succeed?* It explores the ways that crowdfunding platforms derive from, and further amplify, a long and troubled history of selective deservingness in deciding who is and is not entitled to help. This sets the stage for, and justifies, large inequities in crowdfunding campaign outcomes. Chapter 3 explores the terrain and contours of those larger inequities, asking, *Why do some campaigns succeed while others do not?* Data here show how crowdfunding reinforces and normalizes powerful social hierarchies while promoting a false idea of meritocracy and rugged individualism.

The second half of the book looks at the broader impacts and implications of the answers to these questions. Chapter 4 highlights the disjuncture between the myth of opportunity in the crowdfunding marketplace and users' ambivalent realities. It explores the more subtle tensions and cruelties that make it so that crowdfunding is never quite enough: how it reinforces individualism even as it purports to connect us and how it renders real care impossible even as it makes it easier for us to express shallow forms of care through donations. Chapter 5 situates crowdfunding within a wider set of digital technologies for health that are fundamentally altering how healthcare is delivered and where we intervene to help people. By exploring the stories of families trying to use crowdfunding to pay for complex care, we begin to see how this technological solution, even when successful, often obscures the true causes and costs of care. As health systems increasingly turn to "downstream" tools like crowdfunding to provide health coverage and support public health interventions, their adoption has far-reaching consequences. Ultimately, when we choose quick technological fixes, they often distract us from the upstream causes of these problems and can worsen health inequities.

Finally, the conclusion helps us understand where we go from here, offering three different templates for action, using examples from community efforts to mobilize aid in response to COVID-19. The first template for action is the common technology industry approach of "tweaks and fixes," and I show how these will not be sufficient even if pursued with best intentions. The second option is a more radical one of reimagining and remaking—particularly aimed at dismantling the market-based health systems that contribute to crowdfunding's popularity and necessity. Because these are such large reforms, I also offer readers a third set of suggestions for what I call "living in the meanwhile"—everyday efforts that can cultivate better practices of meaning-making, caregiving, and connection as we work toward fairer health futures. These include alternatives to, and adaptations of, crowdfunding that readers can employ in their lives.

Just as there is no single crowdfunding story, there is no simple solution to the challenges crowdfunding presents to us. Stories of crowdfunding experiences are stories about technology, society, health systems, and the complex interweaving between these systems in our contemporary lives. In this book I try to follow, rather than unravel, these interwoven threads to better understand how they work together to fuel health inequities. Ultimately, this book is an invitation: to look beneath the surface of a seemingly feel-good technology that has become an indelible part of our public and private lives, to reflect on what role we want it to play in our societies, and to imagine future alternatives for what care, connection, and solidarity could become.

Welcome to "the giving layer of the internet."[44]

The sham

Extra, extra read all about it.
I need a bunch, and wish it wasn't this much.
Obamacare, Trumpcare, Medicare—
everybody tells us we need it.
But I can't afford health insurance, let alone COBRA.
It's a no for Obamacare because I earn too little.
I applied for care credit cards but even they denied me.
When the cancer got to stage 4, and she lost her job,
we paid for COBRA until it ran out.
If we can just raise 60, maybe 80, thousand dollars
we can keep her alive long enough
to get a transplant and Obamacare.
The basis of the American economy is a sham,
and what I mean by this is
unless you make 50–60k a year
you can't afford health insurance,
even with Obamacare. What's unaffordable
about the Affordable Care Act
are the deductibles, the out of pockets, the premiums.
We pay $500 a month for her insurance,
but the doctors in the ER just laughed,
and said, nobody takes your insurance.
I wish my battle had only been with cancer
but it's mostly been with bureaucracies,
insurance companies, Obamacare loopholes.
With each battle
the cancer keeps spreading.

1

SELLING SICKNESS

In 2018, Lisa started a GoFundMe campaign for her husband, Jason. For years, they had struggled with insurance companies and medical bills because of Jason's type 1 diabetes, which required him to maintain access to several expensive brands of insulin to survive. Though Lisa and Jason were young, in their mid-twenties, they were preternaturally cautious, risk adverse, and worried about the future. They were both second-generation immigrants from troubled families that couldn't be relied upon for support. Eight years prior, when they were just getting started in life, Jason's parents kicked him off their health insurance plan, immediately imperiling his access to insulin. Nearly every major decision Jason and Lisa had made since was shaped by their need to keep Jason on health insurance and continue financing his insulin.

When we spoke, Lisa told the story of their relationship in terms of their frequently changing insurance status, using the acronym-riddled language of someone who has had to become fluent in the complexities of the US health-care system to survive. Lisa and Jason had cycled in and out of HMOs and PPOs based on their employment status and scoured through the healthcare.gov website searching for the least bad coverage option they could afford. Their home state of Texas had rejected the Medicaid expansion offered under the ACA. This left many Texans in what health policy experts call "the coverage gap," earning too much to qualify for Medicaid under their state's strict eligibility criteria but earning too little to afford good healthcare on the marketplace and qualify for ACA tax credits to help purchase insurance.[1]

After they had their first daughter on a PPO plan from Lisa's work, her premiums increased so much that she had no money left over in her paychecks after the deductions. "So, I actually went to my employer and I said, look, I have to become ineligible for your health insurance in order to survive. So, I had to drop half of my permanent shifts at work, in order to drop my hours, to where I was no longer eligible for their PPO plan through Aetna" to potentially qualify for coverage under the ACA. Even then, Lisa reflected, "we've never been eligible for traditional Medicaid, because your entire family income has to be lower than $250 a month" in Texas.

Lisa and Jason are not alone, particularly among their fellow Texans. In 2021, nearly one-quarter of Texans were uninsured, and more than 20 percent were in medical debt.[2] Texas was declared the "uninsured capital of the United States" by its own medical association.[3] The state is ranked dead last in terms of the access and affordability of its health system, in part because it is a notoriously difficult place to qualify for public forms of insurance such as Medicaid.[4]

Consequently, Lisa and Jason built their lives around trying to maintain insurance. They married much younger than they wanted to so that Jason could be on Lisa's insurance plan, and they worried about how the timing of their children's births might make their coverage unaffordable. "We've definitely gone through" all the options, Lisa told me, "I've worked with agents, I've worked without agents, I've looked at Christian health shares. All kinds of different options."[5] With her second pregnancy, Lisa had to switch insurance plans on the marketplace three different times to find one that would cover both her doctor and the hospital her doctor wanted her to deliver at. "It's like crawling through thorns, it really is," she commented. They had put much of their lives on hold simply trying to survive. "I've struggled so hard to start my life," she reflected. "My parents were both drug addicts, I've lived on my own since I was 14, I've paid my way through everything, I wasn't able to go as far as I wanted to educationally, because I didn't have funds. I do really well [with what I've got], but . . . I make about $40,000 a year and we live paycheck to paycheck because of diabetes."

Without insurance, Jason's insulin cost him $900 a month, and that didn't include the costs for purchasing or maintaining an insulin pump or for routine medical visits. For the six months before they started their GoFundMe campaign, Jason was without insurance. A friend who worked as a nurse passed along expired samples of insulin from her clinic when they were available. When that strategy fell through, Jason turned to other friends with diabetes, sharing and splitting their insulin.[6] After several days struggling to find any sources of insulin, Jason went into a diabetic coma while Lisa was at work and ended up in the intensive care unit (ICU). On top of their normally unaffordable medical bills, they knew the hospital stay would land them in severe debt.

What struck me in hearing Lisa and Jason's story was just how many options and pathways they'd pursued to get and keep affordable insurance and to avoid medical debt. Numerous programs and policies had failed them—from the ACA coverage gap to Texas's limited Medicaid eligibility criteria to the federal government's failure to regulate insulin prices.[7] When these systems failed them and their informal networks of support fell through, they turned to the only other option they knew: Lisa started a GoFundMe campaign. On their campaign page, she wrote about the rising cost of insulin, which had more than doubled since Jason lost his family's health insurance eight years prior.[8] She talked about the stigma and assumptions Jason faced as he struggled to manage a condition many people mistakenly attribute to poor health choices. And she imagined what finding a cure for diabetes would mean for them: not only would it end Jason's endless medical struggles, but it would also relieve them of the onerous financial obligations the disease carried.

Lisa knew what it would take to make their lives more stable: they needed to get Jason on a health-care plan that was affordable, met his needs, and allowed them both to keep working. "That's kind of been like the purple dragon that we've been chasing all these years," she said, "but it's been very elusive." Lisa's family was from Costa Rica, and the irony was not lost on her that had they never emigrated to the United States, she would have had access to cheaper and more comprehensive care. "It's like $14 a person a month for their universal healthcare program," she told me. "And when we lived there my grandfather had type 1 diabetes and his insulin was dirt cheap, easy to get."[9]

In the unequal, profit-oriented US health-care system, Lisa and Jason were forced to turn to another competitive marketplace—GoFundMe—for survival. There, they tried to sell their story to potential donors but found that GoFundMe's marketplace also left them behind. "I definitely think that as with many things on the internet these days, there . . . seems to be a certain genre of story or topic on crowdfunding that . . . gets a lot of attention," Lisa reluctantly observed. She recalled that right before they launched their campaign, another family at their daughter's school started a GoFundMe and shared it with the entire school. The other family's situation "was truly a heartbreaking and tragic story," Lisa said, but they were also quite well off financially. She continued, "It made me feel just awful inside on a personal level that this was a family that was already really affluent, and they had no problem taking care of any of their needs financially. And I'm glad that [they] got that support, but it was like, wow, they've already got over $30,000 [in donations], and now everybody at the school is going and donating to them as well and feels bad for them. And it just felt like there's no room or sympathy for our situation."

By comparison, Jason's campaign had "a little bit of a buzz, and some trickle of funds" when it started, but donations quickly died off. It was hard to make a compelling case for a disease that required constant, unending investment with no end in sight. Ultimately, they raised less than $2,000. The funds went to hospital bills and insulin supplies, which they were still paying off when we talked six months later. It made little difference in their long-term financial stability.

In our discussions, Lisa mentioned the widely shared story of Shane Patrick Boyle, who had tried crowdfunding for insulin costs and died before his campaign reached its goal.[10] Shane's friend, graphic artist Ted Closson, told his story in a powerful comic titled "A GoFundMe Campaign Is Not Health Insurance" (figure 1.1).[11] Shane's story has haunting parallels with Jason's. As Closson described, "trying to stay alive, [Shane] leveraged every kind of community he could: Networks of clinics, friends online, social media campaigns, health-care marketplaces. But because caring for each other isn't a quality of the American healthcare system, he's dead." Reflecting on Shane's story, Lisa said it also felt unfair that the media only paid attention to people who had died for lack of insulin: "What about people who are alive and trying not to die?" But she said that she had not given up hope: "I still believe that, I have a hope that [Jason] doesn't die . . . from type 1 diabetes." She talked at length about the promise of new treatment options. "It's just staying alive until then . . . that's the current struggle."

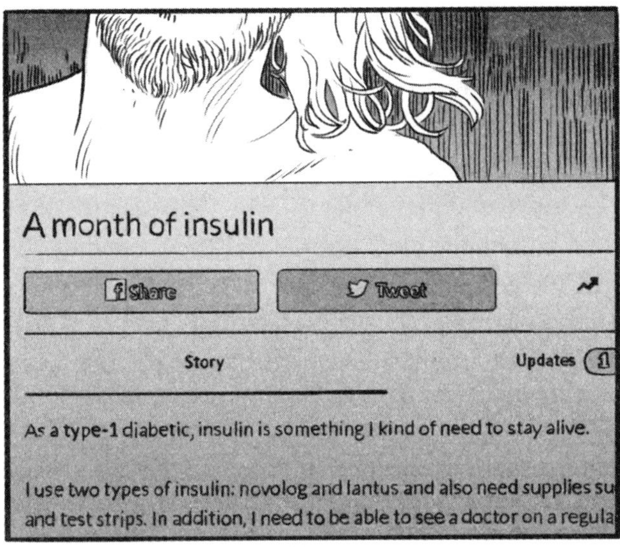

Figure 1.1 A frame from Ted Closson's graphic story, "A GoFundMe Campaign is Not Health Insurance," about his friend Shane, who died from type 1 diabetes while crowdfunding for insulin.

MARKETIZING HEALTH

For many like Jason, struggling to afford care is a life-threatening condition. Health policy expert Elizabeth Rosenthal has observed that in the United States, "we are all potential victims of medical extortion." This extortion causes extensive suffering, financial ruin, and even death.[12] Rather than being the result of mistakes or errors, such extortion is the result of a system designed to exclude people—especially the poor and the very sick—from care. Marketized health systems like the one we have in the United States are built on deeply rooted legacies of excluding people from care while protecting profits and markets. As Lisa found out, crowdfunding is also built upon, and powerfully reinforces, these ideologies.

To be specific, two intertwining ideological legacies have contributed to extremely limited social safety nets and a highly marketized health system in the United States. The first of these legacies is neoliberalism. While an overused and often underdefined term, neoliberalism refers to a political and economic ideology that has been a dominant in places such as the United States since at least the 1970s.[13] Neoliberalism insists governments must act primarily to protect "free" markets and that public goods such as healthcare should be distributed through market forces rather than through government allocations.[14] It enshrines competition among individuals and makes shared social goods scarce by cutting government budgets. Neoliberalism is not only an economic reality but also an ideological one: in a world where market competition dominates, "we internalize and reproduce its creeds," writes George Monbiot. "The market ensures that everyone gets what they deserve"—or so we think.[15]

Neoliberalism reshapes health systems to prioritize corporate profits over peoples' right to health, drawing on market-based tools to maximize revenues and incentivize specific behaviors. In the United States, this means that our primary health goods—insurance, medical services, equipment, and treatments—are all privately owned by profit-maximizing companies, often ones that operate in highly consolidated markets (where there is less competition to drive down prices).[16] Our health system is the most expensive in the world, by a long shot, but it's not buying us better health or care. As Gerard Anderson and colleagues stated bluntly in an assessment of why our healthcare is so costly, "it's the prices, stupid": we pay more—much more—for the same services and goods compared to people in other countries.[17] As Lisa herself was aware, insulin prices in the United States are often five to ten times higher than they are in other high-income countries.[18]

We are told by lobbying firms and politicians who seek to defend this system that protecting market "choices" is the most important priority for consumers and this will yield "efficiency" in our systems. Opposition to health reform often invokes the threat of forced choices and lost freedoms.[19] But even health reform efforts such as ACA legislation prioritize protecting market choices. As President Obama famously said while introducing the ACA's "marketplace" of health insurance options, "if you like your doctor, you're going to be able to keep your doctor. If you like your plan, keep your plan. I don't believe we should give government or the insurance companies more control over healthcare in America. I think it's time to give you, the American people, more control over your health."[20]

It's important to recognize, however, that health-care "markets" don't behave like other markets, in large part because patients lack the kinds of information, control, and agency that would help them to make choices as informed consumers.[21] Take Lisa and Jason, for example: Jason didn't choose to get diabetes, and being reliant on insulin meant he faced a prolonged, forced "choice" between purchasing specific brands of insulin and death. When he went into a diabetic coma, he certainly didn't express a choice about what hospital he wanted to go to or shop around for the cheapest ambulance ride, and he wouldn't have even been able to know the costs of his hospitalization up front. Rather than being able to choose between affordable health plans, Jason and Lisa made huge sacrifices to maintain health insurance, with few if any choices about its cost or coverage options. Situations like these are common, and they demonstrate why Rosenthal describes illness as "medical extortion."[22] Under so-called market conditions, getting healthcare can feel much more like being held hostage than going shopping.

Ironically, the same complexities that make navigating insurance markets so difficult also make our care systems less efficient: it's estimated we spend nearly $2,500 a person on bureaucratic costs per year because our system demands so much administrative labor to manage care.[23] Think, for example, of the hours physicians and hospital staff spend on the phone trying to get treatments approved or processing insurance paperwork. And this doesn't account for the enormous time costs involved for patients and family members like Lisa, who spend years combing through insurance marketplaces, filling out paperwork, managing bills, and finding providers.

All of this amounts to one of the most complex and costly health systems in the world. In 2019, US health expenditures were nearly $11,000 per person, whereas costs in Canada were half that amount.[24] In Costa Rica, where Lisa's grandfather got affordable health coverage thanks to the country's universal health-care system, expenditures are less than $1,000.[25] And our spending is not buying us better health. As my colleague Stephen Bezruchka has observed, "if health were an Olympic event and the race was how long you lived, then the U.S. would not appear in the event as it would have been disqualified in the trials."[26] In terms of life expectancy, the United States ranks well below other high-income countries but also well below Cuba, Lebanon, Albania, Chile, and, yes, Costa Rica.[27]

During COVID-19, the gap between the United States and other countries grew even wider as it bore an inordinately high burden of cases and deaths.[28] If mortality due to COVID-19 over the first two years of the pandemic were a macabre Olympic sport, Peru would win gold, Brazil silver, and the United States would get bronze despite its more advanced and expensive health system.[29] On other key measures of population health, such as maternal and infant mortality, the United States similarly performs well below its peers. And on all of these measures, there are huge racial disparities, meaning that health outcomes for racially marginalized groups are typically far worse than those for White Americans. If the health data of Black Americans were ranked among that of world nations, it would appear in the bottom half of all countries, with a life expectancy nearly six years less than their White counterparts.[30]

While the causes of these inequities and disparate health outcomes are complex, they are not simply attributable to individual health behaviors or genetics. In a landmark study of declining health status in the United States, the Institute of Medicine found that "adverse social and economic conditions matter greatly" in contributing to health disparities.[31] These conditions include high rates of poverty and income inequality, poor investment in social safety nets and public services like education, and inadequate access to affordable healthcare. They contribute to health disparities and cause the greatest harm among the most marginalized US populations. But even Americans with social advantages—those with greater incomes and education and those who are White—face poorer health prospects than similarly advantaged citizens in other countries because of these structural conditions.[32]

While we owe "adverse social and economic conditions" in part to neoliberalism, that's not the entire story. Neoliberal ideologies have been dominant across much of the world for decades now. But the United States has a uniquely abysmal record among its peers of health problems related to poverty, inequity, and limited social safety nets.[33] This is largely because the US government refuses to mandate and implement even the most basic social safety net programs and public goods—like parental leave, affordable childcare, comprehensive unemployment insurance, welfare, and, of course, expanded health coverage—that would provide a layer of protection against such adverse conditions. Reluctance to support safety nets in the United States does not simply stem from neoliberalism but from a second, deeply rooted, and intertwined legacy: racism.

Many scholars agree that we can thank our country's toxic history of racism, segregation, and racialized hierarchies for its weakened and underfunded social support systems, which contribute to particularly poor health outcomes.[34] A powerful current of racial resentment runs through centuries of debates over public goods and social safety net benefits in the United States. From racist portraits of "welfare queens" to the long-standing history of "public charge" rules to deny entry to immigrants who might require public assistance, discussions about social safety nets, healthcare, and public assistance constantly return to racist fears about who these programs are intended to serve and how they uphold notions of equal economic and social rights.[35] We deprive everyone of life-sustaining programs because of White, racist angst over Black Americans and other marginalized groups having equal access to these public goods.[36] As Jonathan Metzl explains, White peoples' unwillingness to build and support more universal safety nets constitutes a "willingness to die for [their] place in this hierarchy."[37] Cedric Robinson observed that racism and capitalism have co-evolved and mutually fueled each other over centuries to create modern economies based on exclusion, extraction, and inequity.[38] While such "racial capitalism" is not unique to the United States, it is particularly powerful in undermining efforts to improve Americans' social safety nets and public goods. Tragically, what we inherit from racial capitalism and neoliberalism are systems that make all of us sicker and more precarious while health inequities grow ever larger.

It's not hard to see how crowdfunding has emerged and thrived in such an environment. Crowdfunding takes many of the logics of neoliberalism and racial capitalism—like competition, scarcity, hierarchies of deservingness, and exclusion—and uses them to transform how charity works. Under the guise of "people helping people" and "democratizing charity," crowdfunding provides a highly competitive marketplace of people in need, competing with one another to appear deserving against the backdrop of racist histories of exclusion that mark many crowdfunders as less deserving than others.

HEALTH-CARE REFORM AND RESENTMENT

In debates over the ACA during both the Obama and Trump presidencies, these ideological legacies were powerfully displayed. In what Abdul El-Sayed and Micah Johnson call an "epic battle for incremental reform," the Obama administration's efforts to improve insurance coverage for Americans faced an enormous uphill battle against powerful corporate interests.[39] Rather than challenge these industries head on, the administration took a consensus-building approach, aiming to develop a health-care reform bill that would enjoy the support of the hospital, pharmaceutical, insurance, and medical provider industries. "The greatest political strength of the ACA was its tremendous effort to win the support of major healthcare stakeholders," El-Sayed and Johnson explain. "But that was also its biggest policy weakness."[40]

Without changing the market forces that powerfully dominate the US health-care system, the administration was limited in what it could accomplish. It achieved some major victories—eliminating coverage exemptions for preexisting conditions, extending the age that young adults can remain on their parents' insurance, and expanding access to Medicaid to a larger group of Americans who fell above poverty guidelines but still earned too little to afford insurance. But the ACA also allowed large corporations to continue setting the rules of the game, choosing where and under what conditions they would offer care and coverage. By offering uninsured Americans an "insurance marketplace" where they could purchase coverage, the ACA preserved the neoliberal, market-driven forces that generally protect profits at the expense of protecting health. In some markets insurers charged high prices for good coverage or offered only extremely poor coverage for affordable rates; within several years insurers were leaving less healthy "marketplaces" to seek profits in healthier states.[41]

The ACA was also crippled by political battles rooted in racial resentment. After the bill was passed, many Republican leaders worked to undermine it at state and federal levels, through both court cases and legislation. Most notably, many Republican-dominated states decided to refuse federal funding for a Medicaid expansion to cover more Americans. Often these decisions were justified using the familiar language of fears about government overreach, limited choice, high costs, and people abusing the system. But as Jonathan Metzl found in focus group research in the Southeastern US, "white populations frequently justified their support for anti-ACA positions not through the benefits that expanded healthcare might have for themselves or their families but through concerns about threats to their status and privilege represented by government programs that promised to equally distribute resources or imagined health advantages" among racial groups.[42] Health insurance reform, crafted by the administration of the first Black president of the United States, "placed white Americans into 'networks' with immigrant and minority populations" and in doing so elicited widespread opposition based on racial resentment and fear.[43]

More broadly, as Jessica Mulligan and Emily Brunson argue, opposition to the ACA was expressed in "resentment narratives" based on "class, gender, sexuality, and immigration status" as well as race.[44] We can see these narratives reflected in the kinds of alternative health networks that many White Republicans turned to as the ACA was implemented, including largely Christian "healthcare sharing ministries," which offer an alternative to traditional insurance coverage by sharing certain health-care costs among networks of members who adhere to "ethical" guidelines.[45] Carolyn Schwarz, who studied these ministries, observed that they deployed and attracted members based on a "mega-narrative" of freedom of choice.[46] However, these groups emphasized a freedom to exclude people from their networks based on race or religion and a freedom to share health resources only with those from similar backgrounds.

It's important to recognize that both proponents and opponents of the ACA reinforced ideas of exclusion. As Mulligan and Brunson argue, "resentment was also baked into the law itself" through policies like those that excluded undocumented immigrants from insurance.[47] These became more entrenched as the law was contested, such as when states rejected Medicaid expansion, thus ensuring the exclusion of large portions of the working poor from subsidies. During the Trump administration, states imposed further barriers to Medicaid enrollment and support, such as work requirements for Medicaid enrollees. All of these measures reinforced "pre-existing patterns of exclusion, often by reinforcing longstanding distinctions between the 'deserving' and the 'undeserving,'" Jessica Mulligan and Heide Castañeda argue.[48]

Ultimately, the ACA was responsible for an enormous decline in the uninsured population of the United States, which dropped from more than forty-five million in 2010 to a low of just under twenty-seven million uninsured people by 2016.[49] Yet significant populations of the United States remained uninsured and thus faced significant health precarities.[50] The ACA reforms did not succeed in lowering the overall costs of care or in simplifying our overly complex health system. Expanding private health coverage to more Americans did not protect many from excruciatingly high costs or the financial crisis that can befall people when they become severely ill. In many places, insurance deductibles and premiums rose after the ACA even as insurance companies made record profits.[51] As El-Sayed and Johnson put it, "in today's America, health insurance doesn't make healthcare affordable, and it doesn't protect you from financial ruin."[52]

KFF Health News estimates that more than one hundred million Americans are saddled with medical debts.[53] More fundamentally, accessing and paying for healthcare continues to be a significant struggle and source of stress. This is most true for Americans with already marginalized identities, leading to experiences of what Mulligan and Castañeda call "stratified citizenship."[54] Rather than establishing a more universal right to healthcare shared by all people in the United States, the ACA largely established stratified, partial, and exclusionary categories of more and less deserving health consumers. Health coverage thus continued to be one of the most contested terrains of politicization, exclusion, and neoliberalism in the United States.

FINANCIAL TOXICITIES AND CRISES OF CARE

In addition to thrusting people into financial precarity and debt, the financial realities of the US health system also, unsurprisingly, lead to significantly worse health outcomes. People who can't afford care delay it or forgo treatments that insurance doesn't cover. "Similar to the subprime financial instruments that made the poor profitable for payday, auto, and high-risk mortgage lenders," observe Mulligan and Castañeda, "the health risks that poor and uninsured populations experience in the United States both worsen their health status and undermine their financial stability, all while generating revenue" for private corporations.[55] Such "subprime risks" of healthcare beget additional precarities of both health and wealth, exacerbating mental health issues, curtailing economic futures, and undermining opportunities to intervene early to reduce the cost and severity of chronic diseases.[56] Researchers recognize that these financial circumstances constitute a kind of "toxicity" that leads to far worse health outcomes for many patients.[57]

Oncologists first coined the term "financial toxicity" to describe the significant side effects that out-of-pocket costs had on patients undergoing cancer care in the United States.[58] Cancer is a notoriously expensive disease, and doctors were increasingly recognizing the need to take its financial and emotional burdens into account when treating patients and in measuring treatment outcomes, including and up to survival.[59] While many people know that getting cancer is expensive in the United States, they may not just how expensive it is until it happens to them. A study of 9.5 million cancer patients between 2000 and 2012 found that within two years of diagnosis, 42.4 percent had depleted their entire life's savings and, on average, had lost nearly $100,000 to the disease.[60] Before the ACA was implemented, researchers estimated that more than 2 million cancer survivors missed necessary healthcare due to cost over a three-year period.[61] And those were survivors: many people diagnosed with cancer simply cannot afford their treatments if they are un- or underinsured or in poverty, and others lose their insurance coverage after diagnosis because they can no longer work. This results in delayed, diminished, or abandoned treatment, often leading to premature death. Cancer survival rates show huge disparities based on insurance status,[62] reflecting the very sobering reality that in the United States, whether and how long one survives with cancer is heavily influenced by one's ability to pay for and maintain private insurance and afford out-of-pocket costs for care.

From a public health perspective, financial toxicities involve far more than just side effects of treatment: they determine how, when, and whether people seek care, and they have long-term impacts not just on patients themselves but also on their families, caregivers, children, and even communities. Rather than thinking about the toxicity of financial circumstances in our health system as a side effect of specific treatments, here I use the term more expansively to describe toxicities in our system that impact population health at large. Much like lead in water or pollution in the air, financial toxicities surround us, are difficult to avoid, and impact our health across the life course. The financial concerns of healthcare impact our health but also often reshape our lives.

Kayla was a completely healthy woman in her twenties when her life was upended by cancer and its many financial consequences. She was happily pregnant with her second child and suffering from what she thought were bad allergies when she was suddenly diagnosed with stage-four lung cancer. She was immediately started on chemotherapy, completing two rounds of it before giving birth to her son, Charlie, prematurely at thirty-one weeks. Charlie's father, Zach, worked for a small, family-owned construction company in Texas, and Kayla was a stay-at-home mom. While finances were tight before her cancer diagnosis, the couple made things work. Zach had health insurance through his employer, but it was too expensive to cover Kayla, so they put off getting married so she could stay on her parents' insurance plan when she got pregnant. This decision made other aspects of their life complicated even before cancer came along: Kayla had a five-year-old son from a previous marriage, and while Zach was eager to formally adopt him, he couldn't do so until they got married.

Suddenly, facing a late-stage cancer diagnosis, these circumstances became far more complex. Kayla was initially only given a few months to live and was desperate to ensure her older son would be cared for. She and Zach decided they had to immediately get married and start the adoption process. This also meant she had to switch over to Zach's insurance, which had extremely limited coverage for her cancer care, charging her about $500 every single time she went to the hospital. Like many cancer patients, treatment required other hard financial decisions. Zach worried about keeping his job while caring for Kayla. In an act of extraordinary generosity, his workplace found out about their situation and kept him on payroll full time but told him not to return to work for a year, ensuring they kept their health coverage while allowing Zach the time he needed for caregiving. Nevertheless, their costs mounted. As Kayla's sister-in-law Susie recalled, "they live out in the country about two hours from . . . the hospital. Having to drive back and forth, and then having to have meals accommodated while she was there . . . also, because this all happened in the summertime, their older son wasn't in school, so they also had to find childcare. And they can't take him into the hospital because it's gotta be a sanitary environment, they don't allow kids there."

By the time Charlie was born prematurely, Kayla and Zach were facing enormous costs, and Susie convinced them to start a GoFundMe. But Kayla insisted they didn't want to ask for too much, that she felt uncomfortable asking for help. They settled on a $2,000 request for "gas money" before Susie convinced them they needed far more than just help with gas and food. Meanwhile, they explored other insurance options. They couldn't qualify for Medicaid without forfeiting Zach's salary even though they were barely above the poverty line. Without better options for coverage, their community pitched in to help: Zach's friends helped retrofit their outdated home so it was safe for Kayla and Charlie, and grandparents stepped in to help with childcare. Within a few months, their campaign raised nearly $6,000. And after several rounds of chemotherapy, Kayla was given more than just months to live. The future was uncertain—both medically and financially—but things were looking better than they'd been.

Kayla was extremely humble about the campaign and kept insisting, "I'm not deserving of any of this!" But Susie was surprised they hadn't attracted more help. After all, she knew the costs had been astronomical for the family, and the $6,000 they raised was but a small drop in the bucket. Plus, in her mind, theirs was a "crazy, sad, emotional" story: "she's never smoked, she's pregnant, and she has stage 4 lung cancer. And then to go through with a premature delivery, and still going through chemo. . . . This is like something you'd see on TV!" The family called radio stations and pitched home makeover TV shows on the idea of remodeling their home. "But I never heard anything. There are just so many people applying. But it seemed like the perfect story," Susie said. Kayla and Zach were extremely wary of asking for what they thought was "too much" help. Zach told Susie, "I don't want to be a beggar, I don't want people to think we're taking advantage of anyone, or the situation, or trying to profit from it."

It's important to interrogate Zach's concern about appearing to "profit from" their tragic story. Kayla and Zach hardly profited from this experience, having borne many of the out-of-pocket costs of their healthcare, childcare, transportation, meals, home renovations, and hotel stays while Charlie was in the hospital. Zach's employer, a small business, also bore enormous costs from covering his lost work hours. Their friends and families bore the cost of being their informal safety net. The main entities profiting were the hospitals, their insurance company, and GoFundMe—which took an 8 percent fee off each donation to their campaign.[63] As Nicholas Freudenberg has observed, a dense network of multinational corporations dominate the insurance, hospital, pharmaceutical, medical device, and private equity markets responsible for driving up cancer treatment prices and also influencing policymaking that protects market-dominated systems.[64] The power of these industries, he writes, led the United States to "[sacrifice] a rational evidence-based approach for a casino mentality where the promise of profit decides which medical avenues are pursued and which are ignored," and which "undermined systemic reforms that could improve access to affordable quality care."[65]

Kayla and Zach's story documents how costly this system is to families and individuals when someone gets seriously sick: it's not just the price of healthcare itself but the massive disruptions to life, jobs, childcare, and networks of support. When neoliberalism undermines public safety net systems, families and societies face what Nancy Fraser has called a "crisis of care."[66] While it has long been the case that "the capitalist economy relies on—one might say, free rides on—activities of provisioning, caregiving and interaction that produce and maintain social bonds, although it accords them no monetized value and treats them as if they were free," Fraser argues that our current economic systems have prioritized profit over social reproduction to such an extent that systems of care are in utter crisis.[67] Our care networks are depleted; they can no longer meet the immense needs that we thrust upon them when more formal systems of support fail us.

As costly as Kayla's cancer was, by comparison with many Americans, she and Zach were quite lucky: they had insurance and were able to maintain it, Zach's employer was exceedingly generous, and their community provided ample support. But imagine what their circumstances might have been had they not faced the financial toxicities of the marketized health system: they could have married when they wanted and not worried over adopting Kayla's older son; they could have focused on getting second opinions, finding the best treatment options, spending time with their kids, and supporting Kayla's recovery. Without these stresses and care obligations, perhaps even Charlie's extremely premature arrival might have been delayed by several weeks, thus giving him far better chances at survival and fewer long-term complications.

Kayla and Zach, like many Americans, struggled with asking for help even during an exceptional crisis in their lives. It's a strange and tragic dynamic in our society that the very systems that make us vulnerable in moments of crisis also make it hard for us to ask for help when we need it. Surely, we think, someone is worse off than we are; at other times, the same categories of exclusion that mark who is more or less deserving of public assistance keep us from feeling we have a right to ask for help at all. Even with what Susie thought was a "perfect story" of deservingness, Zach and Kayla didn't think they were deserving and didn't want to be seen as taking advantage of others.

The feeling that one is not worthy of help is such a common sentiment that it's easy to dismiss as cultural tic or cliché. But it reflects the ways that the financial toxicities of marketized health systems are intertwined with *moral toxicities*—values like the idea that asking for help is shameful or that we must maintain rugged independence during crises. These moral toxicities are so normalized that we barely notice them, but they do real harm to people and communities. As this book explores, moral toxicities like selective deservingness, exclusion, individualism, and market competition are deeply rooted in our health and social systems but also fuel newer "solutions" to our health problems, like crowdfunding. Like financial toxicities, moral toxicities pose real public health dangers, suffusing the metaphorical air we breathe with judgments about who deserves, who should succeed, and what kinds of people are entitled to care. They also undermine our ability to imagine other alternatives, other ways of sustaining ourselves and our communities.

I am keen throughout this book to pause and examine these ideas, to ask why they arise and imagine what life might be like if they were different. What if Kayla and Zach didn't have to feel shame about asking for even a small amount of help? Better yet, what if they didn't have to beg for help at all? What if you didn't need a "perfect story" to get a few thousand dollars from people on the internet to deal with the enormous financial disruptions of late-stage cancer? What if the first thing you worried about when you got cancer wasn't, "How am I going to pay for this?"

PRAYER OF LAST RESORT

There's a term in the health insurance industry—"payor of last resort"—that's used to describe an entity that is responsible for paying for care when all other options have fallen through. Americans who face the financial burdens of healthcare—whether they are uninsured, underinsured, don't have the savings to cover enormous out-of-pocket expenses, or simply struggle to absorb the costs of care—increasingly turn to GoFundMe as the payor of last resort. While Americans crowdfund for all sorts of reasons—and when facing varying levels of financial strain—I have easily seen thousands of campaigns for medical expenses that use phrases like "nowhere else to turn," "exhausted all other options," and "wouldn't do this unless we were desperate." With gallows humor, people joke that GoFundMe is our health insurance now. "Welcome to America your health insurance options are GoFundMe or the Ellen show lol good luck," wrote one commenter on Twitter in 2018.[68] Other times, people make similar observations without the veneer of sarcastic humor. Aliya, a nurse at a safety net hospital who saw lots of uninsured patients, told me, "this is people's insurance now. GoFundMe is what happens when life happens now. Because the insurance we have doesn't take care of you, like, this is what people need."

But this is neither what charitable crowdfunding sites were created for, nor what they provide to users. While some limited research has shown that successful crowdfunding campaigns can reduce the number of medical bankruptcies, it's clear that for many, this is not the case.[69] Roughly 90 percent of campaigns consistently do not meet their goals—even when crowdfunders are encouraged to set artificially low goals at the outset to make it easier to meet them.[70] In 2020, my colleague Mark Igra and I studied the largest collection of US GoFundMe campaigns to date, and we found that the median medical campaign raised $265 from five donors.[71] A third of campaigns in 2020 got no donations at all.[72] Crowdfunding is health insurance like a lottery ticket is a paycheck—it is more like a prayer, than a payor, of last resort.

GoFundMe's corporate executives insist that helping with burdensome medical bills or patching up the social safety net is not what they had in mind for the platform, nor what they want for its future. In a long conversation with Kara Swisher of the *New York Times* in 2021, CEO Tim Cadogan noted that the company was seeing many campaigns related to medical and basic needs arising from the pandemic,[73] saying that "we are happy to help them with that. But we don't view GoFundMe as a substitute for more comprehensive access to healthcare for everybody." While Cadogan dodged the tougher political questions on why GoFundMe had become "America's social safety net," as Swisher put it, he optimistically reflected, "I hope that the needs become more positive like hey, I'd like to take my kid's soccer team on a tour of California." "Those are the old days, Tim," Swisher quipped. Cadogan jumped in to respond: "right, well there's no reason—" he paused and then continued. "We can get back to that. And that's honestly what we would prefer to be there for is to help people with the . . . You name it, right? It can be honeymoons. It can be baby showers. It can be a study abroad trip. It can be mission trips. It can be the local animal hospital. It can be like the search and rescue team, like I used to be a part of. All of those things—we're there for those."[74]

GoFundMe says very little about its corporate strategies or what is most profitable for the platform, but it's clear that the company would prefer its users leverage crowdfunding for more fun, feel-good activities than making desperate pleas for help with cancer care. The brand works hard to project a positive image of itself, routinely reminding users that its platform is "powered by kindness."[75] But this aspirational projection of a feel-good, happy crowdfunding marketplace collides with the undeniable realities of how the platform is being used. Around the time of this interview, Cadogan also published an op-ed asking congress to pass a new COVID-19 relief package.[76] The piece was titled "Hello Congress, Americans Need Help and We Can't Do Your Job for You."[77] GoFundMe walks a fine line here in critiquing the systemic gaps that clearly drive people to its platform. It's hard to tell if this concern is motivated by good will or by concern for its own brand image.

Like other digital technologies, many charitable crowdfunding platforms were first built without a clear idea of how they would be used. Daryl Hatton, who founded the site FundRazr in collaboration with PayPal in 2010, recalled that at the time, they had no idea what people were going to do with their technology: "And we all said we don't know, but it feels like we're getting some requests for [personal fundraising]. And so, we did that. And it was literally a start-up dream, in that we turned the system on, and we had customers that day. And we had people making transactions the next day. And it kept rolling, and growing and growing." Hatton had come up with the idea for FundRazr after trying to collect fees for a youth sports team he was coaching, an eerie precursor to Cadogan's dream of "more positive" campaign purposes. Hatton recalled that in the first weeks of launching, he and his colleagues would print out each campaign story and put it up on the walls of the office, "to try and figure out what the heck they were wanting to raise money for. And it was personal healthcare, and it was animals, and it was car accidents, and it was . . . all the things that we see now were just latent in the market."

With the benefit of hindsight, we can see that crowdfunding platforms such as FundRazr and GoFundMe emerged at a notable time. Both were founded in 2010, in the continuing aftermath of the 2008 financial crisis and in the same year that the ACA passed. In the post-2008 economic context, austerity measures were eroding social support systems and health investments across many countries, while citizens turned to digital media platforms and social networks not just to socially connect but to also increasingly seek out work in the emerging gig economy.[78] Social safety nets were eroding from both sides as governments cut costs and more and more workers became informal, independent contractors with few benefits or workplace protections. Whether or not it was intended for this purpose, charitable crowdfunding aligned with the needs of digitally savvy citizen entrepreneurs rendered precarious by limited safety nets.[79] When gig work couldn't support you, at least you could turn to gig begging.

Needless to say, crowdfunding took off, with GoFundMe quickly leading the pack. GoFundMe was so successful in its rapid growth and market dominance that Hatton recalls "others in the industry, we'd meet and kinda go 'what the heck are they doing? Like, what deal have they made with the devil?' Because you just don't grow that fast." The company worked extensively with local and national media, using armies of public relations agents to identify compelling campaign stories and push them out to media. They learned to partner with celebrities and hired communications experts with political savvy, like Dan Pfeiffer, White House communications director under President Obama.[80] "They schooled an entire generation of [Silicon] Valley experts on how to scale a business" Hatton told me, with equal parts awe and regret.

Ultimately, despite coy proclamations that GoFundMe was never intended for basic needs or safety net care, the company seems well aware that these uses have contributed to the rapid growth of its business and the remarkable transformation of its platform into an eponymous product. During the early months of COVID, the company scrambled to find the best ways to leverage the crisis for further growth, launching huge new campaigns for nutrition support, small business help, and support for health-care workers, often in partnership with big-name celebrities and other large corporations.[81] On a campaign page that GoFundMe started for pandemic-related mental health support, the text read, with startling honesty, "We're in a growth industry: pain. The world is hurting right now—from Covid anxiety, from the quarantines, from economic ruin. And we believe this . . . is going to last a very long time. So, we need to grow."[82]

GLOBAL PLATFORMS, LOCAL PROBLEMS

While GoFundMe was exceptionally good at growing its market share, it exhibited far less control over how its platform was used. Despite starting as a site for charities to fundraise, users consistently turned to it with medical and health needs as well as requests for help with accidents and emergencies, funerals, and bills. Cadogan has been quick to insist, however, that GoFundMe operates in other countries and these issues are not unique to the United States. "We operate in the UK as well. And medical fundraisers are a really big category there too because what the government covers—or the National Health Service (NHS) covers—there's still a lot of additional expenses on top of that," he told Swisher.[83] He's not wrong: charitable crowdfunding has exploded in popularity across the globe.[84] While GoFundMe only allows users in a select number of high-income countries to start campaigns, other platforms have filled its place in other countries. In India, platforms like Ketto use a model similar to GoFundMe and promise to help patients with medical bills. The Kenyan platform M-changa, which leverages the country's popular M-pesa payment system, reports that 40 percent of fundraisers are for medical needs.[85] And in places as diverse as Venezuela and Tunisia, citizens turned to crowdfunding to address acute health-care shortages during the COVID-19 pandemic.[86] As early as 2013 the World Bank heralded crowdfunding as a highly promising technology that could, it claimed, "fuel 'the Rise of the Rest' globally."[87]

In many ways, the appeal of crowdfunding for health needs follows a remarkable shift toward marketized, privatized health systems globally—a shift that began with the introduction of neoliberalism but accelerated in many countries following the 2008 financial crisis.[88] Indeed, as scholars have documented, the United States has been a powerful architect and exporter of privatization in healthcare, both through its own initiatives as well as through its dominance in global financial institutions like the International Monetary Fund.[89] In places like India, users crowdfund for everything from oxygen and sterilized surgical equipment to cancer treatment and transplants.[90] In Kenya it is not uncommon to see people crowdfunding for family members who have been detained by hospitals when they cannot pay their bills after health insurance coverage falls short.[91] Such hospital detentions are not rare across low- and middle-income countries.[92] At a talk I gave on crowdfunding in 2021, a Nigerian gentleman stood up to praise GoFundMe and ask whether he could use it to address hospital detentions in his home city of Lagos. And in the UK, where the NHS has faced significant budget cuts, crowdfunding is increasingly common for individual causes, but citizens have also used platforms to fundraise for the NHS itself, contributing to budgets and raising money for scarce public health goods.[93]

Like any technology, crowdfunding is taken up in diverse and unexpected ways by users across myriad locations, cultures, and social strata. It also resonates with deep-rooted cultural practices of charity and mutual support, such as the Islamic practice of *sadaqa* and the Kenyan concept of *harambee*. But it is clear that it has gained popularity as a technological Band-Aid for trying to cover some of the holes left by market-based health systems. Where safety nets unravel and where healthcare becomes marketized, crowdfunding tends to follow.

There are important differences, however, between how crowdfunding is used for medical needs in the United States verses other countries with better systems of universal health coverage and social support—even where those systems face budget shortfalls, as in the UK. Cross-national studies of medical crowdfunding have found that US campaigns are more likely to aim to address routine and basic care and to substitute for gaps in public health insurance and social safety nets, whereas campaigns in places like Canada and the UK are more likely to focus on experimental or uncovered treatment.[94] Nonetheless, in these places there are also gaps in health coverage and social support systems, and research documents that people commonly seek out crowdfunding to fill these gaps.[95] In the United States, it's simply that the gaps are far larger compared to most of our peers. Even between US states, crowdfunding is more common where medical debt is higher and insurance coverage is thinner.[96]

Unfortunately, the more people must rely on crowdfunding to fill gaps, the more competition there is for attention and support from the crowd. This leads to further inequities in who succeeds and who does not. The more crowdfunding is used, the more it also normalizes a market-based solution to market-based problems rather than challenging the gaps in the system directly. Cadogan can call on US legislators to "do your job," but ultimately, GoFundMe still profits from the political conditions that drive people to his platform.[97] As Jeremy Snyder observed, "GoFundMe is increasingly engaging in a public relations approach of shifting attention from the inadequacies of crowdfunding as an ad hoc social safety net to the failures of the US government, in particular, to provide adequate social supports."[98] These two phenomena are connected: crowdfunding benefits from, upholds, and celebrates the very same values that have undermined efforts to expand health coverage and safety nets in the United States.

EXCLUSION GOES VIRAL

The year 2015 marked the period that, as GoFundMe put it in a year-end report, "giving went viral."[99] The "Saving Eliza" campaign (discussed in the Introduction) reached more than $2 million in donations. Taylor Swift donated $50,000 to a young fan's leukemia campaign, causing GoFundMe to change its maximum donation policy. Overall, campaigns on the site raised more than a billion dollars.[100] Among the campaigns that went viral in 2015 was an unexpected one, for an uninsured South Carolina man with diabetes named Luis Lang. Needless to say, Luis's campaign was not highlighted in GoFundMe's year-end report. Luis started a campaign seeking $12,000 to cover the costs of urgently needed eye surgery due to complications from his diabetes.[101] His story was picked up by local newspapers, which portrayed him as an Obamacare-hating Republican who had refused to sign up for insurance under the new ACA legislation and was now seeking help for a procedure that insurance would likely have covered.[102] The story quickly went viral, picked up by newspapers around the country and scrutinized by liberal bloggers who seemed to delight in Luis's predicament. "See Man Hate Obamacare. See Man Refuse to Get Obamacare. See Man Whine That He Can't Get Obamacare When He Needs It" read the title on one blog post.[103]

Supporters of the ACA flocked to Luis's campaign page, where they donated small amounts and posted comments mocking his decisions regarding insurance. While Luis ultimately raised more than $30,000, he faced enormous derision for his viewpoints alongside ableist and classist criticism of his appearance and spelling errors, even as he explained that "I can not [sic] see very well" due to diabetes.[104] As one commenter wrote,

> Let's re-cap shall we? You have diabetes, yet you continue to smoke. You let two open enrollment periods for the ACA go by without signing up for insurance. You were gainfully employed, yet chose to not purchase health insurance for yourself or your family. Now that you have reaped what you have sown, you expect other people to GIVE you the thousands of dollars you need for your medical procedures, preferably while you keep your $300 k house. And on

top of that, you want to blame Obama for your troubles. How's that "personal responsibility" thing working out for you?

But as Lang himself attempted to clarify in the media storm that followed, he wasn't so much opposed to Obamacare as unable to get it.[105] Like many, he had found himself in the "coverage gap" of the ACA after his state refused to expand Medicaid—making too little to qualify for federal subsidies. He knew he should enroll in insurance but couldn't afford it. He thought if he had a health emergency, he would get help.[106] Luis's wife said that they called Obamacare the "Not Fair Healthcare Act" because it didn't seem to be able to help someone like him—disabled, unable to work, and medically needy.[107] While they unfairly placed blame on the ACA rather than their state legislators for rejecting the Medicaid expansion that would have closed the coverage gap Luis found himself in, they were not wrong about the unfairness of their situation.

While journalists and policy experts debated the many forms of support Luis should have sought or may have been qualified to receive, and as commenters made judgments about his smoking habit and his poorly controlled diabetes, what passed largely unnoticed were the ways his story was used to reinforce the very same moral toxicities of exclusion and resentment that were undermining the US efforts to expand health-care access. Luis was deemed morally unworthy of care for his life choices, his behaviors, his political views, his disabilities, and his ways of asking for help. On his page and across the internet, a particular politics of health was normalized: one in which those with financial resources are empowered as a "crowd" to decide who should and should not deserve healthcare, and to make judgments based on assessments of behavior, ability, identity, political affiliation, and perceived worth. These political values are antithetical to the values of a truly universal health-care system, where even those who do not want assistance or oppose the right to health will find themselves caught by the social safety net, should they end up plummeting toward health crisis. Few of the avowed supporters of Obamacare who commented on Luis's case recognized that they were extolling the very same values of individual responsibility, free markets, and selective deservingness that have been used for decades to oppose health-care reform and expansion efforts in the United States. What they were also doing was reinforcing the new, morally toxic norms of crowd-driven decisions about who deserves, and who does not deserve, access to care.

Luis Lang's story is one marked by moral and financial toxicities, as this chapter describes. Those toxicities predated crowdfunding and were a long time in the making through US politics of racial and class exclusion, health privatization, and neoliberalism. Market-based health systems and inadequate social safety nets constitute what Ruth Wilson Gilmore has called "organized abandonment."[108] But crowdfunding reinforces and popularizes racialized and class-based exclusions under the guise of equal opportunity generosity, as we will see in the coming chapters. Driven by values of the freedom of choice and the "wisdom of the crowd," these platforms usher in a new era of "socially organized abandonment." Even as crowdfunding purports to fill gaps in this broken system, it normalizes and reaffirms its brokenness. As the next chapter explores, a central moral toxicity that crowdfunding emerges out of, reinforces, and ultimately profits from is *selective deservingness*—the idea that only certain groups and people deserve charity and support. As we already saw in this chapter, selective deservingness is deeply embedded in the exclusions that shape the US health system. But as is evident in the case of Luis Lang, crowdfunding popularizes a more extreme form of selective deservingness, empowering largely anonymous crowds of users to decide who is entitled to care and who is not.

Very good people

First of all, we ask for your prayers for Emily's healing.
Emily is a very good person who loves the Lord and her family.

This is the story of a spectacular human,
one of the most tenderhearted, understanding,
    funny, loving, upbeat,
        loyal, ambitious, optimistic,
    charismatic, tenacious,
one of the kindest, friendliest, biggest-hearted,
people on the planet.

The best human being
I've ever known.

A hard worker and good person
who loves his family very much.

A good person with a big heart
who just wants to survive to help others.

Who works two jobs
and takes care of her grandkids.

Who works his hands to the
bone everyday to feed three daughters.

Who never quits, even when
there are many cases of COVID at work.

Who was pulling himself up by the bootstraps
when Big C cut the straps.

We were promised the American dream,
that bad things don't happen
if you work hard, do well,
are a good person.

It doesn't matter to cancer that you've been a good person.
That you're a father, a mother, someone's child
a caring daughter, supportive sister, devoted partner
    a loving dog mom
        a champion of underdogs
a gifted teacher
    an army medic
        a widower

a hardworking tree lover
    a phlebotomist police officer
        a talented and kind lawyer
or that you're only 30 and a very good person,
but can't afford the transplant.

Cancer doesn't care.
It doesn't matter if you're rich or poor,
educated or not,
that you're 31 years old
and the sole breadwinner for your family.

This process
of proving your worth
and your right to claim it
is humiliating
and only sometimes fruitful.

2

DESERVINGNESS ON DISPLAY

It all started when Hannah's friend from church, Allison, posted a frantic note on Facebook that her young son Beckett had been hit and run over by a car while playing outside. Beckett was life flighted to a nearby trauma center with multiple organ failure. Allison "just had a really hard time. She was hysterical for days," Hannah recalled. Hannah kept checking in, asking what she could do, and after a few days she asked if anyone had offered to set up a GoFundMe. "No, no one's even thought of that," Allison replied. She was grateful for the help, exhausted by constantly providing updates and answering questions about Beckett's status and of course worried about the medical bills. Hannah built a crowdfunding page, including pictures of the family's blond-haired kids decked out in matching sports gear, surrounding Beckett's bedside at the hospital. "I think I included [the photos] just to show people that this is the sweetest family, they're doing everything that they're supposed to, their kids are well taken care of, these are good parents," Hannah explained. She wanted the sports photos to show that "this is a kid who has not had any health problems before, he's really healthy, he loves doing all these things."

Hannah's campaign adeptly communicated to an audience of donors that this was a family deserving of help: it was an unfortunate, horrible accident; Beckett was an innocent, previously healthy child struck down by misfortune; and they were "good parents," a "really sweet family." As someone who had struggled with debilitating chronic illnesses for many years, Hannah was no stranger to the silent moral logics that shape whether, and on what basis, people are deemed worthy of compassion. Later, she confided that she would never consider setting up a campaign for herself: "I'm just not the type of person who could do that."

Beckett's campaign ultimately raised about $5,000, and he made a nearly full recovery after several weeks of intensive care. Expressions of support and prayers for recovery poured in from their close-knit community. What many donors did not know, however, was that Hannah and Allison had gracefully withheld more complicated truths about his accident from the public narrative. In a scenario straight from many parents' worst nightmares, it was Beckett's father driving the car that ran him over. Beckett had wandered into the parking lot from the playground as his father was backing up their car. The family was "really scared about people judging them . . . so they didn't really tell many people." Hannah explained. "You see so much on social media of people just shaming other people for accidents like that," she remarked, that they decided to focus on Beckett's recovery and loving family. Hannah insisted they were "not keeping it a secret—if people [asked we planned to] tell them," but she also deleted inquisitive comments on their Facebook page so Allison wouldn't have to answer them.

Hannah thought people would have "understood that it could happen to anybody," but she wanted to spare Allison any public shame and preserve the family's privacy. The family didn't end up needing all the money the campaign raised. It was helpful, of course, but their church had mobilized a large support network to help with childcare and other needs, and they'd already reached their out-of-pocket maximum on their robust, employer-provided health insurance. Ultimately, what the campaign really provided was a place to cultivate social support and reaffirm the story that theirs was a good family whose tragedy arose through no fault of their own.

How does crowdfunding uphold, and reinforce, particular ideas about what it means to be deserving of help? Sites like GoFundMe have become powerful social arenas where ideas of goodness, merit, and deservingness are taken up, scrutinized, and circulated. Hannah's campaign for Allison's family is a telling example of how crowdfunders appeal to these ideas and how they use campaigns to reaffirm their own identities as good people and upstanding citizens. Powerful ideologies of deservingness and meritocracy have been foundational to many charitable and social relief efforts, but online crowdfunding introduces additional dimensions of public scrutiny and reinforces the moral toxicities of these long-standing ideas. It provides a powerful new public stage on which dramas of deservingness distract us from the more fundamental idea that everyone, regardless of problematic assessments of "merit," could be worthy of care and assistance when they need it.

ONLINE MERITOCRACIES

When users consider starting a GoFundMe campaign, they are bombarded by messages of opportunity. The company has good reason to present crowdfunding as a marketplace of equal opportunity, welcome to everyone. But most users quickly ascertain that not everyone is treated equally. As Hannah intuitively sensed, there were many ways that Allison's family appealed to the moral hierarchies of this marketplace. Wholesome, young, healthy, White, Christian, and beset by tragedy: it was an easy story to tell as long as they withheld key details about how the accident had actually happened. The pressure they felt to edit their story comes from the highly competitive economies of sites like GoFundMe, where each campaign must appear more uniquely deserving of aid, attention, and compassion than the next. There is little room for human fallibility here, nor for those who struggle, as Hannah herself did, with chronic health conditions that often elicit blame or assumptions that one's ill health is due to individual behaviors or decisions.

The moral terrain of crowdfunding is fueled by two persistent social ideologies that powerfully shape our social, health, and cultural systems: these are the dual, and intertwined, myths of meritocracy and the "deserving poor." Michael Young originally coined the term meritocracy in 1958, using it to describe Britain's transformation from a society where life chances were determined by one's status at birth to one where status was allocated based on personal achievement.[1] However, he used the term satirically, trying to describe how institutions that seemed merit based in fact rewarded and elevated those who already had the economic and social means to succeed.[2]

Meritocracy, as Daniel Markovitz has written, is a trap: societies, especially neoliberal economies such as the United States, have enshrined a system where people are told that if they just work hard enough they can succeed, but radically hierarchical and racist institutions reproduce and reinforce elitism.[3] When people fail to succeed in this system, it becomes particularly easy to blame their own efforts or characteristics rather than the falsely meritocratic systems themselves. "It is hard indeed in a society that makes so much of merit," wrote Young in 2001 as he reflected on this misuse of the term meritocracy, "to be judged as having none."[4] The ubiquity of our belief in meritocratic systems is evident in the widespread use of phrases like "equal opportunity" and "pull yourself up by your bootstraps." In particular, given the economic, educational, and social impacts of structural racism in US society, meritocracy upholds and justifies racial inequities. As Tressie McMillan Cottom observes, "We do not share much in the U.S. culture of individualism except our delusions about meritocracy. . . . I can talk to hundreds of black folks who have been systematically separated from their money, citizenship, and personhood and hear at least eighty stories about how no one is to blame but themselves. That is not about black people being black but about people being American. That is what we do."[5]

If meritocracy is a relatively recent myth, the myth of the deserving poor is a much older one. Political philosophers have long debated to whom society owes forms of social support.[6] As early as the seventeenth century, poor parishioners in England were given badges to wear in exchange for social support under the Elizabethan poor laws. These were intended to elicit shame and deter a sense of entitlement among the "able-bodied" poor.[7] By the 1800s, poor laws allowed citizens to "lay claim to aid from the state only on condition that they accept inferior status . . . [creating a] distinction between the deserving and the undeserving disadvantaged, between those who are not responsible for their misfortune and those who are."[8] In the United States, nineteenth-century charities upheld similar values: the social policies and programs which grew out of these practices, including health-care safety nets, powerfully upheld this ideology.[9]

As conservative leaders in both the United States and the United Kingdom retrenched postwar social programs in the 1980s and 1990s under the banner of neoliberalism, the "political imaginary of social welfare" shifted, creating dominant discourses that severely blamed the poor for their circumstances.[10] Narratives of a "culture of poverty" and racist, denigrating portraits of "welfare queens" laid the moral groundwork for exclusion from the body politic based on "presumed moral laxity."[11] Ironically, as Gay Becker observes, "deservingness [in US social policies] is related to productivity, and hence, to wealth—in short, to the ability to find the financial resources to pay for medical care."[12] Thus, those who most need financial assistance for care—due to structural racism and histories of economic exclusion—are often deemed the least deserving of it.

These dual myths of deservingness and meritocracy have been particularly powerful tools for upholding gender, class, and, particularly, racial hierarchies.[13] Charity given under such ideologies, Anderson writes, "reflects the mean-spirited, contemptuous, parochial vision of a society that represents human diversity hierarchically, moralistically contrasting the responsible and the irresponsible, the innately superior and the innately inferior, the independent and the dependent. It offers no aid to those it labels irresponsible, and humiliating aid to those it labels innately inferior."[14] As Amson Hagan shows, within the context of neoliberalism and post-Jim Crow racial resentments, deservingness increasingly became a means by which Black people could be scapegoated—with White Americans blaming Black Americans for getting too much support from scarce social programs while also blaming them, rather than structural inequities, for their circumstances.[15] Deservingness served to uphold racial hierarchies and signal that marginalized groups did not belong to the body politic.[16]

Finally, deservingness offers one more advantage to the powerful: it focuses social attention on constructing elaborate criteria by which the poor and powerless can be deprived of resources. These petty public dramas of deservingness distract us from turning our attention toward the rich and the powerful and asking how they came to deserve what they have or whether they have any obligations to redistribute their wealth. Selective deservingness enshrines the already powerful as arbiters of who will get handouts while insulating them from questions about why the powerless are left to fight for unfairly distributed handouts at all.

Meritocracy and deservingness are everywhere on sites like GoFundMe. Many popular campaigns implicitly or explicitly appeal to these values, using phrases like "hardworking," "breadwinner," "hero," and "supermom."[17] The rhetoric of superheroes is particularly prominent, especially among campaigns for children, reflecting the near superhuman characteristics of strength and goodness that crowdfunders must claim to succeed.[18] GoFundMe itself reflects this rhetoric by highlighting the work of "GoFundMe Heroes" and "kid heroes" through a podcast, social media accounts, and "heroes celebration" events.[19] Reflecting the mythology of meritocracy, GoFundMe brands its heroes as "everyday people doing extraordinary things."[20] Most of these so-called heroes are people who have launched projects to help communities or neighbors. Yet this rhetoric excludes a primary way that crowdfunding is used: by people seeking help for themselves in desperate circumstances. While GoFundMe highlights the ways it is "powered by kindness,"[21] its marketplace often quietly rewards campaigns that successfully appeal to the unkind and discriminatory myths of meritocracy and deservingness. While it is certainly not the first charitable system to do so, its wide-reaching platform is deepening and extending these myths in powerful ways.

SPECTACLES OF SELECTIVE DESERVINGNESS

For centuries, assessments of deservingness have been central to charitable giving. The individual virtues or character flaws of those in need are held up to public scrutiny, while compelling stories of misfortune are circulated to potential donors who seek to "save" the deserving poor. It would be impossible to cover the history of these practices in depth here, but their persistence over time provides an important antecedent to contemporary crowdfunding. Below, I present several exhibits of historical charity practices that have particular resonance with today's cultures of crowdfunding.

The Orphan Election Our first exhibit begins with a painting by George Elgar Hicks, depicting an "infant orphan election at the London Tavern, 'polling'" (figure 2.1).[22] In the painting, election posters and pamphlets don the walls of the tavern as colorfully dressed women and men engage in earnest conversation. In the foreground an anxious-looking widow, dressed all in black, clutches a small girl to her legs. In the right-hand corner several men in dark suits seem to be recording election results. Were it not for this painting, the practice of "orphan elections" might have been forgotten entirely. But so-called charity electioneering was a common practice in London society in the 1800s, whereby donors ("subscribers")

Figure 2.1 Hicks's *An Infant Orphan Election at the London Tavern, "Polling."* Source: Museum of London.

voted for those who would receive charity from institutions like orphanages, asylums, and hospitals.[23] Subscribers were allocated a certain number of votes and often campaigned for months on behalf of preferred candidates, using cards and circulars describing their unfortunate circumstances. Hicks's painting depicts an election to decide which infants would receive scarce spots in an orphanage after the death of one or both parents.

While an orphans' election may seem particularly distasteful to us today, its practice reflects dominant social mores of charitable giving. The first of these was the perceived scarcity of aid itself—that charitable aid was a rare gift to be bestowed only on the very most deserving. Deservingness here reflected the already socially entrenched stigmatization of the poor: elections were limited to the orphaned children of "upstanding members" of society. Those who were illegitimate, had deformities or disabilities, or whose families had previously received any "poor relief" would not be granted spots at many institutions.[24] The severe limitations placed on orphan 'candidates' stand in stark contrast with the voting liberties granted to subscribers. The private selection of an extraordinarily slim deserving few served not only as status symbol and entertainment for the donor class but also as a symbolic and political alternative to state-run relief projects.[25]

Queen for a Day The second exhibit brings us to late 1950s America, to a popular televised game show called *Queen for a Day*. The show had an eerily simple premise: several neatly coiffed women would be introduced to a live audience in fairly quick succession by host Jack Bailey, who coaxed each woman into briefly telling their story of woe and need before making a specific request of the show. Frequent commercial breaks featured a relentless series of modern home products marketed to women. The live audience would then vote for their favorite contestant by clapping for an applause meter as the camera zoomed in on the contestants' faces. The winner, crowned "queen for a day," was showered with gifts of modern appliances, outfits, and other prizes that the host promised would make her life easier. And then the "queen's" specific wish was granted—such as a vacation for an overworked housewife or diaper services for a mother of triplets. In one typical episode, Viva Birch, a serious and taciturn mother of a boy with cerebral palsy who had to stop working due to her own disability, wins the audience's favor. As she is crowned and seated on a throne, she looks so uncomfortable that one wonders, peering at the grainy footage, if she is actually crying (figure 2.2).

Even for its time, *Queen for a Day* was seen as crass and materialistic—it was banned in Mexico for its excessive promotion of consumer products as inappropriate fixes for suffering and poverty. As Amber Watts observes, the show offered "a direct correlation between the alleviation of misery and the acquisition of consumer goods, even if the goods were potentially useless for the recipient."[26] In a post-World War II consumerist society, the show's success hinged on the increasing visibility of women as household purchasers—and projected the idea that acquiring those goods could ameliorate social ills that grated against the public's notion of an affluent and generous American state (at least for White citizens).[27] Here we see the repeated motifs of charity scarcity and competition to demonstrate deservingness. Emergent forms of technology—television broadcasting, of course, but also applause meters—elicit a broader participation

Figure 2.2 Viva Birch, *Queen for a Day*. Source: Screenshot by author from: Classic TV Channel, "Queen for a Day—Episode #6," 18 Dec 2019, YouTube video, 22:13, https://youtube.com/watch?v=4YJ30r_dMJs.

than that of the rarefied members of charitable society in nineteenth-century London. But even here, inclusion is limited to the White, middle-class women consumers who serve as the show's primary audience.

Child Sponsorship Around the same time that *Queen for a Day* was airing in the United States, the American Christian evangelist Bob Pierce was working in China as a missionary, where he developed the idea of "child sponsorship," which serves as a third exhibit. Child sponsorship became the cornerstone project of World Vision and other Christian development aid organizations, spreading to nearly every low- and lower-middle-income country around the world. The premise of child sponsorship was simple: Christians in higher-income countries were invited to "sponsor" an orphan or needy child abroad and committed to providing monthly or yearly support for their well-being. Sponsors were sent pictures and information about "their" child and wrote frequent letters in return, encouraging faith, educational commitment, and hard work.[28]

While World Vision has shifted its focus over time from support for individual orphans to families, and eventually to communities, the collection of names of needy children continues to be a primary way that donor interest is cultivated, and recipient communities participate, in World Vision's projects.[29]

Marketing children's personal stories of struggle and orphanhood remains central to World Vision's fundraising and public outreach, as we can see in figure 2.3, which shows the organization's headquarters outside Seattle. Visitors are encouraged to contemplate each child's story and sign up to become a sponsor. As Erica Bornstein shows, the relationships fostered by such sponsorship are intimate but shaped by steep hierarchies between sponsor and child.[30] Many critics cite the program as an example of "poverty porn" and exploitative White savior practices.[31] Its resonance with the London orphan elections is striking, though World Vision's success relies more heavily on the power of interpersonal charity. The opportunities for identity formation, relationship building, and meaning-making practices *for donors* is an engine that drives this model of development.[32] World Vision has also, however, faced persistent critiques from donors who feel the organization has misrepresented the allocation of funds that goes to sponsored children and the impacts donations have on children's lives.[33] These disappointments reflect the norms of a donor-recipient relationship premised on ideals of personal investment and even, perhaps, ownership rather than Christian biblical ideals of charity.

Kiva.org These relational bonds across distance bring us into the (nearly) present day, to the globalized and unequal economies that have given rise to crowdfunding platforms. While many think of project investment platforms like Kickstarter or Indiegogo as the predecessors to donation-based crowdfunding sites like GoFundMe, these platforms all borrow tactics from an earlier model—the wildly popular and remarkably persistent nonprofit microlending platform Kiva.org. Founded in 2005 by two Americans who were inspired by the work of Nobel prize-winning economist and Grameen Bank founder Muhammad Yunus, Kiva connects lenders in primarily high-income countries with mostly female loan takers in lower-income countries, who are given microloans for commercial projects they wish to pursue. Kiva's website focuses on campaigns

Figure 2.3 Child sponsorship pamphlets attached to the wall of a replica mud hut, World Vision headquarters. Photo by author, 2014.

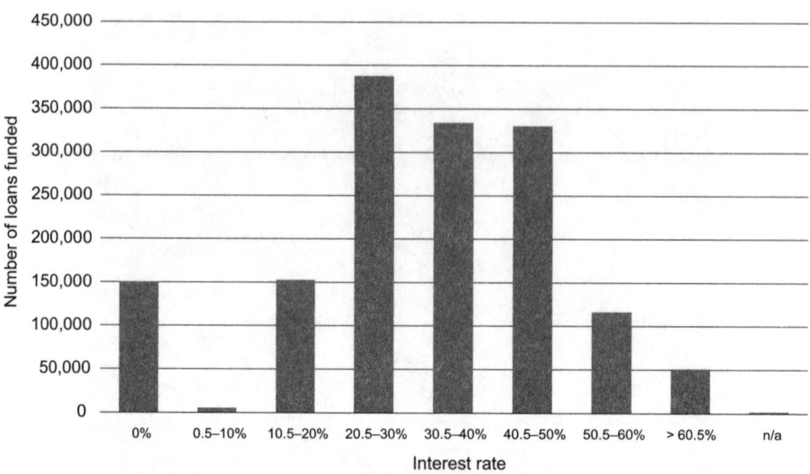

Figure 2.4 Kiva loans, grouped by interest rate. Data source: "Kiva (organization)," Wikimedia Foundation, https://en.wikipedia.org/wiki/Kiva_(organization).

by individual entrepreneurs, featuring their stories and photos alongside statistics about their home country. Lenders are encouraged to "support the causes you care about and make a real personal impact."[34]

Despite glowing accolades from the development and finance communities, experts have warned for many years that Kiva's model is not as straightforward as it seems and poses serious potential harms for loan borrowers.[35] Kiva works through local lending institutions that set interest rates and hold borrowers to account. The interest rates on many loans are extremely high, as depicted in figure 2.4. The net result is that the empowerment goals promised by microcredit loans are undermined by the substantial risks those loans carry and the relative lack of power borrowers have to set terms, create the kind of economic sustainability needed to repay them with interest, or even be the primary household member managing the loan.[36] Studies have shown that women borrowers are more likely to be victims of familial violence due to the ways loans can increase anxiety and gender tensions and cultivate an "economy of shame" for borrowers who feel extreme pressure to pay back loans.[37] As Megan Moodie observes, "microfinance is successful on a global scale . . . because it translates risk into peril . . . [it] operationalizes and sometimes increases social vulnerabilities" for borrowers while radically reducing risk for lenders.[38] The "story factory" of platforms like Kiva creates bonds between borrowers and lenders that, unintentionally, cultivate many of the stresses and harms of the micro lending practice.[39]

Part of the reason Kiva remains so popular is that it marries personalized charitable practices (like child sponsorship and orphan auctions) with technology that further shortens the emotional and geographical distance between giver and recipient. (Ironically, most loans actually do not go to the person that lenders think they are lending to; they often go to the partner lending institutions in countries that have already disbursed loans.)[40] Notably, Kiva has also taken "giving" out of the equation: donors provide loans that are repaid in full so that they risk little in choosing worthy charity projects while retaining power of choice.

These are only glimpses of charitable practices and spectacles across time, but they share common threads. The rights of donors and publics to choose who receives artificially scarce charitable goods stands as a counterpoint to rights-based systems of social support, where citizens have broadly recognized rights to healthcare, shelter, and other basic needs. Those in need must compete—or must have others compete on their behalf—to "win" favor against sometimes great odds. Conversely, for donors, charitable giving provides an opportunity to elevate their identity, relationships, and social status—either through event and spectacle or through intimate but hierarchical bonds between donor and recipient. Storytelling becomes an important way of assessing and judging people seeking aid. As modern health and social systems are increasingly driven by data, numbers, and metrics, these examples show that the "skillful manufacture of stories" is still essential to the affective, relational, and value-laden ways we decide who deserves and who does not.[41]

Charitable crowdfunding is a natural outgrowth of these predecessors, but it makes deservingness and charitable inequity even more challenging for the needy to navigate in several important ways. Technology has increased the specificity, intimacy, and proximity of stories in charitable appeals and has dramatically expanded the size of their potential audience. At the same time, it has increased the marketing and competition among campaigners. Crowdfunding creates an online marketplace that relies on the supposed "wisdom of the crowd" to sort the deserving from the undeserving.[42] But that is not how the market actually works. Instead, visibility, success, and even the ability to craft a compelling story depends to a great degree on who you are, what you need, and who you know. The sheer volume of campaigns and the anonymity of many donors on crowdfunding platforms makes it harder to see these forces at work. What campaigners must offer to compete in this environment and to create connections with potential donors, however, is deeply intimate, and, as Hannah and Allison knew, subject to the scrutiny and judgment that people so often encounter on social media.

Stories are an important way for us to understand the full extent of inequalities between different crowdfunders online and how these are shaped by ideologies of meritocracy and deservingness. Here, I am not referring to the stories that crowdfunders craft for their campaigns but stories of their actual crowdfunding experiences. The complex (and often invisible) dynamics of inequity that shape these experiences are clear in the following two campaign stories. While these stories begin similarly, their fates quickly diverge. They help us to understand just how fiercely competitive, and unfairly selective, this marketplace has become.

DIEGO AND MARIANA

Diego is a twenty-year-old Latino college student from the Yakima Valley of Washington State, a richly productive agricultural region whose economy has been built on steep racial and economic inequalities. A fifth of the population in Diego's hometown lives below the poverty line, and nearly a third reports fair or poor health status.[43] When Diego's eighteen-year-old cousin Mariana suffered a permanent brain injury in a car accident, his family asked him to create a crowdfunding campaign. As a computer science major, Diego was seen as the most tech-savvy member of his family. The campaign he set up offered a very brief narrative describing Mariana's accident and a photo of her before the crash, smiling radiantly. Diego's close-knit family was unwilling to share many details of Mariana's situation via the campaign page. Diego said they didn't want "to seem like they were just trying to get pity." It was hard, he observed, "to just balance the things that they didn't want to share . . . and the things that were sort of important to having [in] the campaign, to make sure people knew the seriousness" of the case.

In our discussion, Diego filled in the gaps in that story in short, stoic sentences. Mariana was not wearing a seatbelt. She flew through a window of the car and stopped breathing at the site of the crash. She had no health insurance, and the driver had no car insurance. She was pregnant at the time of the crash, and doctors told the family they could either try to save her or try to keep her alive to save the baby. Mariana's family made the agonizing choice to keep her on life support until the baby could be delivered; she eventually died at home, though her baby survived. Her health-care costs were astronomical, including more than a month spent in intensive care. "All the financial burden fell on my family," Diego explained; he was sure his uncle, an agricultural worker, would "be in debt until he dies."

Despite Mariana's care costs, Diego had low expectations for the GoFundMe campaign, saying that "we were just hoping to start at . . . a low starting point . . . and see where it would go." Ultimately, they raised $1,200 toward a $2,500 goal, which he thought was "a little more successful than I expected it to be." The family also hosted community dinners and raffles; many in their community preferred these in-person methods of fundraising because of technological barriers and suspicions about online fundraising. "I think people like seeing the things happening in person," Diego observed. "[It offers] a sense of reassurance that you aren't just putting your credit card info on some website." Eventually, the family soured on GoFundMe after seeing that the platform took "a significant portion of the donations." "At the beginning, it didn't feel like such a big deal," Diego said, "because I figured they have to run the website somehow. But at the same time, once I . . . did the math and everything else, I was like, 'that is actually a little more significant than just a few dollars.'"

Diego's family's experience reflects multiple ways that crowdfunding platforms can exclude, diminish, and further disenfranchise already marginalized users. Encouraging campaigners to set low goals and lower expectations ensures that even "successful" campaigns cannot cover relatively small medical costs. Thus, the cultivated effect of campaign outcomes—"it was a little more successful than I expected it to be"—coexists with grief and disappointment arising from debt, loss, and silences. Percentage fees charged by websites (a norm when Diego ran his campaign) can seem most significant in low-earning campaigns where every dollar is precious. Limited trust in technology means campaigners face diminished returns for online labors and more offline labors to raise money. Most importantly, there is the type of narrative that families like Diego's can construct. He notes the care they took not to seem pitiable—and to protect their privacy, likely because of worries about how their family, as immigrants, would be perceived. Their reluctance to share details on the campaign page reveals how disclosure, storytelling, and public engagement experiences can differ across social hierarchies.[44] Their experiences echo hierarchies of deservingness in the United States that limit the claims that campaigners from already marginalized communities can make in public.[45]

SPENCER, MARK, AND SOFIA

The same week that Diego told his story, Spencer suggested we meet at a trendy coffee shop to talk about the campaign he'd set up for his close friends, Mark and Sofia. The couple are married with two children and are recognized as community leaders in the Pacific Northwest. Sofia is originally from South America and works on immigration issues; Mark is a well-known Christian social entrepreneur. A year prior, they had been involved in a serious car accident while celebrating their anniversary in Mexico. Stranded without travelers or rental car insurance, Spencer recalled that "their first fear as they're trying to survive a near-death experience, their first fear was like, can we pay for this, can we get home." While they had health insurance, they worried about what it would cover, and their injuries were severe enough to require medical repatriation to the United States. Spencer repeatedly described their situation as "dramatic," especially their fight to get medical repatriation covered by their American Express card. He also raised questions about the other driver involved in the accident, calling inconclusive police reports "a pretty classic coverup" and a "shady government deal" to conceal evidence.

After Spencer got Mark and Sofia's call from Mexico, he worked all night to set up a crowdfunding campaign on YouCaring. He solicited support from other friends, "gathering people in for their skill sets." Lawyers helped negotiate with the credit card company; others handled media requests. Spencer noted that "all the people on [the] team had either the financial ability to take the time off, or some of them like me. . . . [I'm] in charge of my schedule." They created several social media accounts for the campaign and online forms to organize volunteers. Within an hour of launching, the campaign reached its initial $7,000 goal. From his hospital bed, Mark created a hashtag—#fellowshipofcare—to describe their remarkable mobilization.

The campaign, to put it in Spencer's terms, "blew up." Friends "basically ran a budget on what all the potential expenses would be," from childcare to flying in parents for support to long-term counseling and therapeutic services, and then raised the campaign goal to $75,000. Early success increased exponentially as YouCaring's site algorithms made the campaign more visible. "As far as I know, a lot of [our] supporters were just from YouCaring," Spencer remarked. "That happens more with these larger [campaigns] I think, where it just trends on [the site]." This led to considerable media coverage since the media "just check these sites . . . for things that are starting to trend." In less than two weeks, they met their goal.

Soon, it became clear that their projected costs were grossly overestimated. American Express covered the medical flight, health insurance came through, and friends and family covered other costs directly. "It was a little scary," Spencer recalled. "We were thinking, can we give the money back if we don't need it? How does this work?" Platforms provide little way for fundraisers to do this or for them to redistribute funds to less successful campaigns. Instead, success opened new doors to imagining what care could look like for Mark and Sofia. "That's what I love about the YouCaring concept," Spencer said, "is it can actually help people think . . . long term and actually get the funds . . . to do that self-care." He went so far as to credit the platform's design with their rapid medical recoveries: "What's beautiful about YouCaring is that it shows all of those supporters . . . the design, [with] the funders on the right, where it scrolls down through all the people [who donated] and their little comments . . . that is like an additional boost." He noted that cash donations were evidence that well wishes were "not trite" but showed people were really "there for you." Mark and Sofia recovered quickly after several surgeries. Left with a vast surplus of funds from the campaign, Sofia quit her "high-stress" job and started a community coffee shop in a rapidly gentrifying neighborhood.

Spencer was forthcoming about why the campaign was so successful. First, he credited Mark's and Sofia's identities: "they had already established themselves in the world as people who care." Mark and Sofia benefit from a narrative in which they are blameless humanitarians caught in a situation made worse by non-White, suspicious others. "It was no fault of their own. . . . That's one of the key pieces for me," Spencer explained. "Like if I go climb a cliff, and fall off, because I'm stupid, I'm probably going to feel awkward about crowdfunding for that. . . . [Mark and Sofia's] story was so much more powerful. It was dramatic, it was fast, and it was, like, criminal. And it happened in another country." Mark and Sofia also benefited from significant social capital, the many talented friends who leveraged expertise on their behalf, and the benefit of the doubt given to them by media outlets and donors. Their ability to be perceived as "doing good" in the community is deeply linked to classist, racist, and nationalist notions of who provides help, who receives it, and what doing good looks like.

Spencer credits two other successful campaign elements: first, the outcome was unknown but hopeful, offering the likelihood of a happy ending, and second, he was careful to "keep . . . any of the desperation" out of their story. I wondered whether and how Mariana's family might have leveraged similar narrative arcs. If successful crowdfunding relies on offering narratives of resilience, deservingness, and hope, for whom are these available? Contrasted with Spencer's frequent invocation of the value of "drama," the dramas of Mariana's story remain hidden and even become shameful. Her story was certainly tragic—but not in ways that could be expressed, or find value, online.

"Stark" is a deeply inadequate descriptor for the disparities between these campaigns, which accumulate along multiple axes of inequity—race, immigration status, class, education, social capital, and age. Credibility and deservingness differ not just between Mariana and Mark and Sofia but also in the ways technology is perceived and used. Diego's neighbors and family, who needed in-person fundraisers and eschewed websites that asked for their personal information, show how technology is experienced and leveraged differently across social strata. Beyond the technology, however, these campaigns raise questions about the moral toxicities that shape crowdfunding and health systems: Who gets to be seen as good? What claims do different people get to make about their rights to basic care? When is crowdfunding an opportunity for growth, and when is it an excuse for social abandonment? One final story will help us understand how crowdfunders are internalizing and making sense of these questions and, in doing so, are normalizing the hierarchies of deservingness on crowdfunding platforms.

FROM THE DESERVING POOR TO THE DESERVING POPULAR

Crowdfunding creates a powerful social media culture that upholds, and extends, the moral toxicity of selective deservingness, disguising it within a platform that appears to offer equal opportunities for everyone. The power of the crowd is not that it magically manages to select those who are most in need of help; rather, it powerfully selects for a rarefied group of beneficiaries. Crowdfunding takes the narrow, exclusionary, and discriminatory category of the "deserving poor" elevated by orphan elections and poverty programs and twists it into a new category of selective deservingness: *the deserving popular*. As Mark and Sofia's campaign demonstrates, many of the deserving popular are not even that needy—they have experienced unfortunate crises or setbacks, but instead of providing a safety net, crowdfunding provides them with a trampoline, allowing them to reach greater heights of social status, self-determination, and achievement. Like influencers on other platforms, campaigners like Mark, Sofia, and Spencer leverage hashtags, build connections with audiences, and create a brand out of their campaign.[46] So, too, do campaigns often succeed when their organizers or recipients have already created an online personal brand for themselves with a following that can be naturally tapped into for support.

Troublingly, campaigners, donors, and public audiences have begun to conflate crowdfunding success with goodness and deservingness, adding further weight to the legitimacy of the deserving popular. FundRazr's CEO Darryl Hatton described crowdfunding to me as "an ATM on your karma bank. If you've been depositing a lot of karma into your community over your lifetime, when you have a crisis, crowdfunding lets you make a quick withdrawal when you need the cash." But as crowdfunding becomes more popular and more competitive, the selective deservingness of its economy becomes even more contorted. No longer is it just that campaigns are successful because they are deserving: instead, people are perceived as deserving because their campaigns are successful and popular.

Danny's experience helps illustrate this point. He was already a fairly well-known local media personality in a large urban city when he got hit by a car. Chelsea, his coworker, started a GoFundMe, and it expanded quickly. She recalled, "we talked about it a little bit on air, but we didn't direct people towards it at all. And then some of us who work for the station . . . do have [people] that follow us on social media and probably saw it. There's quite a few communities that he's a part of, [so] it . . . circulated quickly." Chelsea, a producer and social media manager, drew on her skills to craft the campaign and direct attention to it. But it was not a lot of work—the campaign seemed to spread naturally across social media networks, quickly raising more than $30,000.

Chelsea attributed its success not to her skills, nor to Danny's social prestige, nor to the extensive media exposure but to Danny being a "good person": "one thing we learned, and the thing that . . . his wife kept telling me about [was that Danny's reputation] was their insurance. She said, 'you know you've been doing something right in life, when this type of response happens.' . . . And he's just a great person. Danny's a kind person. Nobody complains about Danny. So, I think it was just, it was that." The explanation Chelsea offered for Danny's success disregarded the many social, economic, and media assets that helped his campaign easily achieve success. The focus on individual stories and merits in crowdfunding economies makes it easy to disregard these more structural determinants of success.

Chelsea's reflections demonstrated the ways that crowdfunding economies conflate popularity with goodness, trustworthiness, and deservingness. She talked openly about what she felt was and was not a legitimate reason to use crowdfunding. She admitted she wouldn't use it for herself because "I just like to earn what I get," and she disapproved of people who "rely on GoFundMe for medical" needs because it "gives people the excuse not to save money." At the same time, however, she felt that Danny's reliance on the platform, even as a form of "insurance," as she put it, was justified. Danny and his wife could be trusted with the money, whereas other crowdfunders were less reliable. "Even if [Danny and his wife used the money to] go on vacation, you know what you're contributing to," she argued. In her mind, Danny's socially verified goodness made his campaign far more trustworthy than others even if the funds were used for nonessential expenses.

During our conversation, Chelsea brought up two recent campaigns that had received national media attention; both involved young Black children who had been trying to earn money in their neighborhoods and faced racist treatment from neighbors and the police. But Chelsea did not recognize the racist events motivating these campaigns, or if she did, she avoided mentioning them. Admitting it was a "crappy situation," she argued that they should not be crowdfunding. "I don't necessarily think you should throw money at people that are dealing with that type of situation, whatever it is. . . . [In that situation] I don't think you set up a GoFundMe because the point of [what the kids are doing] is to be an entrepreneur, and earn the money they are making, and you're taking that away by just throwing it at them because somebody complained." Referring to Danny's campaign, she explained, "There's situations where I think GoFundMe is fantastic because it's like, somebody has been dealt a really shitty hand and now they have people in their lives that want to help because they're returning the favor of being around a good person." Chelsea gave voice to norms of the deserving popular that often remain silent on crowdfunding sites but powerfully shape who crowdfunds, how their campaigns are treated, and whether they find help on the site. These norms are rooted in histories of structural racism, class and racial hierarchies, neoliberal ideologies, and the ways that charity has been used as a tool to police who belongs in US society. Crowdfunding platforms conceal these norms under a simplistic veneer of "good people making a difference in other people's lives." Those who get to be seen as good are a rarefied, privileged group of people.

Chelsea's perspective also highlights how crowdfunding is undermining the idea that everyone should deserve access to healthcare when they need it. When popularity—people "returning the favor of being around a good person"—becomes a form of "insurance," we quickly lose sight of a more universal kind of deservingness: the idea that everyone has a right to adequate healthcare regardless of how popular or even how "good" they might be. In crowdfunding's hypercompetitive online marketplace, where the volume of need is overwhelming, donors must use more and more scrutiny to decide who is and is not worthy. Thus, inadequate systems of health coverage fuel the demand and competition that reinforces selective deservingness, which then further undermines public recognition of a more basic, universal right to healthcare. The form of insurance Chelsea and many others embrace with crowdfunding helps the deserving popular succeed, and even thrive, while causing disproportionate harm to those who need help the most.

When health relies on the charity of a digital crowd, it creates and exacerbates deep inequities and undermines claims to more universal, rights-based systems of healthcare. As Ralph Nader argues, "a society that has more justice . . . needs less charity."[47] Crowdfunding shows that the inverse of this statement is also true: more charity means less justice. Ultimately, the spillover effects of crowdfunded care impact everyone: the world of the deserving popular is a very unhealthy place to end up. The next two chapters explore how crowdfunding fuels inequities and disparate health outcomes while reinforcing a perception of the crowd-based economy as "democratic" and "wise." Real-world data reveals just how unequal the crowdfunding marketplace is, particularly for those who need the most help. But more broadly, it shows that the inequities of crowdfunding act like toxins that affect all of us—our health, our sense of what we owe each other, and our visions for the future.

Be the first to donate!

Save baby Ayana

GIGI'S FIGHT AGAINST ALS

Our 34 yr. Old Brother Has A Rare Form of Cancer

Nuestro hijo Daniel contra el Cancer Cerebral

Little Brave Benjamin Needs a Bone Marrow Transplant

Fernando Fights Leukemia

Fort Worth ICU Nurses Need Supplies

Micah needs a new heart

CANCER SUCKS

Necesito de tu ayuda tengo Cancer de Mama

Mom is losing her battle with cancer

5 different cancers all stage 4

We are Asking for any help feel free to contribute

Please Help Carter

AYUDEMOS A JUAN MANUEL

Help save Miguel

Ayuda a Benjamin

Please help us save Adelita's life

Make A Dream Come True

3

THE WISDOM OF THE CROWD?

Crowdfunding, GoFundMe's CEO Rob Solomon once said, is the "great democratizer." "It's the power of people coming together to help each other out," and it's also where people go "to voice their displeasure and put their money where their mouth is."[1] Crowdfunding enables people to "vote with their wallets."[2] In the worldview of Solomon and other supporters of crowdfunding, the appeal of this new technology is that it allows the "wisdom of the crowd" to be instantaneously sought out, amalgamated, and directed toward causes. "The key is," Solomon said, "everyone has equal access and the most compelling ideas win out . . . Each [idea] is evaluated in the clearest terms possible—donations."

Solomon offers an appealing, if oversimplified and erroneous, account about what happens when "the crowd" gets involved in charity. Rather than democratize it, crowdfunding powerfully reinforces the status quo. Many campaigners find themselves "crowded out" of this economy by its steep hierarchies and inequalities. And as crowdfunding normalizes the idea of the "deserving popular," the inequities that shape this economy also become more normalized and harder to discern.

There is a powerful, self-reinforcing dynamic that produces such "crowding out." Deep social and economic inequalities, exacerbated by decades of neoliberalism and centuries of racial capitalism, give rise to crowdfunding and its popularity. These inequalities, as the previous chapter showed, also reinforce ideas of selective deservingness and meritocracy that make crowdfunding more appealing and popular. And as crowdfunding becomes more ubiquitous, it reinforces and reproduces these inequities, generally diverting more resources to those like Mark and Sofia, who already have more social and financial capital, and less to those like Mariana and Diego, who are more marginalized. But to sustain its popularity, crowdfunding must conceal the severity of these inequities and defend why some campaigns do better than others. As industry leaders like Solomon promote the wisdom of the crowd and describe crowdfunding as "democratizing" charity, they further conceal and reinforce the inequities that shape this marketplace.

No two crowdfunding stories are identical, and myriad factors shape any single crowdfunding campaign's outcomes. This makes it particularly difficult to discern how specific factors affect campaigns—their success, visibility, and even perceived deservingness. There is no single, cohesive rule about who succeeds and who does not when it comes to crowdfunding. What we can observe are broad trends, using larger datasets that represent a range of crowdfunding experiences. This chapter summarizes these broad trends alongside insights from individual crowdfunders and industry experts. Taken together, this research documents consistent and egregious inequities within the crowdfunding marketplace. These show up at every stage of the crowdfunding experience, influencing everything from whether someone turns to crowdfunding in the first place to the visibility and permanence of campaigns after they are over. This chapter is organized so that it follows the lifespan of crowdfunding campaigns from start to finish, exploring how and why inequities arise at each stage of the process.

GETTING STARTED

GoFundMe's webpage on starting a campaign oozes with friendly enthusiasm: "Welcome! GoFundMe is the world's largest crowdfunding platform. . . . With a community of more than 50 million donors, GoFundMe is changing the way the world gives."[3] Other platforms similarly inundate users with messages about how easy it is to begin a campaign, often using data to convey how popular these new fundraising strategies are. The personal fundraising homepage for Fundly, one of GoFundMe's competitors, insists that "anyone can create a fundraising page to raise money for themselves or someone in need. People all over the world are creating fundraising pages to help cover tuition, medical expenses, and so much more."[4] Crowdfunding sites emphasize opportunity and ease of use alongside the democratizing and empowering aspects of their platforms. GoFundMe promises users they can "harness the power of social media to spread your story and get more support," while Fundly advertises that with its platform, "individuals are empowered to share their stories and ask for help."[5] Statements like these conceal a more complex reality of uneven empowerment and access.

In an introductory video for first-time users, GoFundMe claims that "creating a fundraiser is a simple and quick process." Indeed, many users have told me that this a primary benefit of using the platform.[6] And yet the video goes on to explain numerous exclusions: GoFundMe only allows people from a small group of wealthy countries to start campaigns, and to receive funds, US users need both a bank account and a social security number. Users also need a smartphone or computer and an email address to set up their campaign as well as reliable internet to access and maintain it. They must be able to craft a compelling, clear, and marketable story, and they are told that fundraisers featuring a high-quality photo or video "are generally more successful than those that do not."[7] And, perhaps most importantly, they must be ready and willing to share their campaign with as many people as possible. "Remember," GoFundMe tells users, "sharing is the key part to getting donations on GoFundMe. If you aren't sharing your fundraiser with your friends, family, and community, then it's not likely to get donations. Using your personal network can help get you closer to your goal."[8]

While crowdfunding may be quite easy for most people to use, for those who are the most marginalized and financially underresourced, there are significant barriers. Many people in the United States still face significant barriers in accessing the internet, social media, and formal banking services. As of 2021, 15 percent of Americans did not have smartphones, and more than 25 percent didn't use any kind of social media.[9] Digital skills and literacies remain a major axis of inequality, particularly for older adults. The Pew Research Center reports that more than a quarter of adults "say they usually need someone to set up a new computer, smartphone or other electronic device for them," and a tenth of Americans report they feel "not at all" or "only a little confident" using personal technology for the things they need to do online.[10]

Because most crowdfunding platforms require banking information and social security numbers, these are also significant barriers, particularly for immigrant and low-income populations. A substantial proportion of people in the United States classify as "unbanked" or "underbanked"—that is, they don't have bank accounts or rely on expensive alternative banking services like payday lenders. While 5.4 percent of US households overall are unbanked, these percentages are far higher—often between 15 and 25 percent—among low-income, less-educated, and Hispanic and Black households.[11] Without access to banking services, most crowdfunding users cannot receive funds from their campaigns.

Crowdfunding disparities arise from both access barriers (e.g., limited technology, internet, social media, and banking access in more vulnerable groups) and complex sociopolitical dynamics that make people with marginalized identities more or less inclined to crowdfund. Education, media literacy, and digital skills shape how easily users can set up and run a campaign and distribute it among their network, as in the case of Diego's family and friends.[12] Older generations, particularly from marginalized racial and ethnic groups, can be more reticent to use crowdfunding platforms. Alejandra, who managed several campaigns for family and friends, told me that many members of her extended Mexican American family distrusted online donations and preferred to do things in person. Instead of raising money online, "you know, we made trays of enchiladas and baked cookies and set up . . . *social night*, where, you know, you come and you pay . . . and hang out with your friends or whatever . . . [it's] probably a bunch of Mexican aunts and, you know, *tias* . . . cooking and raising money." Some of the reticence to use digital crowdfunding platforms is cultural and generational. As another crowdfunder, a second-generation immigrant from West Africa, told me, "It's a very American, Western idea to do that. And so, yeah, there's some cultural [differences]. Even in my culture, my parents [would be like,] no. People will give you money privately . . . if we have someone die, a funeral, people give donations. But not an online [fundraiser] . . . my mom would be mortified. You're not gonna put [our] business online in that way."

Alejandra described how both language and technology barriers contributed to the reticence to use social media platforms in her community. "I think just technologically and with language . . . the understanding with the migrant community of our country is still one generation behind. . . . I'm 36, and I'm using online resources and crowdfunding . . . [while] my mom's generation, she barely understands Facebook."

These barriers amount to more than just generational or cultural differences. I asked Aliya, a critical care nurse in a major public hospital who crowdfunded for a colleague, why more of her patients don't start crowdfunding campaigns. She works at a major trauma center, where many patients can't afford their care, and sees tragic and devastating cases every day. No stranger to health and social inequities in her work, Aliya quickly began listing the many barriers her patients might face in using crowdfunding,

> "I don't think . . . [my] homeless patients, they're not doing a GoFundMe . . . if you don't even have a phone, if you live on the street, how are you going to? Who is donating for you? . . . In my opinion, it's those with families, with strong support systems, with people to reach out to, with 600,000 friends on Facebook. It's those with, I guess . . . some community. . . . If you're estranged from your family, if you're undocumented, if you're, I would even say, a first-generation immigrant, if there's a language barrier. I don't know, is GoFundMe in different languages? Would you think to use that?"

In fact, she reflected, "most of our patients" probably couldn't crowdfund at all.

When it comes to digital disparities, it's important to move beyond overly simplistic, black-and-white portrayals of difference. Rather than think about digital "divides" between people who "have" and "have not" got access to technology, or imagining social media as being simply "good" or "bad" for certain communities, it's useful to think in terms of a spectrum of experiences.[13] The internet is a "system that *reflects*, and a site that *structures*, power and values"—that is, it both reflects existing power inequities and can also fuel them through the new social spaces, opportunities, and relationships to which it provides access.[14] For those in marginalized groups, social media and digital technology use typically comes with higher costs, more drawbacks, and more potentials for disparity than it does for dominant groups. While we tend to think of technology as open and objective, bias and discrimination suffuse many technologies, from pulse oximeters that have been shown not to work on darker skin to search algorithms that amplify racist results.[15] As Ruha

Benjamin writes, new technologies are often a "subtle but no less hostile form of systemic bias."[16]

Disparities also emerge in how technologies are taken up and used. A great deal of research has shown that health technologies, for example, are more easily leveraged, and to more advantageous ends, by people with greater resources and social status.[17] Meanwhile, technologies are also wielded in ways that disproportionately harm, police, surveil, and extract resources from marginalized communities.[18] Finally, as is all too familiar for many these days, social media can powerfully incubate, amplify, and legitimize extremism, hate, and violence.[19]

Reticence in using technologies like digital crowdfunding platforms, particularly among historically marginalized and overpoliced communities, can reflect the excessive surveillance, privacy infringements, and harm that these communities experience as they come into contact with various digital technologies.[20] Crowdfunding campaigns are hardly insulated from these dynamics and likely exacerbate them. But harm is not the only dimension of these experiences: as Andre Brock and other scholars have powerfully examined, the internet and social media also offer spaces for building, strengthening, and celebrating social, cultural, racial, and other dimensions of collective identity and meaning-making.[21] As one of many internet spaces where people seek connection, support, validation, and voice, crowdfunding encapsulates these tensions, disparities, and possibilities.

As the last chapter introduced, ideologies of deservingness, so rooted in racist and classist discrimination, influence who can turn to crowdfunding and find success there. Some users set up campaigns and then never share them due to shame or internalized feelings about their own worthiness, and others never manage to start a campaign at all. As Trevor, the single father with diabetes, explained in the introduction, "I did research to look at other people's GoFundMe pages and I was just like, holy shit. I have no right to be asking for money on this page with some of the [other] stories that I read and what they're going through." Even those who do end up crowdfunding often do so only because someone else sets up a campaign for them. Kayla, the young mom with stage-four cancer from chapter 1, just didn't "want to ask for help" her friend Susie recalled. "I think she almost feels like she's not deserving of it," she said, "and there are people suffering and struggling worse than her. I think she's just very humble . . . she would have been like, 'Seriously, me? Why me, out of all these people?' She doesn't see her own need." As chapter 2 explored, crowdfunding's popularity and visibility spreads and normalizes these ideas of selective deservingness.

Deeply held taboos, particularly among lower-income Americans, about asking for help also impact who is willing to crowdfund and for what types of causes. Nearly everyone I have spoken to about crowdfunding indicated that they felt a deep discomfort about the idea of crowdfunding for themselves and would only do so in the most desperate of circumstances. After crowdfunding on behalf of a charitable organization, Camilla realized she could never do it for herself:

> I was telling my husband, "I . . . don't think I [could] ever do this. I think I'd rather be homeless under a bridge than ask people for money." And he's like, "If it comes down to it, why wouldn't you?" And I—I don't know if it's my anxiety, or what; but I have discovered this year that I don't think I could ever start a GoFundMe for myself, I think it would make me very uncomfortable. If it made me so uncomfortable asking people for money [that] wasn't [even] coming to me, it was [going] directly to the charity, I can only imagine if that money was coming to me.

Others talked about the shame they felt from family and friends when they did decide to crowdfund for themselves. One woman whose home had been destroyed in a natural disaster reported that her own sister refused to share her campaign on social media "because she was embarrassed. I know she was." She spoke of the particular hurt it caused that her sister, despite being fairly well off and having contributed to more public crowdfunding campaigns, had not so much as shared her own plea for assistance.

Finally, creating and narrating a campaign story requires technical, media, and health literacies, especially in order to appear credible and deserving. Successful crowdfunding often requires digital skills, social media literacies, and the ability to craft compelling narratives about complex medical topics. Research has shown that campaigns with shorter narratives, more grammatical errors, and less narration of deservingness have poorer outcomes.[22] In an early study of GoFundMe campaigns, Lauren Berliner and I observed a "double bind of the poor" in leveraging crowdfunding: "the more generalized one's distress or the more complex

Let's show Jackie some love

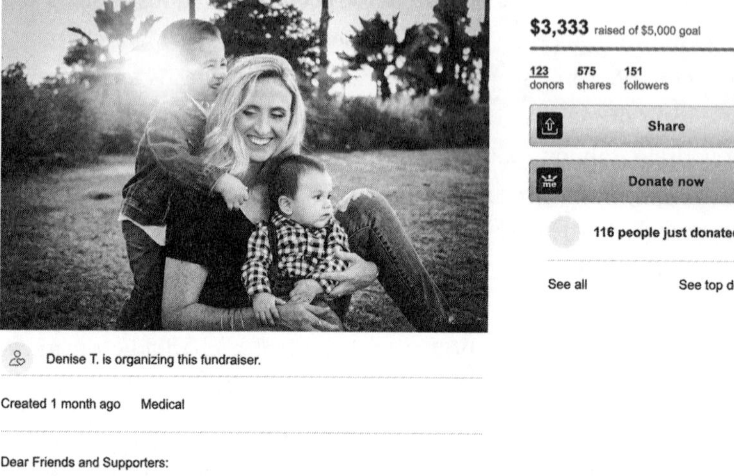

Dear Friends and Supporters:

As many of you know, Jackie is an utterly amazing person: a loving mom to two beautiful little boys, a dedicated wife, a hardworking nurse, and loved by everyone who knows her. She has given so much to her family and community, and now it's time for us to give back to her.

You see, Jackie just got the news we were all dreading - she's been diagnosed with stage 3 lymphoma (cancer). She will need surgery and chemo, and likely be off work for quite some time. While she's got insurance, we all know how medical bills can pile up, and we want to make sure she has as much time as possible to focus on her recovery and her family. We don't want her to have to worry about a thing!

All funds will go directly to Jackie's family. If Jackie has touched your life in some way, please consider giving. Shares and prayers are also welcome! Thank you all so much, and God bless!

Figure 3.1 First anonymized campaign page created for focus group feedback. All identifying details and images from the original have been replaced. Photo used in campaign by Edward Cisneros on Unsplash.

one's needs, the more difficult they become to represent. When the narrator is able to promote a few discrete needs . . . that promise a possible solution to the medical problem, the campaign itself becomes more marketable and compelling."[23] By contrast, "generalized financial distress" was both harder to narrate and harder for donors to embrace as something that could be solved by crowdfunding.

These trends became even clearer in focus group discussions, in which I asked participants to evaluate, and consider donating to, different anonymized campaigns (figures 3.1 and 3.2). One was for a White woman with significant resources (insurance, social support, financial stability) whose friend was seeking to help her out through a period of cancer care

Help us to not be homeless

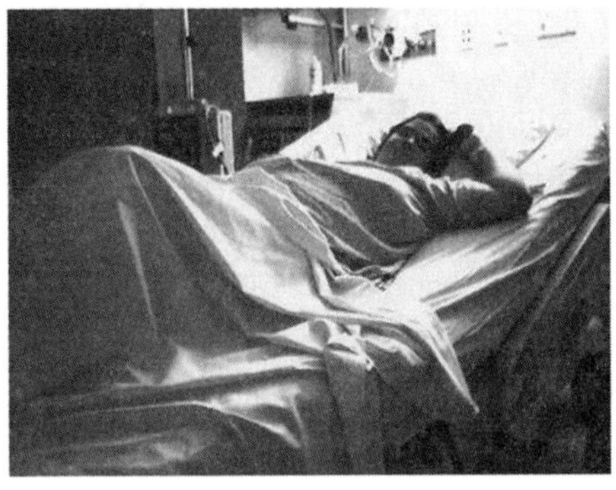

Randy is organizing this fundraiser.

Created August 2021 Rent, Food & Monthly Bills

Hello my name is Randy. The pic above is my son, who is disabled. I've also got disability. But I take good care of my boy and his needs. We are. At risk of losing our home. I'm pass rent more than $2000. Because I had to go to the hospital for heart troubles.

We need to pay up by Friday or we lose our home. Which means we'll be staying in our small car. My son can't live on the street, his medical equipment needs power to run at night. If I pay by Friday we can retain our home. Thanks if you can help, if not may God bless you. And keep you.

Figure 3.2 Second anonymized campaign page created for focus group feedback. All identifying details and images from the original have been replaced. Photo used in campaign by Sharon McCutcheon on Unsplash.

so she wouldn't "have to worry about a thing." The other campaign was for a more complex and extensive medical situation between a parent and their son, both disabled, who faced homelessness. This campaign included grammatical errors, had difficulty explaining the situation clearly, and used a poorer-quality photo.

To my surprise, while viewers often recognized the more severe needs of the second campaign, they were more willing to donate to the first campaign and in larger amounts. Often, participants pointed to the second campaign's grammatical errors and narrative insufficiencies as factors that made it hard to "trust" the campaigner. They talked about how the grammatical errors and writing style made the campaign seem like a scam even when they understood that there could be many factors influencing this aspect of the narrative. "I don't want to judge because maybe they were typing on a small phone screen, [or] messed up their punctuation," said Helen, "[but] it sounds exactly like, 'I'm a Nigerian prince, please send me money.'" Common as such comments are, they reveal the racism, classism, and xenophobia embedded in how the authenticity and deservingness of campaigns is assessed by viewers.

Focus group participants also demonstrated the difficulty that crowdfunders with dire, chronic, extensive, or complex needs face in creating narratives that others find believable and compelling. They noted that given the severity and seeming chronicity of the second campaign's situation, they felt it was unlikely their donations would result in a resolution or improvement. "To me," Tracey observed, "if he needs . . . money to pay rent this month, he's going to need money to pay rent next month. So, it's not like this is a one-time thing that he needs. And that to me is concerning . . . if I give to him this time, is he going to ask me again next month when rent is due again?" Many participants also found the urgency of the situation suspicious rather than compelling. "Like, maybe you could have asked before you got to this point where you'd be homeless on Friday," one observed frankly. These opinions echo the kinds of skepticism and blame that those who do not fit stringent categories of the "deserving poor" often face when they seek assistance.

It's not surprising, then, that there are systematic inequities in terms of who actually starts a crowdfunding campaign. During the early months of COVID-19, my colleagues and I found a higher density of campaigns in higher-income, better-educated areas of the United States, and we observed that these areas were able to more frequently launch campaigns in response to COVID-19-related needs.[24] In Canada, researchers have found crowdfunding use is greater in higher-income areas and regions with more homeownership and educational attainment.[25] In studying campaigns for transgender surgery, Chris Barcelos found that the majority of campaigns started were for people with more privileged identities.[26] In a randomized sample of US medical GoFundMe campaigns, we found that nearly 80 percent of campaigns were for White people.[27] Black and other non-White campaigners were underrepresented by about 33 percent and 25 percent, respectively, and Black women made up less than 4 percent of the overall campaigns.[28] These disparities are especially troubling in light of the higher burdens of illness, poor health, and medical debt among Black people and Black women in particular.[29]

In addition, we found acute gender imbalances among campaign organizers: among those who were starting campaigns for themselves, about 67 percent were women, and among those who were starting a campaign on behalf of someone else, more than 80 percent were women.[30] In essence, women were starting campaigns for other people at more than four times the rate that men were, reflecting new forms of inequitable, gendered care labor online. The barriers and inequities in crowdfunding use are complex, involving both technological and social factors. But research makes clear that crowdfunding is not equally accessible or empowering for all users. Substantial populations are being crowded out and left behind by this new technology.

SPREADING THE WORD

If a campaign gets started, its success largely depends on how often it is shared and with whom. Crowdfunding platforms clearly inform users about the importance of this step in the process. After donors navigate away from a campaign in GoFundMe, a pop-up window reminds them that sharing the campaign online is "worth" $37 in expected donations. Similarly, sharing a campaign on Facebook "can increase . . . donations as much as 350%." Before it was acquired by GoFundMe, YouCaring used similar metrics on its site to encourage sharing. Jessie, who worked as a campaign success consultant for another crowdfunding platform, helped users set up and share their campaigns. She explained to me, "if you take a look at where the traffic comes to for a campaign, it always comes from the social sharing. It doesn't come from somebody just randomly showing up. We can attribute almost every contribution that comes in to some sort of social share that started with the campaign."

The vast majority of crowdfunding campaigns, as Jessie observed, attract donations from a crowdfunder's existing, and primarily online, social networks. This has two important implications. First, it means that success depends on the network with whom a crowdfunder shares their campaign—how big it is, how wealthy and well connected, and how much those in the network are willing and able to contribute to the campaign. Second, it means that what we see of crowdfunding campaigns on social media and traditional media may differ greatly from the typical experience. Stories about crowdfunding that gain traction in the media tend to feature someone particularly in need or down on their luck whose story seems to magically capture the public interest, catapulting them into the spotlight of public attention. Or we are told stories of Taylor Swift, Ellen DeGeneres, or another celebrity surprising a particularly needy fan with a huge donation, seemingly out of the blue.

Both traditional news media and social media tend to focus attention on successful campaigns, and they often contribute to the success of those campaigns by driving traffic to them, thus reinforcing their popularity.[31] Algorithms on social media drive the most popular and visible content toward users, meaning that we are most likely to see popular, trending, or successful campaigns on our social media feeds. And finally, algorithms and editorial decisions on many crowdfunding sites tend to prioritize successful campaigns in search results, social media and blog posts, and in the prominent spots on landing pages.

What this means is that there is an enormous difference between the campaigns we are most likely to see and interact with and the typical crowdfunding experience. As Jessie put it bluntly, for the typical campaign, "there's no anonymous person waiting to crack open their wallet and make a donation to a stranger." She explained the following:

> People tend to not understand how [crowdfunding] works. . . . So, they think it's more like angel funding, where they put up a page and anonymous wealthy benefactors come by and make a donation to them, rather than a tool that they can use to . . . sort of, circle the wagons and get support from where it already exists. And . . . I think the challenge is reframing that, because, you know, people see viral GoFundMe campaigns and other fundraisers where a lot of people who don't know the individual fundraising come out to show their support and they make donations, but that's . . . that's one percent. And 99.9 percent of personal fundraisers are people tapping into people they already know. . . . One of the challenges is just making people understand: This is a tool you can use, but it's not a solution, it's not free money, it's not a grant, it's not an Angel Fund, it's a tool you can use to circle the wagons and get the support you need from the people in your life. . . . I tell people this all the time: Crowdfunding is not about the kindness of strangers, it's about the kindness of your crowd.

Jesse points out that it's the "kindness" of one's own, very personally connected "crowd" that determines success, even as most crowdfunders believe that going viral is their path to success. This creates perceptions of crowdfunding that are frequently mismatched with reality.

These dynamics also impact where donations go and how they are directed. In discussions with crowdfunding donors, most said they had only donated to a campaign for someone they knew. Nationally representative surveys of people who have donated to medical crowdfunding campaigns show similar results: only about 30 percent of respondents say they have given to a campaign for someone they did not know directly.[32] But the campaigns that spread the farthest tend to be for people we don't know personally. This contributes to a bifurcation in crowdfunding realities: a vast majority of crowdfunding campaigns raise small amounts of money almost exclusively from known members of a limited social network, while a much smaller group of highly successful crowdfunding campaigns raises large amounts of money from an extended group of donors who may not have personal ties to them or may only know them due to an outsized social media following or presence.

For those whose campaigns largely reach a small circle of connected donors, social network dynamics powerfully shape inequalities and reinforce the status quo. Sociologists have long observed what they call the "homophily principle" in social networks: people tend to be most connected with others like them. Homophily in networks extends to social and demographic characteristics such as race and class and to ideological and cultural characteristics like political orientation and religion.[33] Put simply, birds of a feather flock together.[34] These dynamics are important in crowdfunding because it leverages social networks to generate resources. Long before GoFundMe existed, philosopher Pierre Bourdieu recognized social capital as "actual or potential resources which are linked . . . to membership in a group," essentially highlighting how social ties constitute links to material resources.[35] These dynamics can powerfully reproduce social inequalities.[36] For example, if I am a low-income person who struggles with chronic illness and is hard hit by the latest recession, it's likely my friends are in a similar financial boat. If I turn to my social network for help, they may have less capacity to help me even if they want to because they are more likely to be facing similar challenges. On the flip side, wealthy Americans are far more likely to have social networks populated with other wealthy people who have more capacity to help them out.

It's not hard to see how this can lead to radically different outcomes in crowdfunding. Imagine two people: John is relatively rich, and Dan is relatively impoverished; both are starting campaigns after a cancer diagnosis. Let's imagine both John and Dan have a network of two hundred people with whom they share their campaign, and in turn one hundred people within each network donate to them. But donors in John's affluent network can give an average of $100 each, and those in Dan's more impoverished network can only donate an average of $20. John will earn $10,000, while Dan will earn just a fifth of that amount, $2,000. However, this scenario *underestimates* the potential inequalities we might see. It assumes that both John and Dan will have an equivalent number of people in their networks who can donate to them at all, and it's very likely that in Dan's network there will be fewer people who can afford to donate to him. In fact, research has shown that even though campaigns are shared more often in poorer counties, in wealthier counties "sharing yielded significantly more donations."[37]

This effect has less to do with different levels of generosity and more with economic inequalities. Researchers often find that those with the lowest incomes are deeply generous and more likely to help others within their social networks.[38] Studies have attributed this behavior to the compassion, awareness of hardships, and commitments to egalitarian values among people in lower-income groups.[39] Unfortunately, this behavior often gets overshadowed by the larger amounts that richer people can and do donate.[40] Though people across different income groups donate roughly the same percentage of their income to charity, in higher-income groups this obviously amounts to larger net donations—and thus attracts far more attention. A survey of people donating to medical crowdfunding campaigns found that 40 percent of donors had household incomes of less than $60,000, and more than a third were out of work when they donated.[41] Sal, a Black focus group participant from Chicago, gave voice to this logic: "I believe [that] what I do to others will be done to me, so I like participating in crowdfunding because I believe that there may be a situation where I will not be able to pay for my medical [expenses], but someone [else] may come through [for me], because I can come through for somebody who [needs it]." Many people spoke of a sense of shared fate when it came to medical expenses in particular because they can be so unpredictable and the financial impacts of serious illness are often so large.

Jessie, who had helped thousands of people in creating and launching their campaigns, was intimately familiar with the effects of homophily and unequal capital in social networks. "It's tricky," she said, "because obviously there are people who are living in poverty and they may have a thousand Facebook friends but if those Facebook friends are all also dealing with poverty, then they can't really turn that into a successful fundraiser." She added that "even if their friends don't have money, they can still share it on social media with their friends, and sort of signal boost it. And I won't say that that's the kind of fundraising that gets, you know, thousands and thousands of dollars, but it usually does get them a couple of donations, if they're savvy about [it]." What's unspoken here, however, is just how much harder someone with a lower-income social network will have to hustle, even to raise a small amount.

The flip side of this phenomenon is that those with a very large online social network can often leverage it toward far greater campaign success. "A millennial savings account is just a twitter account with 10k followers just in case you need to crowdfund for medical bills," quipped writer Alyssa Keiko on Twitter in 2018. Indeed, having a large social media following often helps campaigns get spread by other social media influencers and also picked up by local and national media. For example, Mark and Sofia, whose campaign was discussed in chapter 2, easily had ten to twelve thousand followers across several social media platforms—Facebook, Instagram, Twitter—and their friend Spencer, who founded their campaign, had close to another five thousand on his social media accounts. But they also had friends with expertise in social marketing, public relations, and media relations who were crucial in helping attract attention to their campaign. These socially networked resources enabled them to succeed in an internet-driven attention economy where shares, likes, and followers hold real economic value and can be transformed into cash. While this may not sound so different from the more traditional forms of "social capital" Bourdieu observed, in the social media environment, networks are far larger, the spread is lightning fast, and there is much less friction in the transmutation of connections into cash.[42]

Moreover, the crowdfunding economy, like other social media spaces, rewards certain types of people—and more specifically, people who look a specific way since so much content is visual. "Generally, if you're crowdfunding," Jessie said bluntly, "it's very helpful to be young and thin and attractive. Those are the people that do best, because they can post lots of pictures of themselves, people have generally good associations with them. . . . Generally speaking, the things that are advantageous to us in life are also advantageous to us in crowdfunding." While she didn't say it out loud, racism plays heavily into these biases, as we'll see below.

Jessie articulated the realities of this new economy and how it impacted crowdfunders. "We tell people to think like a marketer," she said. "You're marketing yourself. You're marketing your cause, your fundraiser, so you really want to think of yourself . . . you want to make yourself look a certain way to get the results that you need, as a crowdfunder." Jessie talked about how people used videos, hashtags, and cross-platform integration of their messaging to get their campaigns spreading. But she also acknowledged that such hustle could only take people so far. She said that the campaigns that were hardest to help were those for people who kept telling her "I don't have any friends, my family doesn't have any money" because "those are the things that help a fundraiser to be successful." If someone didn't have an online presence or a social network that they could tap into, it was nearly impossible to get their campaign off the ground. "The really tough thing is the people who have no social network," Jessie said. "There's nothing we can do for them, unfortunately."

WHAT SUCCEEDS

Jessie's observations about crowdfunding as a social media economy raise important questions about what actually succeeds, and how much, in this deeply unequal environment. If we zoom out and look at crowdfunding outcomes on a population scale, we can more clearly see the enormous disparities in terms of who succeeds and who does not. In this section, I refer mostly to crowdfunding outcomes in terms of money raised—that is only one measure of success, and a crude one at that. There are widely different definitions of what constitutes success and many benefits and drawbacks to crowdfunding that go well beyond how much you earn.

But campaign earnings can be a useful quantitative measure for assessing differences across a large number of campaigns.

Much of the research on factors of success in crowdfunding has focused on the things that campaigners do in their campaigns—how many photos and updates they post, how long their stories are, and how many grammatical errors are in those stories.[43] While these factors may be more within crowdfunders' control, there is strong and growing evidence that things outside their control—their race, their education and income levels, where they live, and what kinds of health conditions they have—may be much more important than other factors.[44] In the sharing economy, where the opinions of others have a particularly strong sway over outcomes, biases and discrimination are well documented. Airbnb, for example, has been plagued with issues of racial discrimination against non-White hosts and guests; research has also shown that non-White hosts essentially "self-discount," charging less for accommodations.[45]

Researchers have documented similar dynamics on rewards-based crowdfunding platforms such as Kickstarter: African American men receive less funding, and their products are perceived as lower quality;[46] minoritized producers face price discounting;[47] and campaigners' visually identifiable race impacts their probability of success.[48] Disparities also arise in terms of gender: women are underrepresented on entrepreneurial crowdfunding sites, and they receive less funding.[49] At the same time, if all other things were equal, their campaigns would be expected to outperform their male counterparts[50]—a dynamic that is hauntingly familiar to women in other industries (including academia).

Evidence has quickly mounted that similar biases persist in donation-based crowdfunding. In 2018, Martin Lukk and colleagues looked at a relatively small sample of Canadian education and health campaigns and found that older adults, women, and "visible minorities" had poorer fundraising outcomes than other demographic groups.[51] Barcelos observed that campaigns for transgender medical care seemed to earn far less on average than campaigns for cisgender medical care.[52] Some have suggested that stigma against particular health issues or groups of people may also impact success: a study of campaigns for Canadians seeking addiction treatment found that they raised on average only 1.6 percent of what they requested.[53]

It's clear, however, that race is a major axis of disparity in crowdfunding outcomes. In 2020, my colleagues and I examined campaign outcomes alongside the race, gender, and age of both campaign creators and recipients.[54] We found substantial evidence of racial bias, with recipients who were people of color receiving significantly fewer, and smaller, donations. Black recipients received on average $22 less *per donation* than their White counterparts. In a subsequent, powerful study, Mark Igra tried to answer the question of whether these racial disparities in crowdfunding outcomes arose directly from the racial biases crowdfunders faced from donors or more indirectly from the well-documented racial wealth gap within the United States, which would mean these crowdfunders' networks had less to donate to campaigns.[55] He found that while rates of sharing did not differ depending on the race of the campaign recipient, "Black and Hispanic beneficiaries receive fewer and smaller donations than White or Asian beneficiaries" and differences in the "financial capacity" of crowdfunders' networks could explain most, but not all, of these disparities.[56]

To explore these effects further, Aaron Davis, Shauna Carlisle, and I looked at a subset of the most successful, "viral" medical crowdfunding campaigns: 869 that had raised more than 100,000 in donations on GoFundMe.[57] This group represents a rarefied sliver of the hundreds of thousands of medical campaigns that are started GoFundMe each year. Unlike most typical campaigns, these had earned the outsized attention of a more public "crowd." In this group, we saw much stronger disparities in terms of both race and gender: 15 percent more campaigns were for men rather than for women, and less than 4 percent were for Black people. What was most likely to go viral? Cancer campaigns for White patients, often ones who were in their younger adult years or in childhood. Many in this group were connected to wealth, celebrity, and power through their immediate social networks. Shockingly, only 5 campaigns in the group—0.6 percent of all the campaigns we examined—were for Black women, and two of those were created by White campaign organizers.[58]

While connections to wealth and privilege clearly play a role in these campaigns' success, we also saw evidence of persistent interpersonal racism and sexism in the types of campaigns that went viral. While crowdfunding has been portrayed harnessing the "wisdom of the crowd," among campaigns that get the most attention from such crowds, race and gender disparities grow even larger.[59] At this altitude, the "wisdom" of the crowd sure looks a lot like rampant discrimination.

Social biases intersect with economic and social disparities that also impact campaigns. As might be expected from the prior evidence in this chapter, people in disadvantaged groups and areas may be more in need of crowdfunding, but they end up earning far less.[60] In 2020, Silver and colleagues studied a large group of US cancer crowdfunding campaigns and found that those from counties with higher levels of neighborhood deprivation raised significantly less money (about 25 percent less) and were less able to create campaign texts that "described beneficiaries as worthy of donations."[61] These authors concluded that "although lower-SES patients are at greater risk of [financial toxicity] . . . these patients are the least likely to benefit from cancer crowdfunding as a way to mitigate it."[62] In a small but compelling study, Sumin Lee and Vili Lehdonvirta also found that counties with the greatest needs in the United States—"the poorest, sickest, and least socially-connected"—had the least success with crowdfunding.[63] In 2022, Mark Igra and I looked at the largest-to-date dataset of medical crowdfunding campaigns in the United States, nearly half a million spanning the years of 2016–2020.[64] We found that in areas with more medical debt, higher uninsurance rates, and lower incomes, campaigns earned substantially less.

Finally, it appears that these inequitable patterns of success hold true—and may be even worse—when people turn to crowdfunding during periods of crisis. It's not uncommon for periods of widespread social and economic crisis to widen gaps between rich and poor and to be leveraged by powerful groups to further impose economic austerity measures.[65] But it is surprising to see these dynamics extend to more interpersonal giving. Despite a lot of public shows of solidarity and generosity at the beginning of the COVID pandemic in the United States, my research team found huge disparities between unsuccessful and successful campaigns during the first seven months of the pandemic.[66] Not only were people from wealthier and better-educated communities more likely to be able to start crowdfunding campaigns in response to COVID-related needs, but their campaigns did far better than those started in poorer and less-educated communities.[67] Distressingly, we also found that campaigns for individuals' basic needs—food, rent, cash—were most common, but they also did most poorly, often earning only a small fraction of what campaigns for other pandemic causes (business closures, health-care workers, etc.) earned.[68]

Taken together, these research studies point to extensive and multidimensional disparities that emerge from, and are fueled by, crowdfunding, resulting in those who have the most acute needs being least likely to find help from this charitable marketplace. While sites like GoFundMe cultivate a public image that crowdfunding can be used by anyone to find help when they need it, they play host to and exacerbate inequities that affect who crowdfunds, how they crowdfund, and, ultimately, the help they can receive.

STAYING VISIBLE

One of the most troubling aspects of crowdfunding inequities is how hard they are to track. Crowdfunding companies likely have a vested interest in ensuring these inequities remain largely hidden from public view: after all, if people knew that only 10 percent of campaigns reached their goal, or that campaigns for people who needed the most help did most poorly, it could deter their potential customers from crowdfunding and seriously hurt their public image as do-good, feel-good companies that harness the "kindness of strangers."[69] Companies like GoFundMe handle data, design sites and algorithms, and determine user terms and conditions in ways that conceal many of these realities from the public.

Researchers struggle to get data from crowdfunding companies, who are under no obligation to share their data with the public. Only a handful of studies have ever succeeded in being granted company data, and those studies tend to be quite laudatory about the social impacts of crowdfunding.[70] Platforms do not post or make public some of the most important characteristics that researchers might want to know about crowdfunding users—their income and education levels, their insurance status, and self-identified demographics such as race, class, and ethnicity. Thus, we are left to estimate and measure these features as best we can with the data we have available—but it severely hampers our ability to do more robust or large-scale research.

Troublingly, in 2022, Mark Igra and I found further evidence that GoFundMe was likely concealing unsuccessful campaigns from visitors or researchers. Its site index—a list of all web URLs hosted by the site that is used by search engines like Google as well as researchers to find campaign pages—did not include many campaigns that were less successful, particularly those that had raised $0. As we described in a paper, we also found evidence that unfunded campaigns—those that had no donations at all—were disappearing from the site after a year.[71] There are many possible explanations for this phenomenon—perhaps site administrators want to clear up space and consider these campaigns as having no activity, for example—but the effect is that unsuccessful campaigns are essentially lost and unaccounted for. As an archive of what actually happens in the crowdfunding marketplace, GoFundMe's publicly available data is both woefully incomplete and heavily biased toward successful campaigns.

LANDSCAPES OF INEQUALITY

As a crowdfunding campaign moves from nascent idea to launch, spread, and ultimate closure, it most likely experiences a profound "crowding out," fueled by social inequalities, hierarchies of deservingness, and platform design choices. Far less than reflecting some "wisdom" of the crowd, this process amplifies inequities. Ultimately, only about 10 percent of campaigns ever reach their financial goals, even though campaigners are routinely encouraged by sites to drastically understate their financial goals at the outset.[72] Among all medical campaigns that we could find on GoFundMe from 2020, more than a third of campaigns raised no money—zero dollars—at all.[73]

In figure 3.3 we can see the steeply declining percentage of campaigns that reach 25, 50, 75 and 100 percent of their goals. If we broke up all medical crowdfunding campaigns from GoFundMe into five equal baskets, or quintiles, we would see that the bottom 20 percent raise $0 and the bottom 40 percent raise $65 or less. Eighty percent of campaigns raise $3,000 or less, and the top 20 percent encapsulate an enormous range of outcomes, from a few thousand dollars up to millions. But those that raise more than $100,000 only number in the hundreds.[74] The more we drill down into specific groups, the more we can see who has these poor

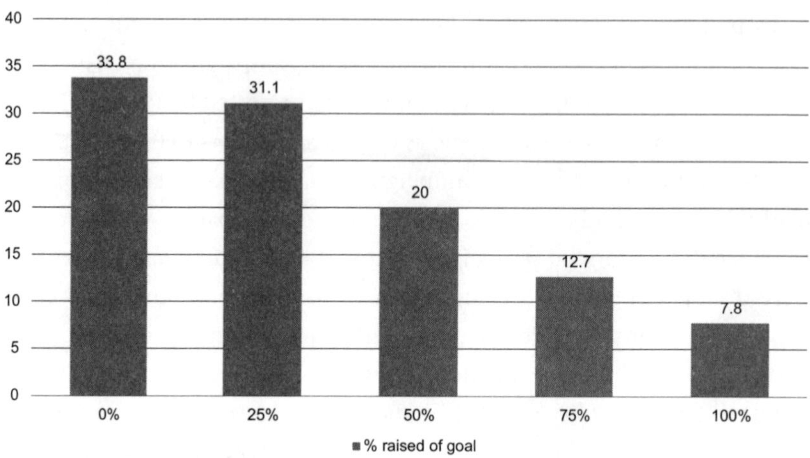

Figure 3.3 Percentage of medical campaigns on GoFundMe in 2020 that reached different percentages of their goal. Source: Nora Kenworthy and Mark Igra, "Medical Crowdfunding and Disparities in Health Care Access in the United States, 2016–2020," *American Journal of Public Health* 112, no. 3 (March 2022): 491–498, https://doi.org/10.2105/AJPH.2021.306617.

outcomes more clearly. In a randomized study of COVID-19 campaigns on GoFundMe, the campaigns for urgent personal needs—rent, food, cash—raised a median of only $20, while campaigns supporting health-care workers raised 20 times more, over $1000.[75]

Even these statistics conceal just how little many campaigns earn. In the same study of 2020 medical campaigns, the median campaign—that is, the one that is smack in the middle of the spread from least to most earnings—raised $265 from five donations, toward a goal of $5,000.[76] Unfortunately, this means that the typical crowdfunding campaign is best suited to minor, short-term needs that can be met by donations from a small circle of contacts. These are not the sort of gains that help alleviate large amounts of medical debt or uncovered medical costs, and they do not provide assistance with long-term chronic health needs. In short, the typical crowdfunding campaign is best suited to provide a small amount of financial help for someone dealing with minor health problems or someone who has other substantial sources of financial assistance. This is hardly the kind of aid that is needed to fill the enormous gaps in health and social safety nets in the United States.

If we thought of crowdfunding outcomes as a topographic landscape with hills and valleys, it wouldn't look like anything we find on earth. Instead, it would look like the landscape of a distant planet or a Dr. Seuss book. And yet, much like broader patterns of wealth inequality in the United States, people tend to radically underestimate the extent and scope of the inequalities between successful and unsuccessful campaigns. In focus group discussions, I always ended with two questions: What did people think the typical medical crowdfunding campaign raised in total dollars? And what percentage of campaigns did they think reached their financial goals? On average, participants estimated that the typical campaign raised more than $8,000 and that 43 percent of campaigns reached their goals. These are understandable, but considerable, overestimates of crowdfunding success.[77]

Even more troubling, many participants indicated that they did not trust, and therefore would not donate to, campaigns that had raised no money. Though this outcome is the reality for more than a third of campaigns, participants struggled to understand how a campaign raised no money, attributing these outcomes to a lack of community endorsements and trust. "If . . . nobody donated . . . [it feels like] there's no credibility here, like is there no network at all that the person had?" one person responded. Another, Tracey, went as far as to compare the situation to online shopping: "When you want to buy something, you first have to read the reviews from the people who have bought it before, so that you can know whether its legit or something. [See] some comments from people. But everything here is zero. No donors, no shares, no followers." Participants seemed to wonder if the organizers of these campaigns truly had no one who could vouch for them. But as we have seen, there is a hidden, complex set of factors that can contribute to the large subset of campaigns that raise no money at all.

Social media has a way of changing how we see landscapes of inequality. At first glance, it seems to give us equal access to opportunities and power, even proximity to wealth and privilege. Anyone can go viral, anyone can comment on a celebrity's tweet, and anyone's story can be heard. At the same time, we see also social media's steep inequalities firsthand—we see the incredible power that social media can lend to celebrities, politicians, or influencers who direct the attention of the crowd. We know that the likelihood of anything a "normal" person posts going viral or finding fame is small. But because digital media tends to obscure barriers to use and patterns of discrimination, inequity, and bias, we are fooled by the great meritocratic lie of the equal opportunity internet. Crowdfunding is a powerful example of that lie and the hold it has on us. As the next chapter explores, that lie entangles us in what Lauren Berlant has called a "cruel optimism" where we continue to strive for an "unachievable fantasy" of success while blaming ourselves, rather than the structural conditions that limit our opportunities, when it is not achieved. The structures that shape who crowdfunds, how their campaign does, and ultimately whether it even remains visible online are powerful forces that transform the cruelties of inequity into a mirage of equal opportunity.

A matter of pride

Hello.
Yeah, I'm still here.
I pray I'll find the right words to tell this story.

I'd never do this but I'm swallowing my pride

This might be the hardest thing I've ever had to write.

But here we are (swallowing pride)

Okay let's try this again. I cancelled the last one
within minutes because . . .
well, to put it simply, pride.

I'm simply trying to survive, pushing past my pride

I have no idea how to do this
without completely debasing myself.

The only thing bigger than his heart is his pride

So many people have asked
how they can help and I
keep saying, "we're fine, we're fine."
But we are not fine.

I am putting our pride on the back burner

That fact I even have to start
a GoFundMe is hitting my pride lol, but
I was told to reach out if I needed help.
Friends, now I need it.

Here I am, with humility and swallowed pride

Desperation makes us do
things we might not do otherwise, but
desperation is now my reality.
It was bad enough to beg for money
the first time, and I'm even more ashamed now.

I've conceded trying to swallow my pride

No one likes to admit publicly they are struggling,
have lost or failed or are in pain.
That we need help.

But I'm coming to you with my pride set aside

It pains me to ask this—
pains, and shames me.

I'm tossing my stubborn pride out the window

For the first time in this battle I am really scared.
My savings are gone and I've no more income.

I've learned the hard way to swallow my pride

Gradually, we've redirected every single
penny to medical expenses
I shouldn't let pride keep me from asking for help . . . right??

Her life is on the line if we can't pay for this surgery.
Our pride's gotta jump out the window

This is how hardworking people end up on the street.
Not sure whether I should be shamed or optimistic
this is not the American dream, it's my American nightmare

It feels greedy to ask for what I need
But I know of no other way.
Maybe we're all in this together, maybe
hardship teaches us to rely on one another.
Anyways, I have cancer. Again.
I am swallowing my pride and gagging on it.

4

THE CRUELTY OF DIGITAL OPPORTUNITY

Illness can be a profoundly isolating event. It can distance patients from friends and family, geographically as well as emotionally, and it can deplete their energies for social connection. Patients often have difficulty communicating about the hard parts of their illness experiences, bound as they are to social expectations that they show strength and positivity, and protect their loved ones from witnessing the full extent of their suffering.[1] And for many patients, particularly those from marginalized or historically mistreated communities, journeys through the medical system can involve encounters that deny their realities, diminish their sense of self, and subject them to discriminatory treatment.[2]

For many patients, digital spaces and online communities can offer support in navigating and narrating illness experiences. Through forums, digital tools, social media platforms, and blogs, patients connect with others going through similar experiences, tell their stories on their own terms, and share ideas of "how best to live on, considering."[3] Such "digital intimate publics" not only provide social connection but also validate experiences, offer access to shared knowledge, and can enable collective mobilizations for recognition and rights.[4] But digital illness experiences are not without drawbacks: for example, online engagement offers young cancer patients a "vital media" that generates a sense of well-being but also asks that these patients produce optimistic and resilient illness narratives for online audiences that limit their ability to narrate other kinds of experiences and emotions.[5]

As crowdfunding has become more popular, patients and their families have increasingly sought such "biosociality" and connection through online fundraising.[6] Anika Vassell and colleagues looked at campaigns for people with Lyme disease in Canada and found that they used crowdfunding to express "what was lost, missing, sought and hoped for" in their illness experiences.[7] Amy Gonzales and colleagues observed that "seeking financial or emotional support online requires that users disclose tragedy or hardships to a broad and unwieldy Internet public."[8] Experiences of disclosing often highly personal information to digital publics can be transformative, and even reaffirming, but also bring significant discomfort and loss of privacy.[9] Among young adults with cancer who used crowdfunding, researchers found that the use of crowdfunding involved a complicated "compromise": on the one hand, it offered important support, both monetary and emotional; on the other hand, patients experienced shame, stigma, and humiliation in having to turn to social networks for money.[10]

Crowdfunding is full of feelings—many of them conflicting: hope, connection, and perseverance coexist with disappointment, shame, and loss. How do we make sense of the ambivalent experiences people have when they turn to crowdfunding, and the disjunctures between the hopes that platforms cultivate, and the all-too-frequent disappointments or vulnerabilities that people find there? This chapter explores those tensions and disjunctures through stories of both more and less successful campaigns, where the promise of crowdfunding as digital opportunity runs up against the complex, often disorienting, realities of its experience. To do so, I will draw on Lauren Berlant's concept of "cruel optimism," which they describe as a situation in which we relentlessly strive for a vision of the good life that remains out of reach and, in so doing, "actually [make] it impossible to attain the [thing] for which . . . [we are] striving."[11]

In addition to the grim probabilities of actually finding crowdfunding success described in chapter 3, this chapter delves into the more affective and interpersonal cruelties of crowdfunding that lie beneath its optimistic veneer. Even as crowdfunding involves turning toward community and connecting across distance, it reinforces an inescapable individualism and individualized resilience. Crowdfunding also creates a particularly precarious means of providing care. This is not to say that crowdfunding does not offer real experiences of care and connection; rather, there are many times when the care and connection it offers is far from enough and where seeking care through the mechanism of digital crowdfunding opens doors to new troubles, vulnerabilities, and experiences of abandonment.

AMBIVALENT SUCCESS

While people talked openly with me about experiences of shame, vulnerability, and loss of privacy while crowdfunding, many also talked about positive dimensions of their experiences. Crowdfunding offered a way to connect with far-flung communities and to talk about what patients were experiencing. It allowed an easy way for networks to offer support and lowered barriers to communication at times when life was disorganized, hectic, or isolated. "In a way it was . . . empowering," Angela, who crowdfunded for her husband's transplant, observed. "Because it was giving us a little bit of control over a situation where we had no control at all." Some crowdfunders spoke explicitly about how it had strengthened their relationships with friends and family. Alejandra, who started a campaign for a family member across the country when she felt she couldn't offer support in person, said the campaign deepened her bonds with family she had left behind after moving to another state. It is important that we recognize these upsides of crowdfunding but also not overstate them. For many people, the crowdfunding is marked by ambivalence—even when it achieves the kind of success that platforms advertise relentlessly.

Crowdfunding platforms have cultivated a public aura of optimism and opportunity that is a key element of their brands and platform cultures. This extends from the ways companies talk about crowdfunding, to the implicit and explicit messages users get about how to succeed to the broader efforts companies make to influence social perceptions of crowdfunding. Taking GoFundMe as an example, the company routinely cultivates and celebrates an image of crowdfunding as tapping into a bottomless well of kindness. With tag lines like "we make it easy to inspire the world and turn compassion into action,"[12] "a global community brought together by a universal desire to help,"[13] and "harness the power of social media to spread your story and get more support,"[14] GoFundMe sells a mythology of opportunity to potential users.

In a blog post, GoFundMe's customer service representatives—who are called "Happiness Agents"—share tips on how to find success.[15] Their advice reaffirms GoFundMe's central messaging about how success on the platform is due to individualized effort. "Persistence," one Happiness Agent says, is key: "Campaign organizers who share their GoFundMe on a daily basis do the best." Another suggests that "what makes donors connect to the campaign the most [is] seeing the effort of the campaign organizer try whatever it takes to be successful." A third offers this advice: "Don't worry about what people will think. Jump head-first into your campaign if it's something you believe in—because if the passion is there, the rest has a way of falling into place." This advice reflects much of the moral economy that GoFundMe has constructed, where temerity, grit, optimism, honesty, passion, and hustle win out. The underlying message is that anyone can find happiness with crowdfunding, if only they try hard enough—but it's ultimately up to them to succeed. Success is determined by personal decisions, stories, and efforts.

These messages resonate with broader cultural values under neoliberalism, which celebrate rugged individualism, responsibility, and bootstrapping success. As this book argues, these are moral toxicities—toxic not only because they are untrue but also because they project a world in which suffering, economic precarity, and even death comes down to individual responsibility. These moral toxicities can be like a fog that conceals from us the broader causes of our struggles but also conceals our connections to one another, and our collective, rather than individual, responsibilities to each other.

There can be a jarring contrast between crowdfunding's cultivated image of positivity and opportunity and campaigners' own narratives of struggle as they try to appeal to these ideals. "Mike was pulling himself up by the bootstraps when Big C cut the straps," wrote one of Mike's friends in his campaign for cancer care. Reflecting research that has shown that positive emotions in narratives improve campaign outcomes,[16] other campaigners often try to project positivity even as they struggle with economic precarity: "Hello!" wrote Makayla, a Black single mom, in the early months of the pandemic. "I am raising money for my son and me I have lost my job due to the Coronavirus disease! I am trying to do what is possible to make everything a smooth transition but it is very hard and sad!" Todd, a father of four who created the campaign "Family in Need," wrote about his sons' multiple disabilities and their family's struggles to pay their bills. In ever more desperate campaign updates over several months, he talked about the looming threat of their home's foreclosure: "Things still haven't gotten any better. I don't know where to turn anymore. Got denied for food stamps and still haven't gotten the kids on ssdi. If I didn't have bad lu k [*sic*] I'd have no luck."[17]

Brett, an Army veteran, wrote about the profound hardship of having to publicly ask for money: "The truth is I have never been so scared and alone in my life. . . . I am going to bite chew swallow repeat until my pride is gone. I'm not sure how everyone is going to react when I put this out there. How many are going to judge, discourage, belittle me, or make me feel worse than I already do." These narratives point to the ways crowdfunding users strive to reconcile crowdfunding sites' "personal responsibility" rhetoric for what succeeds with their own struggles, shame, and lack of success. These are the conditions under which the dual phenomena of what I call *inescapable individualism* and *precarious care* emerge within the crowdfunding marketplace.

CHRISTIE

Christie's story helps illustrate what I mean by inescapable individualism and precarious care. Christie was twenty-six and pregnant with her second child when she started to feel sick—feverish, achy, and generally unwell. Several days later, nearly fourteen weeks before her due date, her water broke. Christie was life flighted to a hospital with a neonatal intensive care unit (NICU), where she found out that she and her baby had a life-threatening infection. Because her baby was in distress, she underwent an emergency C-section. Amelia, as Christie and her husband named their daughter, was whisked away to the NICU, unable to breathe on her own. Amelia was "so very, very early, and very small—two pounds, three ounces" Christie recalled quietly. Amelia had numerous complications, including brain bleeds, and was expected to stay in the NICU for at least twelve weeks.

Christie had a one-year-old son at home and a husband who had been granted only a single week of paid time off from his construction job. She was hospitalized for several weeks due to her infection, and so her husband took a second, unpaid week off from his job to care for their son.

Following her discharge, Christie found herself trying to recover from a C-section, caring for her son, and driving long distances to and from the hospital where Amelia remained in the NICU, all on her own. She had to find a cheap, partial day care for her son so she could visit the hospital NICU, since he was not allowed to go with her.

In the days after Amelia's birth, it became apparent that Christie and her husband couldn't possibly get through the coming weeks without financial help. At the very least, Christie admitted they needed "help with the cost of driving round trip . . . and any bills that might come in." Seven weeks later, the hospital would estimate the cost of Amelia's care, not including the C-section or the life flight to the hospital, at $1.3 million. And Amelia was still not out of the hospital. "This [campaign] is just a really small way to kind of help with our expenses—gas, food, things like that" Christie said when we spoke. Luckily, they did have insurance, a basic Blue Cross Blue Shield plan with a maximum annual out of pocket of just above $13,000. The hospital was trying to get Amelia on Medicaid, a fairly standard option for babies born prematurely, but they didn't know how long it would take to come through.

Christie was insistent that their campaign was not for these larger, looming health-care bills but just the small incidentals they were facing with a multimonth stay at the hospital. "You know, the total medical bill—we'll be making monthly payments on [that] for a *long* time," she said. It was clear she was keeping very close track of the other costs of their stay—the different pricing options for parking, whether and when she was entitled to a free tray of food as a breastfeeding mom, and how much they spent on gas each week. They had some support from family members who were flying or driving in to help for short periods of time with childcare, but she and her husband were shouldering those travel costs too. Having her husband take more unpaid family medical leave was entirely out of the question financially.

While Christie's sister was visiting, she overheard the couple worrying about finances, asking each other "how are we gonna do this?" Her sister couldn't help them out financially, but she set up a GoFundMe on their behalf and told them it was ready to share, if only they would be comfortable asking for help. The couple did agree to the campaign but set a surprisingly low goal of $3,000. "We didn't want to ask for too much and set it too high," Christie explained. She seemed more worried about asking for too much help than about how they would pay off their looming bills. "We didn't want to take too much," she said, sighing audibly. "You know, we didn't want to overshoot because we didn't, you know . . . we weren't asking everyone to pay all our bills for us." She repeatedly emphasized that they just wanted a bit of help with gas, parking, and meals. It was clear she believed the larger burden of their medical debt fell squarely on their own shoulders.

Later, Christie said that if her sister hadn't done this for them, they "would have just kind of suffered through. We have some room on our credit cards, I guess." While she didn't come straight out and say it, their finances were clearly very tight, and they had no idea how they were going to pay back the larger medical debts they owed. Christie said they were "just cutting down on spending on pretty much everything," including with diapers and trying not to use formula, and "just making as much of a payment every month that we can." Most people in their community and social network had limited means, which worried Christie. She said that one of the best things about GoFundMe was that it avoided awkward, more interpersonal conversations asking for help, where "it might be hard for [people] to say, 'Oh, wow, I really can't afford it.'" Christie's least favorite thing about GoFundMe was the fee charged on every donation, which amounted to about 2.6 percent of their overall earnings. While other, more successful campaigners rarely mentioned fees, it was often something that lower-earning campaigners noticed. "It feels like a big chunk when every dollar counts," she said.

For the first few weeks, their campaign had a lot of activity. The emotional support they got from campaign engagement was significant: "It really helped us a lot; just to know that we had so many people supporting us, you know, thinking about us and just being there for us, checking in on us every so often. . . . Sometimes more than the money, a lot more than the money . . . having that support system is vital. [Especially] when you're going to be [in the hospital]—we've been [here for] seven weeks and we're looking at another four to six." Christie started a Facebook page where she could provide more personal updates about Amelia's progress. But her updates there, and on the campaign page, focused mostly on Amelia's positive steps. Even in an update on some really troubling neurological results, Christie wrote, "but [Amelia] is doing so well, though . . . we're so proud of how much she's fighting and how far she's come." Later, she recalled, "we just didn't want people to . . . I don't know, we wanted to ask for help. And let . . . people who already donated know how she was doing. But we didn't want to, you know, we didn't want to seem like we were just asking for money all the time." Often, they asked for prayers instead. She and her husband are both Catholic, and it "was really important for us . . . because we didn't know what kind of problems she was going to face yet, or yeah, if she was even going to make it at that point."

But despite this early engagement, Christie admitted that their emotional and financial support through the crowdfunding page waned quite quickly. Ultimately, they'd only raised about $1,700. "I think people . . . after a little while are like, 'Okay, you guys should be in the swing of it,' and, I mean, [they think] that you don't need help; or they don't think about it as much because now she's stable and you know, she's growing and getting bigger." Christie returned to this experience several times throughout our interview, trying to make sense of it. "I kind of think that people," she said, "you know . . . it's not that they lose interest, really. But they think, okay, everything's going good. And they don't . . . think to go back and look . . . or they don't know about the additional mental stress and the additional costs that have come up and things like that."

At the same time, I thought of Christie's cheery updates and posts and wondered how much people could know when she seemed so committed, as many people can be on social media, to putting an optimistic shine on their experience. Christie noted she was aware that she was not just providing updates on social media; she was creating a public record of Amelia's story. She thought about showing Amelia the Facebook archive when she got older "to show her like, look at this, like, there's so many comments on the posts and stuff like that. And people are saying, 'I'm praying for her' . . . you know, talking about oh, 'she looks cute today!'" These posts could serve as a family archive, curated by Christie, for an Amelia who survived and thrived. In this light, her positive updates became poignant aspirations for a future nostalgia about this time.

What remained unspoken, however, were the family's continuing financial needs as well as their constant worries about Amelia's prognosis. "We still have the same costs as before, we still have . . . to handle everything—my husband's [pay] check has to handle everything here," Christie said. She began listing off all their recent, unexpected costs—like oil changes and new tires because they were using their car a lot. "These are real things," she continued, "that we have to think about. But other people don't . . . they don't see it unless we say it." At the end of our interview, Christie said she knew she had to write another post explaining their ongoing financial needs, but she just couldn't bring herself to do it: "It's just so hard to ask for help."

Though Christie had experienced a serious family crisis, the outcomes of her campaign were not a glaring tragedy; I think she would be rightfully angry with me if I wrote her story that way. Rather, her experience was more ambiguous, limited by her own ideas of what she had a right to ask for, to expect, and to articulate. It's safe to say, though, that she deserved more than she got and that people like Christie should not have to experience the kind of struggle she faced in the wake of an already traumatic birth. If Christie had given birth in any number of other countries with better social safety nets, she would have had access to paid parental leave, to health coverage that left her with few out-of-pocket costs, to more affordable childcare options for her son, and, perhaps most importantly, to future medical and social support for her daughter, no matter what health challenges she faced. In another country, what she raised might have been enough, *really enough*, to help her family through their crisis. In another country, perhaps, she would have felt she deserved those things too.

Christie clearly needed more help than she asked for, but pride—and not wanting to ask too much of others who had very little—held her back. Digital platforms like GoFundMe and Facebook made the experience of reaching out to community easier but also watered down the kinds of care she received, including what people knew about their situation and the kinds of attention it got as time wore on. As Christie projected an optimistic, resilient, largely independent portrayal of her family across these platforms, it became harder and harder to ask for the help they really needed. But, she said, the experience "definitely showed us . . . how strong we are . . . I didn't know I could get through some of this . . . but, um, then you're kind of in it. You just got to do what you got to do to keep moving forward."

In many ways, Christie was experiencing what Lauren Berlant has called the "crisis ordinariness" of late capitalism, where what would normally be considered a singular, traumatic crisis becomes repeated and extended to such a degree that it becomes ordinary—or ordinary enough.[18] One "does what one has to do." One of the most pernicious harms of late capitalist, neoliberal systems is that they provide so little support that precarity becomes normalized, chronic, and ubiquitous. Like those many others in Christie's social network who were so financially strapped they could barely donate to her campaign, "crisis ordinariness" forces us to rely on social relationships for support while also depleting their capacity for support. Care itself becomes precarious—don't ask for too much, don't require it for too long. You end up, as Christie put it, just doing "what you got to do to move forward."

As Berlant notes, under such "contexts where making a life involves getting through the day, the week, and the month. . . . life feels truncated, more like desperate doggy paddling than like a magnificent swim out to the horizon."[19] But what Berlant so brilliantly observes about these circumstances is that rather than producing resistance to them, they produce a dogged attachment to dreams of the good life—to the cruelly dim possibility that we might just be the lucky one whose campaign goes viral, whose story ends up on TV. Or we become committed to finding the positive in the scraps of care we find online. Indeed, in its embrace of hustle and individualism and opportunity, crowdfunding normalizes and celebrates a desperate doggy paddle toward a far-off, perhaps unreachable, shore of safety.

INESCAPABLE INDIVIDUALISM, ENFORCED RESILIENCE

As Christie noted repeatedly in our interview, asking others for help can be a tremendously difficult thing to do. In fact, after looking at tens of thousands of campaign narratives over many years, I think the most common thing crowdfunders say is that they don't want to ask for help, and they've had to set aside their "pride" to do so. We can see the many varieties of the way people talk about pride in the poem that precedes this chapter. Losing one's pride by asking for help online is a major affective dimension of the crowdfunding experience. One of the reasons many people find it so hard is that they have internalized a dominant American ethos of "rugged individualism"—that they alone are responsible for themselves and their families, and any shortcomings in their ability to succeed are the result of their own faults rather than any outside factors. For those who have to admit a significant financial need while crowdfunding, it can feel tantamount to admitting failure.

Trevor, the single dad from the introduction who never shared his campaign with anyone, found himself paralyzed by this ethos. During our interview, he returned again and again to discussions of everything he had done to try to stay afloat financially, to the many jobs he held and how hard a worker he was. But when it came down to it, despite recognizing how hard he had worked, he couldn't bring himself to share his campaign with friends and family: "I mean, my pride's worth more than that to me." I asked him to explain his thinking further. "Because I've always led a life where I lead and try to be an example. . . . I just . . . it would . . . I could never make that something," he said. "It would always have to be something that would just be in the shadows. I couldn't make that public because. . . . I don't feel like mine is worthy of being shared, and certainly not to any of the people that are close to me." Later, he clarified that he would feel fine using crowdfunding "if I ever designed something or engineered something that I wanted to sell or have people invest in . . . if I was designing, like, the new . . . Velcro, I would hammer it out. I'd build a website, I'd have it on Facebook, Twitter, I'd have it on the whole 9 yards. And I'd be bumping it every single day." But crowdfunding for his health-care needs—in the way he had done it, without sharing the campaign with anyone he knew—was futile, he recognized. "Gosh," he said, "that's like looking to the stars and hoping to be the one that someone points out to."

Trevor's reticence about what he thought of as "handouts" extended to other public forms of support. His income was low enough for him to be on food stamps and Medicaid, but he admitted that he still preferred to pay out of pocket whenever he could—including for his insulin, which ran hundreds of dollars a month. "I pay out-of-pocket because . . . I don't know," he said. "I don't know. Maybe I'm just odd or weird in that sense, but . . . I'm the type of person that has a real problem with taking handouts. . . . It's like I'm, it's almost like I'm allergic to them. I try to use them as little as I possibly can." Trevor's outlook is the natural outcome of toxic ideas about individualism and deservingness in the United States, and shows how these cause wide-reaching harm.

Crowdfunding powerfully reinforces these ideas even as it encourages us to turn toward our social networks and ask for help. But as much as we turn to the "crowd" for help, it's really on us to figure out how to save ourselves. As we saw at the beginning of this chapter, companies like GoFundMe promote a story of success that is due to individual grit, passion, and hard work. The flip side of this is that when a campaign doesn't work, we're likely to internalize the message that it's our fault or that we simply don't deserve what others have. More broadly, crowdfunding normalizes, as discussed in chapter 2, a moral toxicity of deservingness that conflates crowdfunding success with inherent goodness. If you do well, it's evidence you're a good person. Again, the flip side of that reasoning is that if you do poorly, you reveal (publicly, no less) that you are not as "good" as someone else who finds success. No wonder, in these circumstances, it's hard for people like Trevor to ask for help.

Contrast these ideas with a broader social ethic of collective responsibility—that we are all responsible for each other, that if we fall on hard times, our society as a whole should support us. Crowdfunding appeals to, and reinforces, an individualist, competitive society with few safety nets, where individual choices determine who gets help. In crowdfunding economies, no one forces us to donate; we can choose what matters to us, who we will support, and who gets passed by. We may come to those decisions with very different reasons, but by participating in this economy we are endorsing the idea that who gets help should be a matter of personal choice, not social obligation.

The COVID pandemic revealed in stark terms the toxicity of a notion that we have a right choose who we care for and who we won't. In countries like the United States that celebrate ideas of rugged individualism, Robin G. Nelson observed, people constantly chose their own comfort and desires over broader social protections, eroding what few public health measures were implemented as quickly as possible.[20] On sites like

GoFundMe, we saw the costs of those positions: the largest proportion of campaigns related to COVID in the United States were for individual, urgent needs—and these campaigns had the least support.[21] By contrast, New Zealand, which had a strongly communitarian, collectivist ethic to its COVID response, managed to implement an array of powerful prevention measures.[22] Susan Wardell observed that campaigns in New Zealand appealed to this collectivist ethic and often aimed to aid communal efforts at addressing COVID.[23]

Toxic individualism arises, ironically, in the context of economic conditions in late capitalism that make simply getting by a serious challenge for most people. Rather than recognize these challenges as shared (and changeable), our continued insistence on holding only ourselves to account leads to truncated, personal requests for charitable support that ultimately do not solve—*cannot solve*—our larger needs. Writing from the context of humanitarian disaster response, Mark Duffield has aptly called this phenomenon the "enforced resilience of abandonment."[24] We frantically doggy paddle, mostly alone, through crisis, thinking we have no other choice. Even when these efforts find success, they can reinforce individualism and abandonment, forms of care that ultimately make us more precarious. And when success is found in the hypervisible, digital public realm of crowdfunding, it can create new and unexpected vulnerabilities as well.

THE DANGERS OF GOING VIRAL

Aliya had a very different experience with crowdfunding than Christie—so different, in fact, that its success nearly upturned her life for a while. In some ways, Aliya's story also upends the data on what shapes success: she is a young, Black woman and was campaigning on behalf of an immigrant family from East Africa. But once we dig beneath the surface of the campaign she created, we find that success can create its own kinds of precarity and danger, particularly for people who are already racially, ethnically, or socioeconomically marginalized.

Aliya was an overbusy but highly competent nurse at a public hospital in a large city when she started her GoFundMe campaign.[25] She arrived at work one day to find out her coworker Amari's wife had been violently attacked in her home, in front of her two young children, and was now in the ICU at their hospital. Amari was one of her favorite colleagues, a kind and attentive but low-paid hospital assistant. Aliya knew that Amari was in for a very hard time—his wife Fatima's prognosis was not good, and even if she survived, Amari would be out of work for quite some time. He was the sole income earner for his family, and as recent immigrants, they had limited family support and access to government benefits. "I knew that there was gonna be a need, and there was really nothing we could do for them, but I knew that money was what they were going to really need," she recalled. So, though she and Amari were not particularly close—they liked working together, but she did not know his family well—she started a GoFundMe for him. Initially, it was intended just for immediate coworkers in their unit at the hospital, to let them know what was going on and get Amari some financial help. She printed up a few photocopies of the campaign page and posted them around her unit, figuring it was an easy way to get out the word among staff, who often worked long and varied shifts.

Aliya was on the night shift, so after she started the campaign, she turned off her phone and went to bed. By the time she woke up, "it was chaos. I had like ten missed calls. My Facebook was shut down. [Normally] you can't see anything on my Facebook, it's super private. I had people in my inboxes, I had reporters on my Timeline, which—I don't even know how they got on my Timeline. I had people pay to try to contact [me] through other people." Aliya hadn't even shared the campaign publicly on Facebook, but the local news had picked up on the story of Fatima's attack. Most of the attention she initially received was from journalists wanting to find out more—not about the campaign but about the violent attack on Fatima. "They weren't interested in the campaign," she said, "they wanted to know details. . . . They wanted information that I really could not give them . . . I'm not the spokesperson for the family so I also didn't feel comfortable inserting myself, in this way. And [Amari] didn't wanna talk. . . . It got to a point where I was like you know what? I'm not the spokesperson. And I really don't want to speak on their behalf." Amari was a deeply private person and also did not have the language or media skills to handle the onslaught of attention.

Once local news became involved, Amari and Fatima's story, and the campaign itself, all became extremely public and linked together. None of them had anticipated this would happen, nor had they wanted this kind of attention. "It was supposed to be a very internal thing, in my mind, when I set it up," Aliya said, "and so . . . there was kind of an intrusion of privacy, for me, that I didn't quite realize. Like, I thought, 'it's my friends, and it's fine' but I didn't realize the public, in that way, would . . ." She trailed off. GoFundMe campaigns are typically set up to be shared, so privacy controls are minimal. But sharing with coworkers and friends of friends is very different than having strangers recognize your name and face at Starbucks or having news reporters posting all over your timeline. And Aliya hadn't anticipated how much the GoFundMe page would feed the media's appetite for gory details on the crime and its aftermath.

Journalists knew that Aliya worked at the same place where Fatima was hospitalized, so they were constantly calling her for updates. She always declined to provide them, but the calls became quite invasive. At one point, journalists "somehow found out [Fatima] was pregnant. And so, the reporters are calling me, like, 'What about the baby?' And I was like, 'what the hell?' . . . I had purposely not told [them] any of those details." Because she was responsible for posting updates to the campaign page, she also became the bearer of terrible, deeply personal news as Fatima's condition became worse. "[It] was horrible," she said, "because one of the things was, yeah, I had to post that—[I had to] let [everyone] know she had passed." She sighed and continued, "Like I said, I just signed up for a whole lot more than I thought I was signing up for. And I can't reiterate that enough. . . . It was terrible."

"And then, the weirdos. Can we talk about the weirdos?" Aliya said sardonically. "Let's talk about the weirdos," I replied. We were laughing but it was clear that Aliya had been through an extremely uncomfortable, and at times unsafe, experience. People were contacting journalists trying to get her contact information or harassing her to give out Fatima and Amari's address. It was hard to parse the people who wanted an address so they could send a check and those who wanted contact information for more nefarious purposes. She noted the creepy irony that she was crowd-funding for a woman who had been violently attacked in her home: "You don't put your stuff online, for safety. But [people] want me to provide information. What about my safety? What about [Amari's]? . . . I didn't know if they wanted the address to know exactly where [the crime] happened, or like? . . . You don't know what to think. Because you don't want, you know, his home to become like a drive-by scene." Aliya was also inundated with accusatory questions from donors who didn't trust her and wanted more information—more than she was willing to give—before they donated to the campaign. Accusations, distrust, and invasions of privacy are often more common for women and people of color online.[26] Certainly, Aliya's experience going viral involved far more accusations, distrust, and privacy invasions than Spencer's experience with Mark and Sofia's campaign, which also got quite a bit of news coverage and popular attention.

Aliya had no idea the campaign was going to go viral. As a nurse, in particular a nurse at a public safety net hospital, Aliya treated victims of crimes all the time; it was hard to explain why this story generated so much attention. She reflected that she saw "sadness every day. So maybe my gauge is totally off, because I'm like, well . . . you know, hopeless stuff happens all the time. . . . And not to say that I'm jaded or immune, but I had no idea that all these [news] stations would pick up [the story]." But it also became clear that Aliya had quite a bit of expertise in knowing how to make social media gain traction. Once the media was interested, she strategically tried to direct attention to the campaign, figuring it would at least provide some help to Amari. "I encouraged everyone in our break room to not only donate," she said, "but to share on their Facebooks. . . . And I shared it on Instagram . . . and so I got people I don't really talk to anymore, but were donating."

She would time the campaign updates to when she knew posts would be most likely to be seen, and she would get her coworkers to do the same, saying "You know Facebook has like algorithms, right? So, you kind of have to try to post at certain times of the day." She had taken note of when her Instagram posts did best with friends in different time zones and would post at those times. Same too with the media—she understood that "you kind of have to strike while the iron is hot, because people move on." Aliya mostly attributed her expertise to generational differences: "My generation, we're pretty good with technology. And you've seen enough GoFundMes to kind of know the drill." She recalled helping older coworkers figure out how to make online donations to the campaign and post updates to Facebook.

Ultimately, the campaign raised more than $50,000. It was an enormous help to Amari, who struggled in the months afterwards to care for his kids and could not return to work. But talking to Aliya, I became aware of the mix of challenging emotional labor, invasions of privacy, and technical expertise that the campaign had involved. She called the experience "terrible" on more than one occasion, describing her extensive work on the campaign as "something between . . . project manager and resource specialist." Other coworkers began coming to her, including one who was going through cancer treatment, asking her to set up campaigns for them too.

The experience also complicated her relationship with Amari. Because the campaign took off so fast, and went far beyond what she intended, she regretted not telling Amari before she launched it. But he had been focused on his wife and only minimally understood what crowdfunding was. She did check in with Amari soon after it launched, and he was deeply grateful for what she'd done. But she felt badly that to get help he'd faced such an immense invasion of his—and his children's—privacy. What had been put up couldn't really be taken down. Even if she took down the campaign itself, all the news coverage, the Facebook posts, and the people who had seen it and donated could not be taken back. "Nobody gives you a handbook" for this kind of experience, she said with some bitterness.

Aliya and Amari's story is an outlier, but I think it's an instructive one. Aliya's social media skills surely aided Amari's campaign but so too did media sensationalism over Amari's deeply personal tragedy. Unlike Mark and Sofia's extensive "fellowship of care," she faced a more unpredictable and hostile crowd even as the campaign succeeded by quantitative measures. Going viral helped Amari financially through an unimaginably hard loss, but it also exposed both of them to privacy invasions, vulnerabilities, and experiences they could not have predicted. Amari was surrounded by care throughout this experience—but not from the campaign, which he was barely even aware of. Rather, it was his deep-rooted, far-reaching immigrant community that ended up caring for him.

"Soooo many people," Aliya recalled, showed up to support him in the hospital. "So many people, always. They took over the waiting room, there were always like 25 people [there]."

Much of what Aliya describes about this experience resonates with accounts of how social media economies demand emotional labors and losses of privacy. Researchers have observed that significant labor goes into generating online traction, spreading media, and building a following and that much of this labor is deeply gendered and feminized, as Aliya found out.[27] Similarly, experiences of online scrutiny and loss of privacy are gendered and racialized.[28] Aliya reflected the carefully honed skills of someone who is comfortable in these realms: she understood algorithms and how to time her posts for maximum impact and what sorts of privacy she could and could not expect from different posts. But these were not enough to protect her. Despite her skills, she felt that she had no "handbook" when it came to a campaign like this, particularly as it attracted attention for its sensationalism. Most importantly, such sensationalism precluded—and made impossible—other kinds of care that Aliya wanted to offer: care that was intimate, private, compassionate, and attentive to the fragility of Fatima's condition and to the enormity of Amari's grief.

PRECARIOUS CARING

Aliya and Amari's experience highlights how crowdfunding is shifting the ways we think about, and provide, care. In contrast to the deeply relational, intimate forms of care that Amari's immigrant community showed up to provide, the care he received through GoFundMe was at times alienating, invasive, inscrutable, and objectifying. More commonly, the care people access through GoFundMe is simply not enough, or too fragile. Social media can make it more difficult to articulate real needs, as Christie found out. The late capitalist system, combined with our particularly diminished safety nets in the United States, means that our society faces a "crisis of care."[29] The demands of everyday care far outpace our individual capacities to carry them out, and, ultimately, this undermines our capacity for "social reproduction"—all the (often gendered) efforts of bringing up, sustaining, and reproducing a socially connected life that holds our society together.[30] At times of acute crisis, these already frayed systems fail to hold us together—there is too much need, too little support, too little to go around. And while affluent people can purchase more care and protection for themselves, there are enormous economic, gender, and racial inequities in terms of who can do this and for how long.[31] Together, these conditions make for *precarious care*—where the care demands are overwhelmingly large, they cannot make up for safety nets we do not have, and those who can best purchase or provide this care are often those who need it the least.[32]

Crowdfunding thrives in, and fuels, this crisis. It lowers the transaction costs of care; care becomes as easy as entering your credit card info, logging into Venmo, posting a comment, or sharing a post. And that's not to say that these don't feel like significant forms of care, especially when campaigns are successful. We live in a moral economy where other forms of support often seem impossible and where our identities, social connections, and energies are very much bound up in social media. It's natural that within this environment, such forms of support would come to feel like a very real thing. Angela, who ran a fairly successful campaign for her husband's kidney transplant, conveyed how much donations meant to them, particularly since they were geographically far from many friends and family. She said it was particularly meaningful "when people donate multiple times to you . . . those folks would stand out for me as like, special support. One of them, we're becoming a little bit closer as, actually just as a friendship, just because they reached out the way that they did."

These forms of connection are meaningful, but platforms also shift what care looks like and how it is both given and received. Receiving repeat donations from people became particularly significant to Angela and her husband, and they began to look forward to donations as tangible expressions of caregiving. "I think it mutually benefited both of us because," she said, "it was something that we could look forward to, like, 'we got more donations today.' And it would be like, 'look, we got another donation,' and then we would get happy. And it was . . . a source of hope, and positivity, and optimism that we would definitely . . . not have had otherwise. [It] really helped us to get through this . . . otherwise totally horrible period of time that he was going through."

As Lana Swartz has observed, payment has become a major dimension of social media.[33] What we pay, how we pay, and who we pay have increasingly become part of our online identities. These are "now part of who we are and where we belong," she says. "Our transactional identities can overlap with our other identities—gender, class, line of work, language, geography—in complex ways. They organize space and our movement through it."[34] But as Swartz notes, there are really important barriers to who can pay in these ways and what happens to those who cannot pay. These "transactional identities," she writes, "are technologies of belonging, inclusion, and exclusion."[35] As Spencer noted in chapter 2, the prominence of donations as primary forms of care in crowdfunding means that when people donate, the actions are "not trite" but show who is really "there for you." GoFundMe made it easier for some in Christie's social network to avoid the awkwardness of telling her they didn't have the funds to contribute; yet this also may have meant they were deprived of the opportunity to offer care and concern, to maintain those connections with her.

Crowdfunding creates new forms of care labor as well. Starting a campaign for someone in need is a significant digital effort, as Aliya found out. Caring for people by starting crowdfunding campaigns means curating a narrative of their story, giving thought to how they are portrayed and what claims to moral deservingness can be made, posting updates, sending thank-you notes to donors, providing transparency as to how the funds are used, and managing the financial information that allows donations to keep moving from the platform into recipient bank accounts. This is far easier for some than others. For Angela, it was intuitive—she was a writer and communication expert: "I do a lot of persuasive thinking and writing. And so, I felt like, *I could do this*, like, I could write something really good. [Something] that's going to empower and . . . inspire people to donate. I felt like, oh this is right up my alley."

While Angela had a fairly positive experience with this dimension of care, for Aliya it was profoundly uncomfortable, even despite her skills. It involved risks to her security, privacy, and professional status that she hadn't anticipated. These new digital labors sit alongside other extensive forms of in-person caregiving that should not be overlooked. For Angela, that meant nothing short of becoming a kidney donor through a match program so that her husband could get his transplant. She had been out of work without pay for months on end, and the recovery, she admitted, was not as smooth as she had hoped. For Christie, the care labors for her family were also enormous and hard to convey to her online audiences. Crowdfunding does not supplant these other demands, but it can sometimes overshadow and conceal them. As digital campaigns become the focus of caregiver attentions, offline forms of care and support fade from view.

If crowdfunding provides opportunities for at least some people to give care that is meaningfully recognized as real and impactful, how does it contribute to this phenomenon I call precarious care? First, when users equate donations with care, they normalize a system where those who do not get donations, or who cannot give them, are seen as undeserving of receiving or giving care. This is a not-insignificant portion of people who are suddenly excluded from networks of care, in a society already facing acute crises of care. Second, these forms of online caregiving and help seeking can make people vulnerable in new ways, whether by exposing them to digital incursions of privacy and rights or by subjecting them to the judgments of themselves and others. Finally, and relatedly, it curtails what is perceived as the motivating issue for campaigns. By focusing our attention on little, solvable, personal crises—such as Christie's need for help with gas, not the fact that she had overwhelming medical debt coming her way and few social safety nets—crowdfunding distracts us from the larger problems fueling our crises. It becomes harder and harder to see, attend to, and ideally act upon the broader social crises that are causing us to turn to crowdfunding in the first place. It's a vicious cycle—the more we turn to crowdfunding, the less we pay attention to broader crises; as those crises deepen, we turn more and more to crowdfunding. As Hannah Zeavin has astutely observed, in digital environments "care is a tool, but it is also, too often, a weapon."[36]

Finally, a grim reality of the crowdfunding economy is that one can only turn to crowdfunding so many times. Angela and her husband ultimately ran two crowdfunding campaigns—one for his transplant and one for hers. Both were fairly successful, but she admitted they should have asked for more to meet their needs. As she reflected, "people now may be thinking, 'Oh, they reached their goal. So, they have what they need,' when in reality, we definitely needed more, we had kind of undercut how much we would be needing." But beyond that, their needs were not over—not by a long shot. And they felt they had exhausted the energies and support of their digital crowd. How many times, realistically, can we successfully crowdfund for the "crisis ordinariness" that many of us now face in our lives?[37] Echoing Berlant, the crowdfunding experiences described in this chapter largely failed to offer users important dimensions of safety, security, or support, even when their campaigns appeared successful. Despite platform successes, crowdfunders and their loved ones remained precarious. The promise of crowdfunding as digital opportunity overshadows the ways it creates new vulnerabilities and ultimately limits us from other possibilities—other forms of caring and other ways of surviving crisis.

OPPORTUNITIES LOST

These stories raise questions about what sorts of opportunities are lost when crowdfunding becomes the primary form of caregiving, rescue, and resilience in a time of crisis ordinariness. While users are told that they "can use GoFundMe for just about anything," what other kinds of social connection, solidarity, assistance, and mobilization are made less possible when GoFundMe is the place we turn to when we need help?[38] This chapter has explored how crowdfunding fosters individualistic responses to crisis and an "enforced resilience" in the midst of late capitalist crises of care. Donation-as-care supplants other forms of care and connection and in doing so reinforces the idea that the many people who do not find crowdfunding success are not worthy of care. We lose sight of a sense of being *entitled* to basic protections, and of deserving certain basic rights, when, like Christie, we must turn to friends and family and ask for the least of what need. These dynamics point to larger social questions: What kinds of communal mobilization are lost when we address social crises whack-a-mole style through individualized, competitive crowdfunding? What could we accomplish—what could we imagine and create collectively—if we were not expending so much energy trying to patch over the many holes in our safety net system with crowdfunding campaigns?

The rest of the book is organized around answers to these questions. In the next chapter, we'll look at how crowdfunding is emblematic of a host of new digital technologies that promise to solve health issues but reinforce a kind of "downstream" thinking about how we identify and address population health needs. Such downstream thinking precludes upstream approaches that can be more effective in addressing the powerful forces that create health inequities and fuel crises. And finally, the conclusion introduces some important alternatives to crowdfunding—and alternative ways crowdfunding platforms are being used—that point to other possibilities for thinking about how we can leverage community, care, and connection to create more transformative change.

Corona took everything

I'm not really sure how to begin, so I'm just going to wing it.
Carlos was a wonderful man who loved his children.
Dad was a dedicated teacher and Amazon essential worker.
Soon he struggled to breath and was rushed to the ER.
Corona took everything we had.
Widow. Unemployed. 4 weeks no unemployment.
I've also been laid off because of the coronavirus.
Please help me pay the rent for my house.
I am razing money to help feed my great grand son.
Lost my job, lost my car, losing my mind, this is not working.
As you think about the purpose and spirit of the CARES Act
ask yourself, how is it possible
for someone in my circumstance
to not get benefits of ANY kind?
This campaign is our last resort.
Anything would and will be greatly appreciated very much.
No matter how small anything will help.
This will take a miracle.
Thank you. Thank you all so much.

5

DOWNSTREAM FIXES, UPSTREAM PROBLEMS

When I teach undergraduate students about what causes differences in health status across the life course, we begin with a very simple, well-known public health parable.[1] I ask students to imagine they are with a friend beside a fast-moving river, when all of the sudden they see someone float by, clearly in distress. Panicked, they wade out into the river and pull the person to safety. But no sooner do they reach the shore than they see another person rushing by, also in distress. Again, they wade out into the river and rescue the person. This continues for hours until they are utterly exhausted, and people still keep floating by. I ask my students, What would you do?

This thought exercise is designed to push us, in public health parlance, to think and act "upstream." How are all these people ending up in the river? Is something or someone pushing them in? Are they unaware of the risks? Are there no guardrails or bridges to ensure safety? To think and act upstream is to identify the kinds of measures that prevent crises in the first place. The parable is also a cautionary tale about the ways that focusing on the "downstream" rescue of individuals is both resource intensive and distracts us from preventing people from falling in the river in the first place.

The stream is also a metaphor for poor health—what factors push us into the stream of illness or injury, and how can they be prevented? Public health efforts often aim upstream, trying to implement preventive measures that are minimally invasive or less costly. We know that it's easier and cheaper to normalize kids wearing bike helmets than to treat numerous cases of head and neck trauma and death. Fluoride, seatbelts, vaccinations, vitamin-fortified foods—these are the unglamorous, underappreciated, but deeply impactful, measures that keep people out of the river. They are not without controversy at times, but they work—often contributing far more to extended life expectancies and improved living circumstances than anything we can do downstream for people once they're already ill.

In public health, we also try to think in political and economic terms about what pushes people into poor health, from failures to regulate clean air standards to economic and social inequities that contribute to poor health and premature death. And public health also concerns itself with health systems, attending to the ways that these systems can prevent or cause harm. Even when medical care rescues someone from disease, the costs of that care in marketized health systems can feel like falling into a whole different river right after being dragged out of the first one.

Chris is one of many Americans who found themselves drowning in health costs and looked to crowdfunding as a remedy. His story helps explain how the downstream solution of crowdfunding—even when a campaign is highly successful—fails to address upstream causes. A well-known Chicano musician, Chris ended up in the ICU after falling severely ill while his band was on tour. He was diagnosed with type 1 diabetes. The causes of type 1 diabetes are complex, and there was little Chris could have done to avoid getting it.[2] But an earlier diagnosis would have saved him the anguish and cost of his ICU stay as well as the financial precarity he faced in the months to come. Research shows that considerable financial toxicity accompanies diabetes diagnoses in the United States: more than 40 percent of people with diabetes report difficulty paying their medical bills.[3] Chris's diagnosis came at an especially vulnerable period in his life. He had gotten sober and was finally touring with his band again, but he had lost his house and was uninsured. After being hospitalized, he had to cancel his band's tour, which was his only source of income.

With tens of thousands of social media followers, Chris's GoFundMe campaign quickly raised more than $15,000. Before we talked, I had hoped that his campaign might be one of the rare ones that provides real help. I'd seen far too many campaigns, especially for conditions like diabetes that are chronic and often unjustly stigmatized, that had raised little, if any, money. "When it first happened . . . we were like, 'Wow, this is so much!'" Chris recalled. But "once we started adding things up, and back rent and bills, and three kids, and house, and hospital bills . . . yeah, it just, it was gone." Unfortunately, while Chris's campaign undoubtedly helped him get through a rough patch, he and his family were still facing enormous struggles when we spoke a year later. Donations went to pay off immediate medical bills and debts, and Chris ultimately had to borrow $13,000 from his record label to stay afloat.

A year later, Chris was still living in a camper with his wife and three children in Minnesota. He said the previous winter had been "really bad" given their living circumstances. Despite two years of appeals, he was still not on Medicaid, in part because finances from his music career and the GoFundMe campaign earnings were so confusing. Several times, hospital financial counselors accused him of lying about his income after seeing his campaign. He followed up on doctor referrals, but without insurance, the "bills . . . were crazy . . . and I got kind of weary of going." Chris hadn't seen a primary care doctor in more than a year and was having serious vision problems. It was hard to get healthy food and cook it, especially relying on food stamps. And while he appreciated the low-cost insulin he got at Walmart, when we spoke, it had been five days since he'd taken one of the two kinds of insulin he needed, due to lack of funds. Despite these conditions, Chris radiated generosity and what he called the "DIY spirit" of his band—sentiments that echoed the projected ethic of GoFundMe as well. He was proud of his sobriety and his kids. "Everything is looking up," he told me, despite "tough times and tough changes." He noted it had been hard to ask for money but that he had also questioned whether he should have asked for more. Mostly, he was trying to focus on the future: "So, our string of bad luck is definitely gonna, hopefully, be reversed, you know?"

As Chris talked, his voice was frequently drowned out by the inevitable noise of three children, two adults, and several cats living in a small camper. The cacophony of Chris's real life contrasted with the easy success projected by his online campaign and his social media posts, where an adoring mass of followers assumed they were saving his career and his life, oblivious to the silent crises he still faced long after the campaign had ended. This audible disjuncture highlighted what is often undetectable to online audiences. Chris' campaign defied the odds, but it also failed to offer enough support and contributed to his difficulties enrolling in Medicaid. Crowdfunding can reinforce what Beza Merid has called "health insurance precarity," failing to substitute for yawning gaps in the social safety net.[4] As researchers have found, crowdfunding campaigns for insulin cannot provide the kinds of meaningful, long-term assistance that people reliant upon this therapeutic need.[5] After his campaign, without consistent access to healthcare or medicines, Chris remained at constant risk of falling back into that river of ill health.

Crowdfunding campaigns like Chris's are most often a downstream digital fix for complex problems—problems that require much more than a one-time infusion of cash. As this chapter explores, crowdfunding can undermine efforts to address problems upstream, joining a cohort of popular digital technologies that reinforce downstream fixes. As many scholars have noted, the embrace of these technologies can often reinforce and exacerbate health inequities while also undermining the complex, long-term, hard work of upstream public health initiatives.[6]

WAITING FOR THE SHIT TO HIT THE FAN

"You go from, y'know, just perfectly normal life and all of a sudden you're in over your head," Sabrina said as she began telling the story of her family's crowdfunding campaign. Sabrina was a successful, driven college student, but her family had deep financial and health troubles, and their "perfectly normal" life was on a shaky foundation even before her dad's stroke. Her mother, Debbie, had a host of mental health issues, including obsessive-compulsive disorder, bipolar disorder, and anxiety, which had kept her from being able to work for decades. "For the longest time," Sabrina said, her dad, Glen, had supported the family by working temporary clerical jobs. These forced him to live many hours from home and meant he had no health insurance. "So, money has been really low for quite some time," Sabrina said matter-of-factly.

Her dad's severe stroke, which paralyzed him and left him hospitalized for nearly a month, upended their precarious financial balance. With no money coming in, no insurance to help with the medical bills, and long trips to and from the urban hospital where her dad was being treated, her family was just watching the debt accumulate. "And we were trying to think of *anything* we could do," Sabrina said. "My mom really didn't want to attempt any type of crowdfunding because she was very . . . not secretive, but she just doesn't like . . . people knowing that we were in such a period of struggle. But from our perspective there was nothing else we could do . . . there was just no money anywhere."

Sabrina researched campaigns for similar causes and wrote a clear, compelling narrative for Glen's campaign that emphasized his positivity and sense of humor. She said, "I really wanted to let people know that he was really strong and doing all he could." She talked about how exposed it made her feel asking for help: "I mean, of course there's the concern that you're going to write it and not raise any money. That's the biggest concern. Um, and also, I mean, you do feel really vulnerable, because you are reaching out to people for help because you can't help yourself anymore, and that, that's a really tough thing to do. To say, I'm at the bottom, and I need help. Like, it's harder than you would think to ask."

Sabrina really wanted to make the campaign as successful as it could be. She considered trying to get news coverage or posting printed flyers around the community. Aware of campaigns that got lots of community attention—"not so much [those for the] homeless, but . . . little kids saving to go [to] their baseball national [playoffs] or whatever," she wondered what would happen "if you went somewhere public and just made a big thing of saying, 'Help'?" Ultimately, however, she did not pursue this strategy, saying "I mean, it already took a lot of courage [just] to post the GoFundMe." I asked if she had an expectation for how the campaign would go, and she demurred: "I didn't know what to expect, honestly. Um, because I could picture it really taking off, and I could picture no one doing anything." She said she was just trying to be "very hopeful, and grateful for anything that did come through."

Sabrina's family raised just over $3,000 from about thirty donors. She said it was "very helpful, and I'm grateful for the amount that we did receive. But it also didn't completely blow me away." She paused for a moment. "Like, it was a good amount," she said, as if she was trying to convince herself of this fact. The campaign also offered some of the only support they got during her dad's crisis. The hospital offered very little financial counseling, and her dad's case manager was, in Sabrina's words, "absolutely horrible." The family was eager to find additional support and had lots of questions, but "she really didn't have any answers. She pretty much said, 'Well, y'all need to figure out what you want to do. Because he needs to leave here.'"

The family was also struggling to find a rehab facility for Glen since he was still uninsured, and the money their campaign raised couldn't begin to cover the costs of such care. They were signing up for Medicaid, disability, and other social supports, but these processes were painfully slow. With an insurance status of "Medicaid pending," only two facilities in the region would accept him. "We chose the best of the two, but um, it definitely was not a good place for him to be," Sabrina said. "They did not take very good care of him." When we talked, Glen was back in critical care, having developed terrible bedsores, which then became infected and gave him sepsis. His infection turned out to be MRSA—a staph infection resistant to many antibiotics that is notoriously hard to treat. "Things are not getting better," Sabrina said flatly. They were hoping to rent him a special bed to help with the bedsores since the staff at the rehab facility wasn't turning him enough. The bed cost $8,000 a month to rent.

Meanwhile, much of the money they earned in their campaign was going to Sabrina's mom, Debbie, "just so that she can [eat], so she can keep the electricity running, and gas to go back" and forth to where Glen was hospitalized. Sabrina and her sister were trying to get Debbie on benefits as well, but most of the benefits she qualified for would imperil Glen's Medicaid status, under lesser-known rules in these programs that penalize people who are disabled and married.[7] Sabrina admitted that most of the important medical and financial decisions were being "ignored" because neither of her parents were in a place to cope with them, nor did they have the resources they needed to address them. "I think that we are . . . kind of waiting for the shit to hit the fan at this point," she said. "Because . . . yeah, a lot of things have been thrown to the wayside. We all know very well that my mom is going to be losing her house. It's a matter of when." Even if they filed for medical bankruptcy, her mom was still out of work, unable to get benefits and unable to make their house payments. "I don't know where she's going to stay," Sabrina said. "Um . . . I can't picture her moving into a homeless shelter . . . but she can't help herself . . . I'm in college, and I can't really—I couldn't have my mom living in the streets but at the same time. . . . it would be a very big problem. I can't support my mom. I can hardly support myself right now."

Compared with what most campaigns earn, Sabrina's family indeed raised a "good amount." Recall that in chapter 3 we saw that only the top 20 percent of campaigns raise more than $3,000.[8] But this apparent success could not even begin to resolve their financial precarity or debt. It's not uncommon to hear people talk about GoFundMe as an "informal safety net" that catches people where more formal safety nets do not. As Sabrina's story makes abundantly clear, even when relatively successful, crowdfunding cannot adequately fill in where formal safety nets fail. Had these safety nets been more robust, they could have prevented much of Sabrina's family's suffering. It's always hard to engage in "what if" scenarios, but we can see how being insured might have helped Glen get an earlier diagnosis and treatment to prevent his stroke, or how getting Sabrina's mom benefits and mental health treatment earlier would have made her less precarious when Glen got sick. If the disability and health coverage they both needed were easier to get and less punitive toward people in their situation, they would have better navigated the challenges of Glen's rehabilitation and Debbie's housing. And, of course, with better health coverage, Glen would have avoided further complications and suffering arising from the subpar care he received in rehab. It seemed likely that the long-term financial and educational impacts for Sabrina and her parents would be substantial, threatening to perpetuate a cycle of precarity. Her crowdfunding campaign felt something like trying to put a Band-Aid on a bullet hole.

Stories like Sabrina's are not what crowdfunding companies want us to hear. Each year on Giving Tuesday, GoFundMe releases its annual report, touting how much of an impact the company has had. The numbers of campaigns started, donations received, and people helped are often enormous, and these figures are picked up by media outlets as a feel-good holiday story. In 2022, even as GoFundMe's report detailed continued increases in campaigns for basic needs like gas, groceries, and baby formula, the company emphasized stories of doing good and making change. "Every act of help makes a difference," it declared. "Your help is powerful."[9] It's easy to get caught up in the sentiment of these messages, to read about campaigns that have transformed lives. But behind the glossy reports are stories like Chris's and Sabrina's, where even successful campaigns did not, *could not*, fix systemic problems. And behind those campaigns are the vast majority that do not find even limited success at all.

THERE'S A GOFUNDME FOR THAT

One of the most powerful impacts of crowdfunding sites is the way that they change how we think about the problems we face, where they come from, and what we can do about them. As digital technologies have become immersed in our lives, it's increasingly common to see people embracing technological "innovations" to solve complex problems and fill gaping holes in the systems that are supposed to support and protect us. "There's an app for that," Apple famously repeated in its early iPhone advertising, ushering in a digital era of apps that appeared to solve problems but often did so by "disrupting" existing systems of care and protection. Uber and Lyft provided cheap and convenient alternatives to taxi services but turned entire local markets into gig economies without job protections, benefits, or organizing rights. Airbnb did the same with the hotel industry, in many areas raising rental prices and drastically decreasing the supply of affordable housing.

Tech disruptors soon turned their attention to the United States's enormous, marketized health-care system. From the private acquisition of enormous troves of personal health data, to tracking and surveillance devices, to telehealth innovations, corporations sought to marketize, speculate, and privatize, all while promising greater freedom of choice, ease of use, and innovation.[10] While the emergence of crowdfunding is adjacent to this evolution—GoFundMe was not built with healthcare in mind, per se—it has emerged alongside it and profited from the systems tech has disrupted. If the tag line of the early smartphone era was "there's an app for that," the tagline for the era of economic fallout that followed could easily be, "there's a GoFundMe for that."

The emergence of new digital technologies and their encroachment into healthcare raises numerous issues, which fill the pages of many excellent books and articles on these topics.[11] What I wish to explore here is how our turn toward technologically enabled downstream solutions shifts the way we think about, and provide, broader systems of health and social protection. What happens upstream when the downstream answer is always, "there's a GoFundMe for that"? To answer this question, we'll turn first to a different, lesser-known platform that brings such techno-optimistic solutionism—and the way it changes how we think about healthcare—into clearer view.

When Chase Adam strode onto the stage at Y Combinator's Startup School in 2013, he looked like any other Silicon Valley techie or "thought leader," dressed in a dark T-shirt and sneakers.[12] Adam's organization, Watsi, was the first nonprofit entity to ever be supported by Y Combinator, which is widely recognized as Silicon Valley's most prestigious start-up incubator. Adam had been invited to this forum because he founded what has been described as the world's most successful "global health start-up," a crowdfunding platform that promotes and funds the medical needs of patients in other countries. With the help of "medical partners"—nonprofit organizations, often founded or based in the Global North, who provide medical services in countries in the Global South—Watsi identifies patients in need of medical interventions, helps write patient narratives that will appeal to donors, and posts them to its online funding platform. Using its well-curated website, as well as ample social media outlets and partnerships with for-profit companies, Watsi solicits donations from media-savvy donors across the world to support the costs of treatment for featured patients. Most campaigns focus on technical, biomedical interventions for patients in need of critical care, such as reconstructive surgeries, advanced orthopedic care, or even acute malnutrition treatment. As a result, quick, biomedical fixes are prioritized for fundraising, and communication focuses on the "success" of each campaign.

Branding itself as the "kickstarter for medical treatments," Watsi took a relatively clichéd model for global charity—similar to World Vision's strategy of child sponsorship—and remade it as something new, evocative of the path-breaking technical power of Silicon Valley.[13] Watsi promised users "radically transparent" giving "powered by technology" and novel data-gathering practices. The organization successfully claimed the center of a growing Venn diagram with global health on one side and Silicon Valley on the other. But Adam was at Y Combinator that day to participate in a beloved Silicon Valley tradition: telling his start-up's origin story. The story provides an important glimpse into the ways crowdfunding companies think about healthcare and what the tech industry seeks to disrupt when it comes to charity and social goods.

Adam told the audience that he initially came up with the idea for Watsi while serving in the Peace Corps, traveling on a public bus in Costa Rica. He explained that the impetus for the idea came not from Costa Rica but from an earlier break in his Peace Corps service, when he returned to the United States and visited San Francisco:

> Before I [returned and] saw my friends, I thought they were all going to be miserable. I was the guy that had spent the last five to seven years with nonprofits traveling around the entire world; I figured they were living the *Office Space* life, working dead-end jobs in cubicles in San Francisco, day in and day out. But that wasn't the case. My friends were all happy. Every single one of my . . . friends had an awesome apartment, they actually had girlfriends and boyfriends, they went out, they got to date, they were having fun. . . . But beyond that, they were working for companies and building products and solving problems that they cared about. They were happy; they had found a way to do good and do well. And in contrast, the six years I had spent traveling around the world working for nonprofits, it seemed slow, it seemed bureaucratic, it seemed underfunded—it didn't come with the same energy and optimism and innovation that San Francisco had.

Adam's narrative reflected many of the prominent suspicions and anxieties with which nongovernmental organizations (NGOs) and governments are regarded, particularly within the technology sector, and these mingled with more personal anxieties and feelings of inadequacy that Silicon Valley's success projected for young people who found themselves outside its gilded orbit. Adam recalled that before he left San Francisco, he told "every single person I knew" that he was "done with" working for out-of-date NGOs was no longer "going to sell my soul." At this point in his talk, he was interrupted by enthusiastic applause. He smiled and then laughed. He explained that he vowed to "come back to San Francisco and . . . find a way to do well and do good."

Adam's idea for how to "do good and do well"[14] came to him on that bus ride in Costa Rica as a woman boarded the bus and asked for money to fund her son's medical treatment. Adam "immediately" ignored her requests, noting that such appeals were commonplace on public buses. But then he realized that others on the bus were actually giving this woman money. He said he could not figure out "why all of these local people trusted this woman when they had never trusted all of the women who had come before?" He realized that she "had her son's medical records with her. She was passing it around the bus . . . they were grilling her with questions about the doctor or the hospital or the condition." Adam tells his audience that this moment sparked his idea for crowdfunding that would support medical care in developing countries. Yet it is also a moment that reveals the core values at the heart of Watsi's work: a commitment to accountability, proof, and transparency that will lift the veil of pessimism and doubt through which people in Adam's position regard appeals for charity and the work of nonprofit entities in the Global South. An attendee who posted notes from the start-up school summarized Adam's talk in a three item, bullet-pointed list.[15] The first item on the list read "Fuck non-profits."

Wasti, which is in fact a nonprofit, developed a model of crowdfunding that repackaged downstream health interventions, using digital technologies to make them appear more streamlined, transparent, and accountable. For example, critiquing the opacity among many nonprofits as to where money goes, for a long time, Watsi used a "transparency" link on its homepage to direct visitors to a public Google spreadsheet where it listed every single patient the organization had given money to, including their name, age, and medical issue and where they sought care. The organization published strict rules about who could seek support and under what terms: patients had to be seeking care with one of Watsi's nonprofit "medical partners" in one of the designated countries where it worked, and the cost of their care could not exceed $1,500.[16] Watsi encouraged its partner organizations to put forward patients with treatable conditions that "have a high probability of success."[17] Often, this translated into standalone surgical procedures with low risks and high rewards—hardly the stuff of upstream interventions. Watsi stated its "mission is to fund low-cost, high-impact healthcare. While we would like to eventually work in the United States, we currently focus our efforts in low income countries because it's more frequently the case that a relatively small amount of money stands in the way of someone receiving life-changing care."[18]

Watsi repeatedly emphasized the need for care to be "life changing" to be worthy of crowdfunding. Such justifications appealed to a growing Silicon Valley elite interested in so-called effective altruism as well as everyday donors who wanted to see significant human impact with small, short-term donations.[19] These parameters, as they were interpreted by Watsi's partners and conveyed to me in interviews, not only excluded patients with chronic, ongoing medical needs and unsolvable health problems but also excluded the kinds of preventative, population-level interventions that might reduce the need for expensive surgeries and treatments in the first place.

There is much to unpack in Watsi's model and Adam's narrative, and I have done some of that work elsewhere.[20] But what is immediately striking about Watsi is that it created a very successful model of crowdfunding by marketing a set of technological, downstream fixes to complex health problems. Watsi's platform does not just focus on the downstream rescue—it actively distracts us from upstream possibilities. Through carefully curated lists of patients in need of specific kinds of care, it asks us to focus on what is fixable—and fixable on the cheap: cleft palates, broken limbs, fistula surgeries, and acute malnutrition rank among some of the most popular causes. These are the kinds of standalone treatments that offer compelling narratives and make donors feel like their contributions have sizable impacts. But what donors don't see are all the health needs that remain uncovered, falling outside of Watsi's strict rules for eligibility or the kinds of services its medical partners provide. Chronic conditions, long-term treatments, and routine preventative care are all missing, as are more population-level public health initiatives that might prevent some of the downstream health crises like acute malnutrition that pull so heavily on donors' heart strings.

There are narrative elements missing here too. Often, the origins of patients' ailments are not conveyed, nor much of their treatment aftermath. Each person's story is presented solo—as if they are the only one experiencing malnutrition or fistula and they alone are worthy of our attention. We get no sense of how they came to need these interventions, what they might need in terms of follow-up care, or how their condition relates to broader social determinants. There is often little mention of country health systems, why patients must seek care from a nonprofit, or why care is so cheap in their countries. We also know little about whether and how patients consent to their pictures, biographical details, and names being shared on Watsi's website and in its "transparency" documents.

Notably, Watsi has engaged in some well-intentioned efforts at making crowdfunding fairer. The platform asks donors to contribute to a central fund in addition to individual campaigns; these funds along with grant money ensure that every person on the site will get fully funded care. For a while, rather than allowing visitors to choose which campaign they wished to support from a long list, Watsi's website would show one campaign at a time, seemingly in random order. These are not insignificant alterations to the way crowdfunding works on other platforms. But for Watsi, as with GoFundMe in the United States and other platforms around the world, the solution put forth is still stuck downstream, unable to catch people before they fall in the river. The bigger these platforms become—and the more they attract our attention—the more they distract us from what is happening, and what is possible, upstream.

Ultimately, the shift toward thinking of crowdfunding as a solution to public health problems is occurring at an enormous scale. Entities ranging from nonprofits to research institutions to governments are all turning to crowdfunding for public goods. In 2018, Zimbabwe's finance minister went on Twitter to crowdfund for the country's cholera outbreak despite the government's failure to protect citizens and prevent the outbreak by providing safe and adequate water supplies.[21] In the UK, Ellen Stewart has described how communities have crowdfunded for MRI machines in underserved areas.[22] Among the Venezuelan diaspora trying to aid families and friends struggling to survive during the country's prolonged financial crisis, crowdfunding through social media has become what Michaelanne Dye calls "infrastructural care."[23] When Russia invaded Ukraine in 2022, governments around the world offered support through crowdfunding efforts, and Ukraine's own government crowdfunded for supplies for both civilians and the military. The US State Department, struggling with how to direct charitable donations to Ukraine given the rapidly unfolding crisis, announced a new public-private partnership for collecting and directing donations.[24] Their partner was GoFundMe.

It's clear that crowdfunding has become a prominent solution to health and social challenges in the minds of many across the world. But as Watsi shows, a reliance on thinking about crowdfunding as a solution to public health challenges is a powerful form of "misdirection," blinding us to the things it does not fix, cannot address, and will not change.[25] This is what critical science and technology scholars have called the "solutionism trap"—the "failure to recognize the possibility that the best solution to a problem may not involve technology."[26] The solutionism trap also produces failures of imagination and political will: it keeps us from being able to envision and advocate for the kinds of systemic changes that might render our knee-jerk reliance on crowdfunding for basic needs and widescale crises obsolete.

TECH FOR HEALTH EQUITY?

In public health, we talk a lot about the "determinants of health"—large-scale social, economic, and political forces that powerfully shape population health, though often in ways that are complex and hard to track. Social determinants of health include such things as poverty, racism, ableism, and social connection and privilege, to name just a few. Commercial determinants of health research tracks not only how various corporations and industries directly affect health but also the strategies these actors use to influence policy and the broader economic ideologies, like neoliberalism, that promote commercial interests above those of public health.[27] These approaches recognize that the factors causing people to end up in the river of poor health are complex, power-laden, and societal forces. Such challenges require long-term, structural, and multi-dimensional solutions.

Increasingly, my colleagues and I have been arguing that we also need to recognize digital technologies as a determinant of health.[28] In the health and medical fields, practitioners have generally taken a pretty optimistic view of new technologies, and research focused on health technologies that are used for individual, biomedical interventions: new digital diagnostic tools and treatments, personalized medicine approaches, and improvements in recordkeeping and diagnostic decision-making.[29] But we haven't paid enough attention to the broader ways digital technologies—including social media and the internet—shape physical and mental health and influence the kinds of healthcare we access. Certainly, there are plenty examples of how technology helps improve population health—but we need to pay attention to how technology influences, for better and worse, our health and the ways we access healthcare and information on a broad scale.

This includes acknowledging, as I have tried to do in this chapter, the ways that a specific technology can shift *how* we think about health and healthcare. Take, as one example, the widespread push in US medicine to collect and record social determinants of health data in electronic medical records.[30] This is an approach informed by both concern for health disparities and the tendency of biomedicine to overlook the social and economic conditions that often make people far more susceptible to health issues. As interest in this approach grew, numerous digital technology companies created platforms, apps, and algorithms for collecting, tracking, and quantifying these determinants of health. Articles advertised that the "social determinants tech field" was "wide open" for business.[31] But despite all the investment and heady optimism, in many places it was utterly unclear how companies would take all the data they were collecting on people's living circumstances, education, income, race, and other factors and actually transform it into interventions to address these determinants.

Instead, by focusing attention on data collection and modeling, many health tech firms depoliticized and personalized the very thing they were trying to tackle and thus neutered approaches to addressing *social* determinants.[32] If a patient reported to a doctor that they were behind on rent, their provider could now record that information and the data could be fed into increasingly complex databases, but it wasn't clear if the patient was being linked to assistance with rent or housing, let alone if this data was being used to advocate for fairer or more affordable housing at broader levels. This technological appropriation of the determinants of health weakened its conceptual meaning as well, medicalizing and individualizing these social, political, and economic challenges. Such technological tools rarely help tackle housing policies, wage inequities, or renters' legal rights—things that would actually help to address the social determinants of health at a societal level.[33] Ironically, as more and more private digital technology companies collect and own people's health data, it becomes harder for providers, activists, and policymakers to access and leverage this data for political advocacy on issues such as housing policies.

"HERE'S A FEW BUCKS, SORRY FOR RACISM"

As I have argued throughout this chapter, digital technologies can change the ways we think about, and address, big social problems. Daryl Hatton, FundRazr's CEO, explained to me that he believed one of the big contributors to the growth of charitable crowdfunding were changing expectations among "digital citizens" who wanted immediate and definitive proof of the impacts of their donations. Much like Chase Adam, they were frustrated with the slow pace and limited transparency of traditional giving. "The feeling of making a direct impact overpowered the logic of investing in fixing the root causes of problems," Hatton told me. Crowdfunding offered an "emotional consumer experience" that appealed to many, but distracted from adequately addressing upstream problems.

This phenomenon became particularly clear during the spring and summer of 2020, in the wake of the police murder of George Floyd. As talk of racial justice and the need for reparations circled, many people took to social media to advocate for donations to Black businesses, nonprofits, and social justice organizations. And then a strange thing started happening: Black people started getting digital payments via Venmo, PayPal, or other platforms from colleagues, friends, and even strangers. These donations were not solicited, and they were often for extremely small amounts of money—$5, $10, $20. "Grab a cup of coffee on me" one of the messages with these payments read. "Some variation [of this] has been happening to everybody I know," Emmanuel Dzotsi, who investigated this phenomenon for the podcast *Reply All*, disclosed.[34] "White people have been sending Black people Venmo payments in these really bizarre ways—often completely out of the blue, and frequently, completely unsolicited." Dzotsi referred to them as "the weirdest form of reparations, as if to say, 'here's a few bucks, sorry for racism.'" Exasperatedly trying to figure out what this was about, one Black artist told Dzotsi, "if that was a charity donation to me, that's mad insulting. If that was [for my business] that's *really* insulting. What was that? What was it?!"[35]

Indeed, what was going on here? In one sense, this behavior is an outgrowth of a digital culture that has crept up on us, insidiously changing the way we think about caring for one another.[36] This cultural shift involves our increasing tendency to think about digital money transfers as a means of social belonging and to think of donations as a form of care, advocacy, and action.[37] Crowdfunding is emblematic of these shifts. But what's also shifting is how, and under what terms, we think about social problems and their solutions. Electronically giving a few dollars to the first Black friend you can think of is a quick, technologically enabled, downstream "fix." To best understand what's really happening here, I find it useful to think through what is *not* happening. This is not a political action nor even a public one, and it certainly is not a form of reparations. These are not collective actions or solidarity-building exercises. They reek of downstream solutionism. Racism? There's an app for that. Reparations? There's a GoFundMe for that. These phenomena reveal how quickly digital payments have become a means of *not* dealing with our broader problems or recognizing our greater social obligations to one another.

Small cash payments, like donations to many crowdfunding campaigns, also represent a particularly thin way of connecting and showing care. They seem to work better at relieving our guilt or sense of collective responsibility to each other than enabling actual care. The way that Dzotsi describes these digital encounters reflects care*less*ness: "Here's a few bucks, sorry for racism."[38] Or, in the medical crowdfunding version, "Here's $20, sorry you're uninsured." I'm sure Venmo-ing a few dollars to a Black person made some White people feel a lot better; similarly, crowdfunding donors almost universally tell me that giving to campaigns just feels good, affirming their sense of self and their ability to contribute to helping fix a problem. But these downstream actions often don't solve problems, and they quite often distract us from the real reasons people need to crowdfund in the first place, ultimately making those problems harder to solve.

DIGITAL SPECTACLE AND THE PUBLIC SQUARE

None of this is meant to imply that crowdfunding platforms, like other digital platforms, do not have significant political and social impacts. It's as important to pay attention to where these platforms direct our attention and energy as it is to observe social and political issues they cannot address. Crowdfunding campaigns, particularly popular ones, can evoke a great deal of emotion and engagement precisely because they resonate with broader issues of structural inequity and violence that can feel intractable. At other times, campaigns become organizing spaces for broader social movements. And, like other platforms, crowdfunding sites can also become key spaces where hate, extremism, and antidemocratic visions of the future gain traction and spread.

In July 2022, I was meeting with a focus group of people from the Pacific Northwest. Mostly we spoke about campaigns they had started or donated to for loved ones, friends, or coworkers. But when I asked about more popular campaigns they had seen or interacted with, Jax, a young nonbinary person, nodded, eyes downcast, saying "Well, there's dozens of them, for those kids . . ." Jax was talking about the children and families in Uvalde, Texas, where a teenage shooter had recently killed nineteen children and two teachers and wounded dozens of others. The horror of the shooting was still raw, and news stories were coming out nearly daily detailing the ineptitude and willful cruelty of police who refused to engage the shooter for more than an hour. Everyone was absolutely silent as Jax continued quietly, moved by grief, "I mean, those kids deserve to have their life set with all the money . . . they absolutely should be doing those GoFundMe campaigns. . . . I mean, society failed those children. And most of them will have lifelong trauma. . . . That's probably the least society can do for them."

The other participants in the group nodded. "Okay, so it feels almost like a debt is owed to them?" I asked. Akhil nodded avidly: "Yes . . . the way you summarized it, I feel completely connected with it, that . . . a debt is owed to them . . . [because] they suffered so much . . ." Akhil clarified that these sorts of campaigns were different from others he had engaged with. Even if they raised huge amounts of money, he still felt he owed the recipients something because of how they had suffered. "[In cases] where the victims suffer a lot," he said, "and they get a severely unfair deal from the society, in those cases, I'm strongly motivated to donate and even if their goal is many times oversubscribed. I feel that it is good, and they deserve it."

As I listened to Akhil and Jax, I was struck by their descriptions of crowdfunding as a way to address societal debts. Here, deserving-ness wasn't as much about appearing to be a good person as it was a recognition of suffering—profoundly unjust suffering, the kind that lays bare our social ills and implicates all of us as guilty. As Jax said, "society failed those children," and even though it was "probably the least society can do," crowdfunding offered a way to do *something* in the face of that injustice. Indeed, the Uvalde families had been inundated with charitable gifts and donations from across the country, from scholarships for students to custom-made coffins. GoFundMe's webpage for Uvalde fundraisers became a central place to express grief and assuage guilt.

This discussion raises some important questions about what crowdfunding has come to evoke in our society, particularly as it gains wide public engagement as a reaction to crisis or suffering. Campaigns like the one for Uvalde may have more of an affective than practical purpose, reflecting what captures attention and emotion in an increasingly polarized and digitally connected public realm. But like other examples in this chapter, such campaigns also lead to questions about what they cannot solve: they have not prevented violence or suffering, nor do they work to diminish the likelihood of future traumas through policy or social change. By serving as an outlet for collective guilt, they may both diminish the public's sense of being able to actually do something greater to address these injustices and may also divert attention from the upstream factors that continue to cause them.

When that focus group met, a series of high-profile campaigns for victims of horrific, often hate-fueled violence in the United States had punctuated the past few months. Just a week prior, a shooter had terrorized Highland Park, a suburb of Chicago, during its Fourth of July parade. A GoFundMe for a young boy who lost his parents in the shooting went viral and raised over $3 million. Before that, a racist shooter targeted Black patrons of a grocery store in Buffalo, New York, killing ten. The "Buffalo 5–14 survivors fund" on GoFundMe raised more than $5 million.

At the same time, crowdfunding had also become a means of mobilizing around, rather than in response to, hate. In February of 2022, the so-called Freedom Convoy, which originally aimed to protest vaccine mandates in Canada, quickly became a magnet for far-right extremists of many flavors, at times violently facing off with citizens and police. Again, crowdfunding was central to its mobilization, both in generating funds to support the demonstrators and in attracting attention to their cause.[39]

When GoFundMe ultimately shut down the campaign, it only further outraged and drew attention to the demonstrators.

As far-right organizers have sought to channel the energies of the internet's outrage machine, crowdfunding campaigns and their removal from platforms has become an increasingly powerful, attention-grabbing maneuver. In the wake of the violent, White supremacist "Unite the Right" rally in Charlottesville in 2017, neo-Nazi organizers were kicked off platforms like Patreon and Kickstarter.[40] They responded by setting up crowdfunding platforms like counter.fund, Hatreon, and Goyfundme. While many of these platforms were short lived, their purpose was not just to finance hate speech and far-right organizing but to also elevate fascist ideologies. Counter.fund, in particular, proposed a model for a future fascist government in which seats in a "House of Lords" would be awarded to those who were most successful at crowdfunding on the platform. Here, crowdfunding took up the dual meanings of "platform" as both a technological creation and political organizing tool. It offered a space for transforming hate into governance, and imagining a future where crowdfunding popularity was indistinguishable from political power. These trends continued with Kyle Rittenhouse's campaign for legal defense fees after shooting protesters in Kenosha, Wisconsin, which was removed by GoFundMe for being against the site's terms of service.[41] His campaign was quickly moved to the little-known conservative Christian fundraising platform GiveSendGo, where it raised more than $600,000, lending the fledgling site enormous credibility.[42] Within days, the campaign page was brimming with thousands of incendiary and hateful comments. While such examples can seem exceptional, it's clear that crowdfunding has become a host to dominant and often divisive public conversations in the United States. It can be a receptacle for guilt but can also fuel hate and provide a platform for organizing.

Often, technology platforms try to defend themselves against the negative social consequences of their technologies by claiming they are a neutral platform for the ideas, mobilizations, and actions of others.[43] But as platforms have increasingly become hosts to rampant misinformation, hate, discrimination, and even violent organizing, such defenses become harder and harder to justify. Platforms make decisions every day about what to allow, moderate, endorse, amplify, and remove, and these decisions have huge social and political consequences, though they are rarely subject to government regulation or scrutiny. GoFundMe itself has had to make tough and impactful decisions about what to host, what to take down, and how to justify these choices, including on content related to hate crimes, police violence, and abortion.[44]

What we know is that platforms have political and social "affordances": they shape how people think about things, connect with one another, and imagine and carry out political actions.[45] We also know that people, in turn, shape platforms, leveraging them toward specific means or ends, even in ways companies do not anticipate. GoFundMe has been more active than other platforms in removing hateful content and communicating and enforcing content moderation, but much of this effort has been reactionary, in the service of preserving its image as a site for doing, and feeling, good. Shutting down far-right campaigns after they have already gained traction only fuels their notoriety and organizing power. What the company has yet to publicly grapple with are the broader questions about how its technology is changing the way people think about, act on, and understand the larger social issues that drive traffic to the site.

As crowdfunding becomes more and more prominent as a primary tool for social response—the internet's "take action button" as Rob Solomon put it—it has major social and political impacts even when the solutions it offers are very downstream.[46] Crowdfunding powerfully shifts our thinking about what it is we are supposed to be taking action on and how we should go about doing it. These shifts have significant social and political consequences. As Tamara Kneese observed in her study of funeral crowdfunding campaigns, "individuals who perceive themselves as disembedded, charitable citizens may ignore the broader systemic problems inherent to late capitalism."[47] Rather than being a tool of justice, the spectacle of campaigns flitting across our social media feeds distracts us from real, upstream injustices and the efforts it would take to meaningfully address them. Lauren Berlant has argued that such spectacles of pain, violence, or suffering "give citizens something to do in response to overwhelming structural violence."[48] But the "something" we can do does not alter the structural violence itself. "What," Berlant asks, "does it mean for the theory and practice of social transformation when feeling good becomes evidence of justice's triumph?"[49] What they mean by this is that spectacles allow us to substitute *feelings* for actions that could actually prevent and address such suffering. With crowdfunding, we're often not even successfully pulling people out of the river anymore, as the stories of Chris and Sabrina (as well as the numerous campaigns that raise little or nothing each year) show. We're standing on the bank of that river, watching in horror as someone drowns, shouting about how awful it is.

If crowdfunding has become the world's "take action button," then what are we supposed to do when we want to take action in meaningful ways?[50] And what does this mean for all the heartfelt effort that we put into crowdfunding to help those around us? The next and final chapter explores these questions, offering different strategies for how we can use the energies, passion, and connection that crowdfunding has popularized to better address health inequities and systemic injustices.

6

CROWDED FUTURES, OR MUTUAL LIBERATION?

In April 2020, the community of Jackson Heights, in the Bronx, was gripped by fear. COVID had swept through the city, leaving hospitals and morgues full and thousands of people sick in their homes. The thoroughfares and subway lines of Jackson Heights—a bustling community of working-class immigrants and people of color—were eerily subdued but for the relentless whines of ambulance sirens. Caught in the "epicenter of the epicenter," residents watched family members, neighbors, and community leaders get sick and, sometimes, die.[1] In April, Victoria Jimenez's mother, Maribel, died from COVID; in May, the virus claimed her father's life as well.

By June, Victoria had created a GoFundMe campaign titled "COVID's Angels." While the acute wave of cases and deaths had receded in New York City, the economic fallout was devastating, leaving people in dire need of food, cash support, and other forms of assistance. Pandemic relief measures were slow to come and particularly hard to access for those in Victoria's community who were undocumented or working under the table. Victoria felt compelled to help. She wrote, "The pain and loss that COVID-19 has brought upon our communities has been devastating. . . . My mother and father . . . are victims of this pandemic. The immense pain of loosing [*sic*] both my parents weeks apart has brought out a positive plan. I want to give back to my community of Jackson Heights and help feed those families affected by this horrific virus."[2] She vowed to raise enough money to support one hundred families in her community with weekly grocery deliveries.

While the scale of Victoria's campaign may have paled in comparison to the multimillion-dollar pandemic response initiatives that GoFundMe featured on its homepage at the time, her effort was no small thing. It was a symbolically, materially, and emotionally rich gesture that aimed to transform her own grief and loss into an act of solidarity, care, and resilience. While much of this book has discussed the inadequacies, unfairnesses, and larger ramifications of crowdfunding, the meaning and impact of efforts like Victoria's cannot go overlooked.

Victoria's campaign is an impressive act of generosity and resilience, but she is not alone in turning toward sites like GoFundMe with a heartfelt intention to do something good in the face of overwhelming hardship and crisis. Indeed, the vast majority of people I have spoken to about their experiences with crowdfunding have said that donating to campaigns, or starting campaigns to help other people, has given them a sense of purpose, helped them feel that they had an impact, and reinforced a positive sense of themselves. This echoes decades of research showing that doing charitable, kind, or selfless things for other people has considerable mental and even physical health benefits.[3] Doing good feels good, and yet we also know that the intentions behind, and the impacts of, a desire to help can be complex and sometimes harmful.[4]

This book is not meant as a critique of individual people's efforts to help or of the intentions they may bring to such activities. Rather, it is meant to critique the broader ways that crowdfunding is changing how we address the needs of ourselves and others in a time of growing, and deeply inequitable, precarity and crisis. I've tried to offer a humane look at the complex role that crowdfunding has come to play in our lives as we seek and provide help: why has it become so popular, and what social and political changes has it brought about? It's clear that despite well-intentioned, even selfless, efforts like Victoria's, the broader social impacts of crowdfunding, particularly for health or medical needs, are deeply troubling.

It's also clear, however, that crowdfunding's popularity is partially due to the good feelings it can engender—a desire to help, a sense of purpose, the opportunity to build and strengthen social connections. But many people also feel deep discomfort at the kinds of appeals they see on sites like GoFundMe—appeals that reveal yawning gaps in our social safety nets. These seemingly divergent reactions actually point to a more cohesive set of desires and concerns than we might assume. Crowdfunding is an immoral and ineffective way of addressing people's needs, and yet we turn to it as we yearn for collective, purposeful action that might address the causes of others' suffering.

How can we better mobilize these desires and discomforts? In this final chapter, I offer three templates for action based on the lessons from previous chapters. The first template is the one we most commonly encounter when it comes to technology. It's also the action that crowdfunding platforms would be most likely to embrace. This is the realm of what I call "tweaks and fixes"—the smaller changes that platforms typically make to maintain their market share, popularity, and public image. As Ruha Benjamin has so eloquently described, such fixes uphold, rather than alter, technologies' power in our lives and allow structural inequities to persist and deepen.[5]

Once technology has gained a footing in our everyday lives, in our ways of orienting to each other and the world, it's not easy to substantially change, regulate, or remove. However, tech does become obsolete, on a fairly regular basis. The second template for action that I offer aims to make crowdfunding—at least in the ways it is commonly used to address acute needs and crises—less ubiquitous. This involves much more extensive efforts of "repair and remaking"—larger projects that aim to change the structural systems of market-based health and charity that create the moral and financial toxicities in which crowdfunding thrives. Working toward such projects of repair and remaking won't make crowdfunding obsolete, but it would dramatically change the conditions under which crowdfunding exists and the reasons people turn to it.

These are the large and necessary projects of creating fairer health futures, but they are also daunting, lengthy, and resource intensive. As a final template for action, I offer suggestions for "living in the meanwhile"—everyday efforts of working toward meaning, connection, and justice while slow-moving progress toward larger shifts continues. I look at examples of people who are using crowdfunding as an accessory to their broader efforts to shift mindsets about care, charity, and connection. These efforts offer insights into how we can do the work of what Benjamin calls "viral justice" as we unlearn moral toxicities and strive toward more systemic change.[6] I also offer pragmatic suggestions of meaningful alternatives to, and adaptations of, crowdfunding that can be employed by people in different scenarios.

I anchor these templates for action by drawing on stories of how people and communities have responded to COVID in the United States. The emergence of COVID in 2020 was associated with an enormous growth in crowdfunding and changes in how and why people crowdfunded.[7] While many people sought help with basic needs, others like Victoria turned to crowdfunding out of a sense of grief and frustration in the face of governmental failures to respond adequately to meet people's needs.[8] While the early months of the COVID crisis saw an outpouring of efforts to mobilize and offer help, as the crisis continued, it revealed Americans' deep divisions and lack of regard for others. Over time, many people repeatedly chose their own comfort over the protection and safety of those in their communities, particularly the most marginalized. As Eric Klinenberg observed, COVID revealed our inability to create the kinds of solidarity that actually promote public health and collective well-being.[9] At the same time, efforts of solidarity building and collective action, like those of mutual aid groups across the country, grew and persisted even as the pandemic stretched on far longer than most could have anticipated. COVID held up a mirror to both the remarkable generosity and the dark moral toxicities of American society, and it provides a particularly salient historical moment in which to examine the role that crowdfunding can and should play in our response to future crises.

TWEAKS AND FIXES

In 2019, the *Wall Street Journal* posted a column by Alexandra Samuel that, as its title suggested, promised to explain "how to make health-care crowdfunding work for everyone."[10] Acknowledging the substantial inequities present in current crowdfunding models, Samuel proposed a number of fixes to medical crowdfunding that she felt could make it fairer and more equitable. The suggested fixes included something called "the crowdfunding equity extension"—a browser extension that would alert users to other deserving but less successful campaigns. By drawing on data from social media profiles and other online sources, this "little watchdog for all your online giving" could "ensure that these matching campaigns come from people" from different neighborhoods, income groups, or racial and ethnic groups than your own. Alternatively, Samuel suggested, platforms could apply a "10% solidarity surcharge" to all donations that would go to less successful campaigns. Such solutions, Samuel claimed, could make crowdfunding "a more inclusive part of the health-funding picture."[11]

It's tempting to think that small technological fixes like widgets and surcharges could alleviate the enormous equity concerns that arise with crowdfunding. These solutions seem painless, easy, and straightforward. And indeed, some companies like Watsi have tried to implement changes like these to address concerns about equity. But as we saw in the last chapter, downstream fixes often overlook upstream causes. Samuels's proposals don't account for the many inequities in terms of who can and cannot start a crowdfunding campaign, or platforms' considerable interest in drawing attention away from the vast majority of campaigns that do not reach their goals.[12] Samuel overlooked considerable data here and elsewhere showing that people are quite unwilling to give to the crowdfunding campaigns of people they don't know directly or indirectly.[13] But even a perfectly calibrated widget cannot fix the reasons why people turn to crowdfunding for help in the first place, nor the overwhelming needs that crowdfunding campaigns—even successful ones—cannot fully address. Indeed, the "widget" or "equity extension" that would redirect resources to meaningfully address these issues is called progressive taxation. It's called robust social safety nets and universal health coverage.

In her book *Race After Technology*, Ruha Benjamin warns against the appeal of "technological benevolence" in the form of digital fixes, particularly fixes that promise to address or ameliorate racial inequities.[14] "This is the allure of tech fixes," she writes. "They offer pragmatic inclusion in place of political and social transformation. . . . [These] fixes are a permanent placeholder for bolder change."[15] Similarly, while applying tweaks and fixes to crowdfunding might seem like the easiest option, it's dangerous on two levels: first, it's unlikely to address the financial and moral toxicities that drive health crowdfunding, and second, it's likely to distract us from those bolder changes that Benjamin describes. Much like offering "thoughts and prayers" in the wake of yet another mass shooting, responding to health needs with crowdfunding does little to address the reasons people seek crowdfunding or the inequities they face when they do. Shares and prayers, repeated in the face of innumerable unjust crises, begin to sound not just disingenuous but like a willful refusal to act on the real causes of people's suffering.

REPAIR AND REMAKING

While Jackson Heights was one epicenter of the early pandemic surge in the United States, the Navajo Nation was another. By May of 2020, the infection rate in the Navajo Nation had surpassed New York City's to become the highest in the country.[16] Native people faced particularly cruel vulnerabilities as this new virus spread. The legacies of settler colonialism and oppression had created numerous physical and mental health conditions, from poor nutrition to high rates of diabetes to immune deficiencies, that made them more susceptible to complications and death.[17] The Navajo Nation was also victim to extreme forms of organized abandonment at the hands of the US government, resulting in severely depleted health and social safety net infrastructures with which to respond to the pandemic.[18] Residents found that store shelves were empty of the most basic supplies and that COVID testing was far from home.[19] Other tribal nations and groups faced similar challenges: in Washington State, the Quinault Tribe's nearest testing facility was two hours away.[20] When the Seattle Indian Health Board put out an urgent request for medical supplies amid an early surge in cases, they received instead, three weeks later, a shipment of body bags.[21] Abigail Echo-Hawk, the board's director, observed that this was "a metaphor for what's happening" to Native communities across the country.[22]

At the same time, a heart-warming viral story was spreading across social media about how Irish people were donating in droves to GoFundMe campaigns for Navajo and Hopi COVID response efforts. "Irish Return an Old Favor, Helping Native Americans Battling the Virus" read one headline.[23] Though the history is more familiar to many Irish than it is to Americans, in 1847, only two years after they had gone through the Trail of Tears, the Choctaw people gathered together money and donated $170 (about $5,000 in today's dollars) to Ireland to help people suffering from the potato famine. "It's time for [us] to come through for them now," wrote Irish journalist Naomi O'Leary on Twitter.[24] Ultimately, nearly $3 million was donated by Irish citizens to the Navajo and Hopi nations, reviving a long history of solidarity between Irish and Native communities.[25] A year later, when India faced a terrible surge in COVID cases and severe shortages of medical supplies, Navajo leaders organized shipments of personal protective equipment to be sent to the country.[26]

At a time when headlines were particularly grim, these acts of global solidarity—what some even called collective anticolonialism—captured the hearts of many. Others noted that such displays of solidarity were both inspiring and troubling. Sriram Shamasunder and Priti Krishtel pointedly observed that

> this chain of donations is akin to a crowdfunding campaign for a medical bill that should be covered through a strong social safety net, not by asking those with the least to scrounge together what little they have. The burden of helping marginalized people in need in our global community belongs to those with wealth and power—in this case, wealthy nations like the United States—and not to those who have borne the brunt of systemic oppression and economic disenfranchisement.[27]

They noted that such solidarity was occurring even as the United States and other wealthy countries relentlessly (and unapologetically) hoarded medical supplies and vaccines. And despite such generosity, the pandemic brought exorbitant suffering and too many deaths to communities without access to necessary goods, including the Navajo Nation. Stories of viral solidarity also conceal the many places and people where help does not come through. At the time the Navajo campaign was going viral, I was fielding inquiries from representatives of Native groups whose campaigns were floundering, who were wondering how they, too, could attract such largesse.

This story, as it traveled across social media, gained more than a hint of White saviorism as well. Much credit was given to Irish generosity rather than to the solidarity and generosity of Native organizers, most of them women, who had started and sustained the campaign almost entirely with volunteer labor. In fact, the Navajo-Hopi fundraiser began as a community initiative in the earliest days of COVID, months before it gained social media fame, when leaders recognized the many vulnerabilities of their communities in the face of a novel virus.[28] Organizers drew from existing community organizing structures to rapidly mobilize efforts even as strict lockdown orders limited their mobility. Similarly, Diné mutual aid networks drew connections between historical experiences of pandemics (the 1918 flu in particular), contemporary systems of oppression, and the immediate needs of their communities.[29] These forms of nonheirarchical mutual care were deeply rooted in Diné kinship and belief systems.[30]

In the years since, these efforts have enabled the Navajo Nation to organize highly effective responses to the pandemic as well as to gain political victories on some of the structural vulnerabilities brought into stark relief by the pandemic. Far outpacing trends across the United States, the Navajo Nation quickly mobilized a highly effective vaccination campaign in early 2021 that, by April, had resulted in nearly 90 percent of adults receiving a first dose of the vaccine (compared with only 40 percent of the US population at the time).[31] After experiencing the acute impacts of pandemic-related food insecurity, which worsened already entrenched issues of food insecurity in the Navajo Nation, movements for food sovereignty and food justice gained momentum.[32] While these efforts began before the pandemic, they gained new support and urgency during this time: "It took a deadly virus to make people realize just how important this is, how important it is to grow your own food," one activist observed.[33]

Similarly, after COVID underscored the urgent need for better clean water access, particularly for hand washing, sanitation, and food cultivation, communities doubled down on efforts to fight for improved water rights.[34] These efforts have begun to yield significant successes even as major drought makes water even more scarce in the southwest.[35] In 2022, Native advocates won a major federal victory to support more sustainable funding for the Indian Health Service (IHS), which is perennially underfunded. The Biden administration included $5 billion in advance appropriations for the IHS, in part because of recognitions that inadequate health service funding contributed to the excessively high COVID mortality rates among indigenous Americans.[36] And finally, New Mexico, led by Native groups, was the first state to create a state-wide memorial of COVID deaths, an explicitly political project to contest the organized abandonment that led to excess deaths and to address the collective trauma of COVID.[37]

Though we wouldn't know it from what gained traction on social media, crowdfunding is not the central feel-good story here. Rather, what we can learn from the Navajo/Diné response to COVID is a more complex, slow-moving, but deeply impactful story about collective organizing to address immediate needs while also mobilizing against systemic oppression and organized abandonment. This is a story about successful solidarity but also a haunting record of excessive harm and profound loss. The losses of COVID, particularly of older Native generations, echo other forms of generational trauma and ongoing structural violence.

Crowdfunding, at its best, is an expression of our human desires for connecting, giving care, building solidarity, and working toward systematic change. The Navajo-Hopi campaign is evidence of those desires at work. Crowdfunding's popularity speaks to the desire that many people have to be engaged in these activities. These activities are also essential for imagining and building more just health futures. But if we only participate in crowdfunding by donating to the odd campaign, we get a very superficial, fleeting taste of what these kinds of care and connection are and could be. If we only focus on the Navajo-Hopi GoFundMe campaign, we miss all the other forms of impactful, resource- and time-intensive effort that preceded it, grounded it, and lasted long after the campaign had faded from public memory.

Steven Jackson offers the concept of "repair" as a "broken world" way of thinking about slow-moving, connected care for things and people, asking what it offers us in terms of thinking about whom or what we repair, how we do so, and what kinds of world-making or -remaking it might enable.[38] Jackson argues that focusing on activities of repair offers an opportunity to observe creative, generative efforts that do not simply rebuild things to the way they were before but remake them anew. Acts of repair are part of a broader ethics of care marked by both "chains of mutual entanglement and dependency" and "political claims making."[39] In a time in which so much seems to be broken and breaking around us, and crises accumulate with little respite, repair offers us a pragmatic, collective means of working toward structural change.

In the context of medical crowdfunding, what does repair look like? At an individual level of need, repair assesses how and why things are broken. Rather than embracing individual pride and resilience, it invites us to share our needs without shame. Repair calls on different forms of care, expertise, and resources, cobbling together the skills and parts that are needed to not just address immediate needs but also build long-term resiliency. Repair does not ask for debts of gratitude or proof of deservingness.

At a more collective, societal, and even political level, repair requires a humble, even scathingly honest, survey of our cracks and weaknesses. It is a collective practice by which we assess these broken parts and imagine how they might be remade into something stronger, more resilient, perhaps even more beautiful. In the context of medical crowdfunding, what is broken in our health and social systems and drives people to turn to this form of fundraising is obvious. While repairing these systems is profoundly complex and arduous work, repair helps us begin by asking, What would it look like if this system were repaired? Work on the human right to health helps us envision what this might look like. Put very simply, in the words of the World Health Organization's director general Tedros Adhanom Ghebreyesus, the right to health means that "everyone should have access to the health services they need, when and where they need them, without suffering financial hardship. No one should get sick and die just because they are poor, or because they cannot access the health services they need."[40] Repair also helps us aspire beyond this baseline to begin envisioning what our systems might look like if they did not just prevent unnecessary sickness and death but supported human flourishing and connection.

My favorite part about the concept of repair, however, is that it invites us to take one step at a time. As someone who can find big structural change both inspiring and intimidating, repair allows me to move beyond the paralysis of trying to envision massive change and instead assess what can be tinkered with, remade, and reimagined right now. It is an experimental approach where not all efforts will succeed, and some may be very messy, and that is okay. There are no shortage of people and organizations that are engaged in the work of repair when it comes to our health and social systems in the United States, from patient advocacy groups to health policy advocates to community clinics and clinicians. And these efforts of repair and remaking have a long history in the United States, spearheaded by groups as diverse as the Black Panthers, ACT UP, labor unions, and Physicians for a National Health Program. Repair has been, and is, happening all around us.

When it comes to crowdfunding as a digital technology platform, repair may not always be the goal. Technologies do not have a good record of reforming themselves. Once a technology has become ubiquitous, there is often too much money to be made—and power to be accrued—by defending the status quo. But repair in other domains, such as in our marketized health systems, can make crowdfunding, at least in its current form, less ubiquitous. And it can perhaps make campaigns for basic medical and health needs obsolete. Repair here might also involve reimagining what collective action online could look like if we were not constantly responding to urgent needs with donations-as-care. This is also what crowdfunding executives like Tim Cadogan say they want.[41] They don't want GoFundMe to be "America's safety net"—they want it to be used for honeymoons, birthdays, soccer teams, and charity events.[42] It's time to allow ourselves to imagine a future in which companies like GoFundMe are not primarily profiting from, and reinforcing, health injustices.

LIVING IN THE MEANWHILE

These are, admittedly, big dreams. A consequence of the late neoliberal project is that our economic, social, and technological realities have become so entrenched that imagining change feels impossible. As Angela Davis observed, "dangerous limits have been placed on the very possibility of imagining alternatives. These ideological limits have to be contested. We have to begin to think in different ways. Our future is at stake."[43] One of the architects of neoliberalism, Margaret Thatcher, so frequently used the phrase "there is no alternative" to describe her economic and social policies that she was nicknamed TINA.[44] As Paul Farmer describes in the forward to Salman Keshavjee's *Blind Spot*, the mental hegemony of neoliberalism limits our ability to recognize the value of more collective and just health systems. "The commonweal," Farmer writes, "the sense of shared opportunities and misfortunes that bind us together—after all, what is 'pooled risk' if not sharing?—is often one of the first casualties of hard-core neoliberalism."[45]

"What is the alternative?" is a question that invites hopelessness rather than imagination. Dreaming up alternatives can be an act of resistance and a pragmatic strategy for beginning to remake and reimagine our current systems. At first glance, we might think of crowdfunding as a convenient, time-saving alternative to dealing with the complexities and costs of the US health-care system. It fills a gap, conveniently. But this book has shown that rather than being an alternative to the moral and financial toxicities of our current health system, crowdfunding reinforces both its functions and its values. Recall the case of Luis Lang, who sought support for his diabetes after supposedly refusing to enroll in Obamacare. Rather than use his page to challenge state legislation that had deprived him of access to care, Obamacare's own supporters used it to reinforce the same toxicities of individualism, responsibility, and deservingness that undermined a right to health. At other times, crowdfunding papers over the challenges of our system with a veneer of kindness and opportunity, distracting us from upstream causes. Rather than being an alternative, it distracts us from alternatives and diverts our attention and energy away from fighting for them.

In this final section, I offer some thoughts on meaningful alternatives to, and adaptations of, crowdfunding that might otherwise be hard to imagine. This is by no means a comprehensive account of alternatives but rather an invitation to engage in a more collective project of imagining and creating other ways to connect, care for each other, and cultivate repair in a time of crisis. I offer these alternatives with the recognition that we all must figure out "how best to live on, considering."[46] We are all living, as it were, in the meanwhile—in the aftermath and rubble of accumulated (and persistent) crises, and before the kinds of change we would hope to see have come to pass.

Living in the meanwhile is not about surrender or accommodation but engaging in the smaller acts of repair, change, or care that can add up to something bigger. As Benjamin explains in *Viral Justice*, "all the great transformations that societies undergo rely on the low-key scheming of everyday people."[47] So let's get scheming.

Perhaps the most obvious alternative to crowdfunding is to give time, money, attention, or efforts to organizations that are engaging in health advocacy and equity work. This allows individual resources to go much further, to be directed upstream, and to be more equitably distributed. For example, several programs in the United States allow people to buy back (and thus pay off) the medical debt of those most in need at highly discounted rates. Often, debt can be bought back at a rate of about one hundred times the donation's value.[48] But donations can also go to organizations fighting to prevent medical debt by advocating for health policy reforms or by addressing health inequities at the root in communities. Those who don't have their own money to give can use their voices on social media or public media platforms to talk about upstream issues and causes, advocate for the right to health, and resist the draw of simplified problems and solutions.

One of the most important things all of us can do is build and diversify our community connections and practice forms of caregiving that do not rely on donations. These are important muscles to develop, and they take practice, particularly for the many Americans whose social networks and offline communities are shrinking. By building more robust and inclusive social networks, and by practicing forms of collective caregiving, we make it less likely that those around us, or we, will need to turn to online crowdfunding in a crisis.

However, many of us will continue to be asked to donate to crowdfunding campaigns, and this raises important questions about what we should do when that happens. It's a question I've struggled with myself as I did this research. Depending on one's own access to resources, alternatives here could look different. For those who have additional resources to share, matching what you give to the campaigns of friends or family with a donation to an organization or fund that addresses broader health equity issues is one step you can take. For those who don't have extra monetary resources to share, exploring nonmonetary donations that can be made to friends and family in need (as well as health justice organizations) is especially important. In interviews with crowdfunders, they often recall these nonmonetary gestures with as much, if not more, gratitude even if they were in substantial financial need. Such gestures can include providing childcare, offering places to stay near hospitals, offering to drive or lend a vehicle for trips to and from medical visits, providing meals, running errands, helping with household chores, or helping to deal with hospital billing offices or insurance companies.

Finally, most crowdfunding sites make money by charging or asking for a "tip" or percentage fee on each donation. Donors should think carefully about whether they want to contribute this and, if so, how much to give. Donating offline or off the platform is almost always an option as well.

In the early months of the pandemic, many people in the United States also began practicing mutual aid. While not at all a new practice, mutual aid became far more popular during the pandemic, aided by workshops hosted by organizers like Mariame Kaba and Rep. Alexandria Ocasio Cortez and by books like Dean Spade's *Mutual Aid*.[49] Mutual aid is premised on several key principles. First, it addresses people's immediate needs while also raising consciousness about the structural causes of their needs. Second, it uses a "solidarity not charity" model, rejecting hierarchical, racist, and classist practices of charity that buttress economic and social inequities. Third, it explicitly engages in social mobilization, solidarity building, and political advocacy; and fourth, mutual aid organizing is participatory, nonhierarchical, and rooted in mutuality.[50]

As Tamara Kneese pointed out early in the pandemic, these principles stand in stark contrast to those of crowdfunding. As Kneese wrote, "a GoFundMe can be one tool used in the spirit of mutual aid, if it is verified by the community and by organizations that were already there putting in the work. . . . This is different from brands, institutions, or businesses raising funds on behalf of others, or campaigns that ask for money without advocating for broader social justice. The distinction between these two models is crucial, particularly at a time when sending resources and organizing through digital means is one of the only routes available." Thus, the experiences of mutual aid organizers in trying to build alternatives to the moral toxicities of crowdfunding, while also sometimes relying upon it, can be particularly instructive.

As cases of COVID first emerged in the United States in the spring of 2020, many colleges and universities scrambled to quickly respond, often making hasty decisions to close down campuses right before or after spring break. This left students who did not have the financial means to return home, or have safe homes to return to, stranded. Cal, a first-generation, low-income, nonbinary student at a wealthy northeastern liberal arts college, found themselves in just such a situation. They were already housing insecure before the pandemic and then lost their job and only source of income when campus closed down. Cal knew they were not the only student in this situation but also that the culture of their campus was one where low-income students often struggled in silence. They were determined to figure out a way to help students and started collecting information from all students, asking them to rank and describe their needs. Initially, Cal thought the responses would be minimal and they could circulate the appeal to alumni and more wealthy families connected to the school to see if people were willing to support students. Cal was floored by the response, though, with hundreds of students expressing high levels of need.

Cal quickly realized they would have to mobilize a larger organizational response, and set up a GoFundMe, while also making sure student leaders and administrators at the college were brought on board to help. Unlike the typical crowdfunding campaign, Cal didn't use the GoFundMe page for trying to demonstrate needy students' worth or pulling at heart strings. Instead, they used it as a transparency document, explaining, often in great detail, how the mutual aid campaign would work: how students in need were identified, how the funds would be allocated and tracked, who would manage various steps of the process, and a setting a timeline for handing over control of the funds and fundraiser to a community advisory board with administrative and student representatives.

With only minimal experience in mutual aid and community organizing, Cal built a robust, transparent, and fair system for getting money quickly to the neediest students at their college. They attributed the success of these efforts to their own knowledge of what it was like to be economically precarious at college and to their willingness to speak openly about their own financial distress with others. "Honestly the thing I was most proud of," Cal said, "was I was so happy to have low-income students *see* each other . . . to trust [each other] with these experiences and talk to about these things is powerful in itself."

Within a short period of time, the campaign raised hundreds of thousands of dollars to support students with both acute (i.e., transportation back home) and long-term (i.e., food insecurity, housing insecurity) needs. Major support came from fellow students rather than wealthy alumni, as Cal had expected. The college's student council donated its entire remaining budget to the campaign. Once the college reimbursed students for their room and board fees for the spring quarter, organizers put out explicit requests that students above certain income levels donate their entire reimbursement to the campaign. With help from a college resource officer, Cal developed a plan for managing the campaign payments and eventually transferring the financial management and day-to-day operations to the university. They also set up a long-term community advisory board composed of students and staff to manage the funds going forward. The student government decided to allocate $10,000 of its budget per year on an ongoing basis to support students in financial distress.

It would be easy to attribute the success of Cal's campaign to the economically and socially rarefied group of students at their college. While certainly a factor, Cal's efforts mirror hundreds, if not thousands, of other community mutual aid efforts that emerged across the country in response to the pandemic, seeking to support community members without judgment and in a spirit of "solidarity not charity." From teachers supporting low-income students in Virginia, to author Ijeoma Oluo organizing to support out-of-work BIPOC artists in Seattle, to a Black pastor in Portland helping food-insecure households, to young people in Arkansas mobilizing pandemic relief, mutual aid seemed to emerge everywhere, all at once.

While many of these initial efforts used platforms like GoFundMe as a way to quickly raise money, crowdfunding did not define what they did, nor could it possibly describe the extent of these organizing efforts. With campaigns like the one Cal started, ordinary people were learning and experimenting with a long-standing and widely practiced, but too often forgotten, tradition of mutual aid.[51] Their work involved tinkering, subverting, and challenging; it required reflection on their own histories and privileges and vulnerabilities; it was scrappy, exhausting, and often messy.[52] But it was also work that challenged the toxicities of selective deservingness, rugged individualism, meritocracy, artificial scarcity, and late capitalism. Because these toxicities are so embedded in the ways that many Americans have experienced charity, social assistance, and philanthropy, unlearning them is difficult work, and for mutual aid organizers, it was not without significant challenges. But as Emily Hops, Amy Hagopian, and I learned from mutual aid organizers around the country, this work of unlearning was happening with intention and commitment, and amid the constant challenges of responding to a pandemic while simultaneously trying to survive it.[53]

When successful, these practices of unlearning moral toxicities and remaking how we care for each other are generative, spreading through networks and relationships and changing the way people think about infrastructures of care and community.[54] As Dean Spade explains, mutual aid is not just about meeting people's needs but about challenging the systemic, upstream forces that create precarity, strengthening collective consciousness about those forces, and building the social fabric of connections and trust that can hopefully, in the long term, challenge and change them.[55] One mutual aid organizer from Arkansas described what this kind of work entails in their group's everyday interactions, that it involves saying to people who come in asking for help, "we're all here to help one another and, don't be ashamed . . . you know your current need isn't any . . . sign of your value or your worth."[56] And also, "you know, I hate that our current economic system has put you in this position."[57] What this organizer described is a very explicit, intentional way of interacting with and alongside those who have certain needs to disrupt the moral toxicities that many of us carry into situations of asking for, or giving, help. These actions also educate through and with care, teaching a different way of being in the world and understanding structural inequities.

It's clear from these examples that crowdfunding is not necessary or sufficient for the work of mutual aid and that mutual aid cannot be defined by crowdfunding.[58] Mutual aid efforts offer lessons about what care, solidarity, and collective action can look like while we are living in the meanwhile. When thoughtfully and critically carried out, these kinds of mutual care help us relearn how to give and ask for what we need in fundamentally different ways and to strive for a kind of mutualism that disrupts normal hierarchical dynamics between givers and receivers. These practices recognize and address urgent needs but have their sights set on bigger upstream changes. They are teaching people how to be in community with each other, often spanning and disrupting social divides.

None of this work is infallible, and it is certainly complicated, but what is remarkable is that it has persisted. Many people, like Cal, started mutual aid efforts thinking that COVID's acute impacts would last a few weeks, maybe a couple months. But these efforts developed a persistence, a stickiness, that has created more long-term forms of care and support. People learned new ways of challenging systems, building community, caring for each other, and understanding their mutual interdependence. As Spade notes, this work "has the potential to build the skills and capacities we need for an entirely new way of living at a moment when we must transform our society or face intensive, uneven suffering."[59]

Mutual aid joins many other kinds of organizing and advocacy efforts that, over centuries and across many different countries, have envisioned, struggled for, and achieved steps toward more just and healthy lives for people. Competitively crowdfunding for individualized health needs represents the antithesis of these movements and threatens to undermine what they have achieved. The moral toxicities of crowdfunding—individualism, market competition, selective deservingness, and downstream solutionism—will only worsen the crises that are likely to frequently punctuate our future. A better future for all of us is collective, collaborative, solidaristic, and focused upstream. We are capable of so much more than just "the giving layer of the internet."

APPENDIX: METHODS AND APPROACHES

This book represents knowledge, stories, and insights gleaned from nearly a decade of research on crowdfunding. This research involved multiple methodologies and often included faculty and student collaborators at the University of Washington. While much of this book has been written with general audiences in mind, this appendix provides a more detailed account of the research methods used in gathering and analyzing much of the data used in this book. Because this book summarizes data and insights from nearly a dozen different studies conducted over this time span, even this appendix may fall short of providing the sorts of detailed methodological information that some readers may be seeking. For those readers, I include references to published papers from these projects as well, whose methods sections will include greater details.

Studying a relatively new social phenomenon like medical crowdfunding is both exciting and onerous. With this project, it always seemed as if there were more questions than I could possibly answer, and I also felt a certain responsibility to pursue the research questions that held the most impactful answers for public audiences, including clinicians and policymakers. Over time, my collaborators enriched these projects through their wide-ranging expertise and diverse disciplinary perspectives, taking the project questions in directions I could not have imagined had I undertaken this project alone.[1] My own foci throughout this project's life span have been questions of health, equity, and politics: how and in what ways was crowdfunding impacting US health-care seeking and provision, what impacts did this have for health equity, and what broader politics of health did crowdfunding reflect and contribute to?

Given these questions, I had several methodological goals that spanned various research projects. First, it was essential to try to understand what was going on "behind the website" and beyond the often carefully constructed narratives and photos that crowdfunders were posting to places like GoFundMe—and that by and large, researchers like me were relying upon for data. Like any form of media, crowdfunding pages are constructed with particular messages, identities, and audiences in mind, and I wanted to attend to not just what was on the page but also the broader social contexts and stories of people's lives and health experiences as they turned to crowdfunding. I tried to also remain cognizant of what was not visible in the data gleaned from crowdfunding pages: what might be missing, obfuscated, inaccurate, unspoken, and so on. And I drew on digital ethnographic methods to better understand the architectures and algorithms that shaped crowdfunding sites—and also shaped what was visible and prominent for viewers (and researchers like myself).

My second goal, related to the first, was to ensure that our sampling methods across multiple projects were constructed in such a way that we could accurately observe and document inequities that might be occurring. While no sampling method is ever perfect—and certainly not when one is studying a new phenomenon—we strove throughout these projects to obtain the most representative samples possible. From the beginning, we faced a fundamental methodological challenge in our sampling: we simply didn't know what our "sampling frame"—or the population from which we were sampling (i.e., people using crowdfunding)—looked like. We couldn't assume that people using crowdfunding were the same as the US population as a whole—it was likely there were self-selection factors and barriers to use at work—and we couldn't get reliable data from crowdfunding companies about what their user population looked like. Consequently, our early studies emphasized trying to develop the widest possible sampling frame and then selecting for randomized or criteria-specific populations, depending on our broader methodological approach (more on those below). In our later work, with the expertise of Mark Igra, we were able to refine our sampling methods and use much larger samples that helped us to better understand the larger population of crowdfunders. We also remained cognizant that we were likely studying a changing population of crowdfunders as this form of digital media became more popular over time and as its use expanded to broader categories of help seeking. In addition, crowdfunding platforms also changed dramatically over time, impacting our sampling methods as well as the kinds of data we were able to access.

My third goal was to care for the data about crowdfunders and their experiences as ethically as I could. I quickly realized that crowdfunding sites seemed to demonstrate a kind of "carelessness" when it came to crowdfunders' data and stories. There were few privacy safeguards, high incentives for crowdfunders to share intimate details about their lives, and no publicly available information about how crowdfunders' data was used, sold, or profited from. In all of my work I aimed to offer crowdfunders a greater measure of privacy than they were granted by platforms, and I did this by using pseudonyms and protecting identifying data. Because crowdfunding campaigns are public, this meant sometimes anonymizing additional data or changing small details about campaigns that could be used to identify the people involved in them. For example, all text quotations, images, and identifying data from campaign pages in this book have been put through multiple "reverse searches" on internet search engines to ensure that these quotes cannot be used to trace back to original campaigns.

Unfortunately, institutional ethical guidelines for research often do not offer many protections to data that is considered "public" on the internet. In all research that involved collecting data from public crowdfunding pages, we upheld more stringent data protections than was required—storing data carefully, stripping it of identifiers before sharing it, and ensuring all people who handled the data were trained in human subjects research ethics. For both the interviews and focus groups described below, ethical approval from the UW Institutional Review Board was sought and granted (STUDY00001846, STUDY00004253, and STUDY00015020), with protocols for protecting the identity and data of research subjects as well as minimizing the potential harms of the research.

EARLY QUALITATIVE AND QUANTITATIVE STUDIES

In 2014, I was deep into writing on my first book but found myself drawn, again and again, to emergent crowdfunding websites, where people seemed to be primarily fundraising for medical care needs. At the time, these websites were clunky and relatively unknown; I could find only one brief commentary about this phenomenon in the scholarly literature.[2] I turned to my close friend and colleague Lauren Berliner, a media scholar, to help make sense of this fascination as I had little experience understanding or studying online digital media cultures. Lauren quickly became equally interested in the phenomenon, and together we applied for a grant from the UW's Simpson Center for the Humanities to bring together a diverse group of scholars for a symposium in 2016 titled "Crowdsourcing Care: Health, Debility and Dying in a Digital Age."

Lauren and I had been thinking about, and studying, crowdfunding platforms and campaigns for quite some time at this point, primarily engaging in discourse analysis and platform analysis. However, frustrated by the lack of empirical research on this topic and the ways that platform search engines shaped what we could see on these sites, we realized we needed to get a more representative sample of "typical" campaigns. This was no small task as it was difficult to answer even the most basic questions about the population we were looking at: how many medical campaigns were there in the United States on major platforms? Where was crowdfunding happening? And who was doing it? Answering these questions required surveying a huge number of crowdfunding campaigns, which we didn't, at the time, have the resources to do. But we realized that if we could generate a more complete list of campaigns from one site, we could compute some basic statistics about this unknown population and then generate smaller random samples of campaigns for more in-depth study.

We experimented with different ways of searching the platform GoFundMe, which even at that time was the industry leader, and realized that by doing targeted searches using zip codes, we could generate long lists of search results from that zip code and nearby ones and then compile these together, eliminating any duplicates. Ethan Abeles developed an automated program to query the site for every US zip code and compile results in a spreadsheet. For each zip code, we were able to get five hundred search results—and for the vast majority of zip codes, this was far more results than there were campaigns within that zip code. But it's likely that in highly populated urban zip codes we did not find all of the campaigns that were on the site at the time. Nevertheless, this process yielded 165,925 campaigns from the "medical and illness" category of GoFundMe from which we could draw much more representative samples.

In 2016 we used this list to create a small, randomized sample of two hundred campaigns, which we then studied in depth, using a detailed textual analysis to understand themes and discursive strategies used by campaigns and also collecting quantitative data on campaign performance and coding for campaign demographics and characteristics. Jessica Cole, a graduate student, and Aimee Desrochers, an undergraduate student, provided assistance with this analysis. In early 2017, we published the results of this analysis, the first randomized study of medical crowdfunding in the United States.[3] We also pulled a larger randomized sample of about eight hundred campaigns to study, using similar mixed-methods approaches. Jessica Cole did much of the heavy lifting on the qualitative analysis of this sample.

This larger sample was later used as the basis for a study of gender, race, and age inequities in crowdfunding campaigns, the first randomized sample study to look at these factors.[4] For this study, Fatima Mirza and Anjelica Mendoza provided data coding for demographic factors. Zhihang Dong and Anne Montgomery assisted with data analysis, and Anne Montgomery and Emily Fuller assisted with the write-up of the analysis.

QUALITATIVE RESEARCH, 2017–2022

Beginning in 2017, with support from the UW's Royalty Research Fund and the Simpson Center for the Humanities, Lauren Berliner and I began conducting interviews to better understand the crowdfunding industry and crowdfunders' experiences in it. We started with key informant interviews of people involved in the crowdfunding industry, including company executives, customer service representatives, medical personnel relying on crowdfunding, and experts in crowdfunding success. Following my interest in more global crowdfunding platforms, I extended these interviews to include people involved in platforms like Watsi.[5]

At the same time, we were constantly tracking crowdfunding uses and discussions across our media feeds, in the broader local, national, and international news and within our own social circles. Our attention was to the ways that crowdfunding was showing up in private and public life, how people were using it, and how it was entering broader discourses about health access, deservingness, and social media. We kept track of trending campaigns on prominent platforms; followed content on those platforms' public relations, blogs, podcasts, and social media feeds; and observed how platforms' design, operation, and functionality changed over time.[6] To keep track of all of this, we archived extensively, using screenshots and field notes for recordkeeping. Given our disparate disciplinary interests, Lauren and I often focused on different things but frequently brought these observations together in dialogue and shared them via notes or emails. Christine Hahn and Emily Fuller helped us keep track of these and did the heroic work of trying to keep it all organized.

While this work continued for several years, we also began interviewing crowdfunders themselves in earnest. Given what we already knew from our studies of platforms and more randomized data on crowdfunding outcomes, I felt it was imperative that we use a more rigorous sampling process for these interviews that emphasized diversity, and I ensured we spoke to people whose campaigns reflected the broad spectrum of crowdfunding experiences, from highly successful to unsuccessful. Based on our data to date, we developed target percentages for sampling criteria that included gender, race, age, geographic area, religion, income level, education level, and campaign outcomes. We used data from campaign pages and interview responses to ensure that we were meeting minimum percentages of representation in each category and used this to guide further sampling criteria as we went along.

We then determined specific search criteria for identifying potential campaigns to contact on several platforms (GoFundMe and YouCaring, until YouCaring was acquired by GoFundMe). We emphasized search criteria that would be specific enough to allow us to receive search results on the sites for less successful and active campaigns. Initially, we targeted our search to campaigns that mentioned trauma center hospitals with highly diverse patient populations in two very different urban areas. Lauren and I conducted two years of qualitative interviews with crowdfunders in these sites, and key informants in the industry. I then continued conducting interviews on my own for another 1.5 years, expanding the sampling criteria to include campaigns for some specific, more chronic conditions like diabetes and capture wider geographic areas across the United States. To lessen the extent of recall bias, interviews were only conducted with people whose campaigns were less than a year old.

One challenge throughout the sampling process was simply getting campaigners to respond to our inquiries. Often, we were reaching out to people who were in periods of severe crisis. At other times, people were reticent to speak about crowdfunding experiences that involved shame, disappointment, or loss of pride. For each person who agreed to an interview, we often had to reach out to hundreds of people who never responded. It's likely that despite our stringent sampling criteria and efforts to diversify the sample, our interviews still represent certain unintentional biases. If I had to guess, however, our sample most likely reflects a bias toward more successful and more positive campaign experiences, along with people whose situations were less dire.

Given these challenges, we focused on quality and depth of qualitative data over quantity. Before each interview, we combed through campaign pages, public social media accounts, and any news stories about the campaign, writing notes and compiling questions. We then conducted either one or several hour-plus-long interviews with the crowdfunder, depending on their situation and the depth of information they were willing to share. We followed these up with additional questions if we had them. We would then request an interview with the person being crowdfunded for and, when willing, interview them as well. Christine Hahn and Emily Fuller both provided crucial assistance to the painstaking process of sampling and recruiting for interviews over several years. Emily Hops joined me for several interviews focused on mutual aid crowdfunding, and both she and Cadence Luchsinger assisted with transcribing interviews.

In total, I was able to interview people from about three dozen different campaigns. While this was less than I had initially hoped to interview, the range of experiences and perspectives in these interviews was broad but began to reach what qualitative researchers look for as "saturation" point—when similar experiences, perspectives, and attitudes begin to be heard repeatedly. While this number may seem small to researchers used to much larger quantitative samples, it was quite a bit larger than experts find is necessary for reaching saturation, even within a highly diverse sample.[7]

To complement this data, in 2022 I conducted a series of focus groups with people from around the United States who had donated to medical crowdfunding campaigns. The purpose of these group discussions was to develop a better sense of perspectives on crowdfunding from people who had interacted more intermittently with campaigns as donors, to assess how they view campaigns, choose which ones to support, and the kinds of feelings donation elicits. Sasha Kramer provided invaluable help in recruiting, arranging, and helping to conduct and transcribe these focus groups. Over the summer of 2022, we conducted eight focus groups with a total of thirty-seven people. Again, we used demographic category target percentages (for gender, race, political orientation, and geographic area) to ensure diverse representation. We recruited participants online and through two national research participant databases (Research Match and ITHS Participate in Research), targeting participants over eighteen years of age who had donated to at least one medical crowdfunding campaign in the past two years. We organized focus groups by geographic area and political orientation, aiming for a mix of gender and race representations in each group.

All qualitative data from interviews and focus groups was transcribed and then coded using a two-stage thematic coding process. In the first stage we used inductive coding to develop large categories, and then in the second stage, these categories were refined and expanded as we examined the data more closely. I also kept field notes throughout this process, writing analytic and descriptive notes about my impressions of interviews and focus groups as well as everyday observations of crowdfunding in the news, on social media, and in conversations with others.

QUANTITATIVE RESEARCH, 2019–2022

As we were conducting qualitative research, I was becoming more and more frustrated at the lack of reliable, large-scale research on medical crowdfunding in the United States, in particular research examining how social demographics and other factors might be influencing who crowdfunds and how campaigns perform. Our qualitative research was demonstrating that inequities seemed to be a major factor in the crowdfunding experience, yet there was little national-level data to explore this more comprehensively. As someone trained largely in qualitative and ethnographic methods, I knew that I would need to bring in others with quantitative and even geospatial expertise to begin answering these questions, and I would also need help with data collection from someone who had programming skills.

I lucked out when a colleague connected me with Mark Igra, a doctoral student in Sociology at UW who was doing his master's thesis on crowdfunding and who also had extensive programming experience. Mark and I were interested in many of the same questions and had homed in on similar sampling strategies for generating more representative samples from crowdfunding platforms. We also recognized that without getting demographic data from platforms themselves, any large-scale analysis of crowdfunding data would likely have to rely on estimating demographic characteristics using the attributes we could find on crowdfunding pages—geographic location data, names, photos, and story narratives. Leveraging the geographic data, in particular, would benefit from the expertise of a geographer expert as well, and we invited my colleague Jin-Kyu Jung, a creative geovisualization specialist, to join us.

In 2019 we received support from a few sources (a National Science Foundation convergence accelerator grant headed by Rastislav Bodik, Kyle Crowder, and Sarah Chasins, and a seed grant from UW Bothell) for this joint work and began collecting and organizing larger medical crowdfunding datasets for analysis. Then, in early 2020, COVID arrived in the United States, and we realized we needed to pivot to better understand how people were using platforms like GoFundMe to respond to the pandemic and its many socioeconomic consequences. With the help of two graduate students in public health, Emily Hops and Cadence Luchsinger, along with Aaron Davis, an undergraduate student, we began collecting and analyzing data related to COVID on GoFundMe. This resulted in several studies of campaigns from the first seven months of the pandemic: a quantitative analysis of 164,122 campaigns headed up by Mark Igra that examined race, income, and educational factors of campaign creation and outcomes;[8] and a mixed-methods analysis of a smaller representative subset of those campaigns (n = 919) to understand crowdfunding motivations and outcomes during the early pandemic.[9]

These studies yielded some important results about how crowdfunding relates to existing social inequities that we wanted to examine further on a larger sample of medical crowdfunding campaigns from across the United States. Mark Igra helped us to collect the most comprehensive dataset of US medical campaigns on GoFundMe to date, using targeted zip code searches. This yielded data on 437,596 campaigns from 2016 to 2020, which we examined alongside income, health insurance, and medical debt data. The methods and results of this research are available in a paper published in the *American Journal of Public Health*.[10]

During this time, and with my support, student collaborators took up various parts of the data to explore more fully as well. Aaron Davis examined a subset of highly successful medical crowdfunding campaigns to look at race, gender, and age discrepancies in this group of rarefied campaigns. Aaron, along with Kimberly Bui and I, coded this data, and then my colleague Shauna Carlisle lent her expertise to the data analysis and Aaron's mentorship as we worked toward publication.[11] Cadence Luchsinger examined a subset of COVID crowdfunding campaigns from Washington State for her master's thesis, developing a geospatial analysis of inequities with mentorship from Jin-Kyu Jung and I. And Emily Hops worked independently in her master's thesis examining the experiences of mutual aid organizers across the United States, with mentorship from me and Amy Hagopian.[12] These projects deepened and extended our collective exploration of crowdfunding phenomena in important ways.

Finally, with support from a Digital Humanities Fellowship through the Simpson Center for Humanities, Jin-Kyu Jung and I spent two years developing more creative and humanistic ways of working with this data and compiling it into an interactive website that aims to help people explore, and better understand, how crowdfunding is related to social and economic inequities.[13] Mark Igra was a frequent sounding board for this site and helped organize much of the data on which some of the visualizations are based. Ugbad Mohammed and Luna Bae, undergraduate students, worked to help us develop some of the data visualizations and narratives for the site. And Hayley Park, a master's student in library and information sciences, helped us pull the disparate experiments and data visualizations into a comprehensive and well-functioning website, which was not at all a small feat.

FINAL NOTES

No research is a solo project, but the broader contours of this project have been particularly collaborative, and the contributions of these collaborators are likely too numerous to list in such a short appendix. This research has been indelibly shaped by their involvement, expertise, and disciplinary perspectives, and for that I am deeply grateful. While I led many of these collaborative projects, this book was a solo endeavor, though it builds from our shared work and learning. In addition, this book does not encapsulate the many excellent research trajectories that collaborators have pursued based on work that we began together. I've tried as much as possible to give credit to the efforts of collaborators throughout, but I bear sole responsibility for any errors, omissions, or oversights in this book.

ACKNOWLEDGMENTS

At its heart, this book is about striving for the kinds of connection that sustain, uplift, and inspire us. I am awash in gratitude for the connections, both personal and professional, that have sustained, uplifted, and inspired this project from its earliest days. The generosity of so many has made this project possible and served as a constant reminder of how powerful deep care and collective effort can be.

My first and most profound thanks goes to the people who shared some of the hardest parts of their lives with me and whose stories make up not only the scaffolding of this book but also how I have come to understand crowdfunding. I was often asking people to speak with me during profound hardships and disruptions in their lives and to think through the complex affective dimensions of their crowdfunding experiences. Their honesty and insights awed me, and it is my sincerest hope that I have told their stories accurately and compassionately. I am also indebted to the hundreds of thousands of people whose crowdfunding campaigns' data is included in the more quantitative work featured in this book. It is often too easy to lose sight of the actual people behind such large sets of data, and I have tried to never forget that each piece of data comes from a unique story of need. Thank you for helping me to understand this complex new online world. I am also deeply grateful to the experts from the crowdfunding industry who shared their knowledge and experiences with me and to the many people in my life who shaped my understanding of crowdfunding through their own experiences, both big and small.

There are several key people to whom I not only owe gratitude but without whom this book would not have been possible. Lauren Berliner co-hatched this project in its earliest stages and, as I describe in more detail in the appendix, was a crucial and deeply valued collaborator. While we have taken our research on crowdfunding into different disciplinary arenas and projects, her expertise on all things related to online life and culture nurtured this project from infancy and gave me the confidence to leap into a research topic that felt like an entirely new ecosystem. I am also grateful for her friendship and solidarity through several tough years of tenure-track hustling and parenting babies and young children. Many of the earliest ideas of this project were hatched while we bounced and held each other's babies, and I sincerely hope this book reflects the generosity of care Lauren is so quick to offer.

Later stages of the project owe a great deal to Mark Igra and Jin-Kyu Jung in particular. Mark's patient expertise with all things coding and data related, as well as his eye for methodological rigor, made much of the quantitative work cited and described here possible. Anyone who tolerates an ethnographer bumbling through large quantitative datasets and analyses deserves a prize for patience, but I am also lucky to call Mark a coauthor and peer. He has helped me to think through questions of crowdfunding in new ways and brought a keen sociologist's sensibility to many of these questions. Jin-Kyu Jung has been a joyful coconspirator for several years as we worked on more geospatial and creative dimensions of our data analysis. Our collaboration pushed me to develop many of the more creative data elements—like the poems and fabricated campaign pages—of this book. Jin-Kyu's stunningly expansive and interdisciplinary thinking widened my own perspective on this project considerably. In addition, work with coauthors and collaborators along the way, including Shauna Carlisle, Megan Carney, Johanna Crane, Aaron Davis, Amy Hagopian, Anjum Hajat, Emily Hops, Adam Koon, Emily Mendenhall, Anne Montgomery, Katerini Storeng, Lynn Thomas, and Marco Zenone, contributed deeply to my thinking on this topic and the joy I derived from working with such lovely and insightful people.

One of the most rewarding parts of this project was the opportunity it provided to work with several generations of undergraduate and graduate students. Luna Bae, Kimberly Bui, Jessica Cole, Aaron Davis, Zhihang Dong, Emily Fuller, Christine Hahn, Emily Hops, Cadence Luchsinger, Anjelica Mendoza, Fatimah Mirza, Ugbad Mohamed, Hayley Park,

Chelsea Rios, and Wanjiku Wainaina: I am so deeply thankful for the care you showed for this data, these stories, and the work we did together. In addition, my gratitude goes to Sasha Kramer, who provided crucial help organizing, cohosting, transcribing, and interpreting data from focus groups throughout the summer of 2022. Many hands have helped shape the data that informs this text, but any errors are mine alone.

Several people are particularly responsible for helping me take a disorderly set of studies and thoughts and coaxing them into book form. My gratitude first goes to Matthew Wade and the team of excellent editors and staff at the MIT Press. In addition, the excellent anonymous readers who carefully reviewed the proposal and full manuscript not only undoubtedly improved this book but also provided the encouragement I needed to complete it during a particularly busy time in my life. Before all of this, Audra Wolfe helped me refine the book's general structure and outline. I am thankful for her keen sensibilities and frank encouragement. Participating in Laura Portwood-Stacer's excellent Book Proposal Accelerator in 2021 was an excellent jump-start to the book writing process.

Over a number of years, this project received grants and institutional support that provided both material and intellectual sustenance. My deepest thanks goes to Kathleen Woodward and the University of Washington's (UW) Simpson Center for the Humanities, which supported various iterations of this project over a nearly ten-year time span. Kathy was an early believer in this work, even before the topic was very well formed. Through a collaboration studio grant, Lauren Berliner and I were able to bring together an especially generous and supportive group of scholars to begin thinking through "crowdsourcing care" in 2016. Thank you to Brian Goldfarb, Kalindi Vora, Janelle Taylor, Jose Alaniz, Gina Neff, Sasha Su-Ling Welland, Chrisoph Hanssmann, Lynn Thomas, Jenna Grant, Tamara Kneese, Johanna Crane, Daisy Yoo, Melissa Pritchard, Marieke van Eijk, David Ribes, Ariel Duncan, Chris Wade, Melissa Liu, and Tiffany Williamson for lending so much to this conversation. A later collaboration studio grant supported some of the work on Watsi included in chapter 5. And I was lucky enough to participate in the Digital Humanities Summer Fellowship in 2021with Jin-Kyu Jung, Beatrice Arduini, Juliet Shields, Maya Smith, Yandong Li, Hope Reidun St. John, Ayda Apa Pomeshikov, Gözde Burcu Ege, whose creative and wide-ranging projects both inspired and awed me. I am particularly thankful to the summer fellows, and Caitlin Palo and C. R. Grimmer, for critically nurturing the experiments with poetry from crowdfunding narratives, which resulted in the poems included here.

Thanks as well to the UW's Royalty Research Fund, which supported many of the interviews on which this book is based, and to the National Science Foundation (Proposal 1936731), which supported novel data collection techniques as well as research time for me and several collaborators under the leadership of Sarah Chasins, Kyle Crowder, and Ratislav Bodik. The UW Bothell School of Nursing and Health Studies offered considerable institutional support to this project over the years, as did the UW's Center for Demography and Ecology (with support from a Eunice Kennedy Shriver National Institute of Child Health and Human Development research infrastructure grant, P2C HD042828). The content of this work is solely my responsibility and does not necessarily represent the official views of the National Institutes of Health. Several stays at the peaceful and generative UW Whitely Center on San Juan Island allowed me to write large portions of this book without the distractions of normal life.

This book is the result of deeply productive conversations with scholars from across many fields and spanning many years, to whom I owe a great debt of gratitude. I am particularly grateful for the camaraderie and conversations with fellow crowdfunding researchers while we attempted to make sense of a new phenomenon. Jeremy Snyder, Eric Schneiderhan, Marco Zenone, Tamara Kneese, Martha Lincoln, and Chris Barcelos helped shape my thinking, hone my methodological approaches, and share the frustrations of this work. Various stages and pieces of this work benefited from the generosity and critical engagement of numerous colleagues, including those at the West Coast Poverty Center, the UW School of Nursing, the Ethics and Conflicts of Interest in Public Health Network, the Collective on the Political Determinants of Health at both the New School and the University of Oslo, the UW Population Health Initiative's Pop Health talks, and the UW GIS Day Symposium as well as the students and faculty of the Digitalisation, Health and Society course at the University of Oslo, the American Anthropological Association annual conferences, the Valuing Health Conference at the University of Edinburgh, the Society for Social Studies of Science conference, the American Society for Bioethics and Humanities conference, and the American Association of Geographers conference. My own colleagues in the School of Nursing and Health Studies also deserve thanks for their continued engagement with and support of this project, including their early encouragement for me to focus centrally on questions of equity and disparity in this research. Finally, I was lucky enough to engage with dozens of journalists and writers who covered this topic, helped me to translate my research for a public audience, and asked excellent and unexpected questions. This book is so much richer for the engagement of these many people as well as others whom I'm sure I have forgotten to list here.

Permission for some of the materials used in this book has been graciously granted by other institutions and individuals. An especially heartfelt thanks to Ted Closson for granting permission to use an image from his beautiful comic in Chapter 1. The Museum of London granted permission for use of the painting by Hicks in Chapter 2. Some data that appears in the book was previously published in *Medical Anthropology Quarterly*, *Globalization and Health*, *PLOS One*, and *Medicine, Anthropology, Theory*. My thanks to these publications for enabling me to share this work, and to *Medical Anthropology Quarterly* in particular for granting permission to republish parts of my work here.

While writing a book is often compared to birthing a baby, I was also the mother of a real baby (who is not at all a baby any longer) while doing much of this work. Deep communities and friendships sustained me while juggling these dual responsibilities. I am profoundly grateful to close friends who provided community and co-parenting before, during, and in the wake of the pandemic. Those who cared for, taught, and nurtured my daughter in our home and then through preschool and kindergarten have my lifelong gratitude and recognition.

Ethan's presence, encouragement, and love runs throughout this book, from endless conversations about its contents, to generous time offered to write it, to expert help in collecting early datasets. A special thanks as well to our extended families for their unwavering love. Finally, this book is dedicated, in part, to Josie, who has kept me smiling and hopeful through many dark moments of this research. May you maintain your unwavering sense of both optimism and justice as you grow.

NOTES

INTRODUCTION

1. "Crowdfunding Breathes Life into Malawi's Covid Fight," France 24, January 23, 2021, https://www.france24.com/en/live-news/20210123-crowdfunding-breathes-life-into-malawi-s-covid-fight; Francesca Ebel, "Tunisia: Citizen-Led Initiatives Rally to Bridge Gap in Tunisia's Covid-19 Response," Middle East Eye, July 15, 2021, http://www.middleeasteye.net/news/citizen-led-initiatives-rally-bridge-gap-tunisias-covid-19-response; Arnaldo Espinoza, "GoFundMe: Venezuelans' Lifesaver against COVID-19," Caracas Chronicles, April 15, 2021, https://www.caracaschronicles.com/2021/04/15/gofundme-venezuelans-lifesaver-against-covid-19/; Pooja Bishnoi et al., "Medical Crowdfunding and COVID-19: Awareness and Perception of Healthcare Professionals and Role of Crowdfunding Platforms in India," *International Journal Of Community Medicine And Public Health* 9, no. 4 (March 2022): 1884, https://doi.org/10.18203/2394-6040.ijcmph20220869; Susan Wardell, "To Wish You Well: The Biopolitical Subjectivities of Medical Crowdfunders during and after Aotearoa New Zealand's COVID-19 Lockdown," *BioSocieties* 18 (September 2021): 52–78, https://doi.org/10.1057/s41292-021-00251-7.

2. Here and throughout, I use pseudonyms to protect the identities of crowdfunders and other research participants. In some cases, I withhold or slightly change other details that could be used to identify participants. For a much more detailed description of how data is anonymized—as well as the challenges and ethical considerations involved in anonymizing data that is often publicly available on the internet—please see the appendix.

3. Adrienne M. Gilligan et al., "Death or Debt? National Estimates of Financial Toxicity in Persons with Newly-Diagnosed Cancer," *The American Journal of Medicine* 131, no. 10 (October 2018): 1187–1199.e5, https://doi.org/10.1016/j.amjmed.2018.05.020; S. Yousuf Zafar and Amy P. Abernethy, "Financial Toxicity, Part I: A New Name for a Growing Problem," *Oncology* 27, no. 2 (February 2013): 80–81, 149; Veena Shankaran et al. "Risk Factors for Financial Hardship in Patients Receiving Adjuvant Chemotherapy for Colon Cancer: A Population-Based Exploratory Analysis," *Journal of Clinical Oncology: Official Journal of the American Society of Clinical Oncology* 30, no. 14 (May 2012): 1608–1614, https://doi.org/10.1200/JCO.2011.37.9511.

4. Ainsley Harris, "How Crowdfunding Platform GoFundMe Has Created a $3 Billion Digital Safety Net," Fast Company, February 13, 2017, https://www.fastcompany.com/3067472/how-crowdfunding-platform-gofundme-has-created-a-3-billion-digital.

5. Lauren S. Berliner and Nora J. Kenworthy, "Producing a Worthy Illness: Personal Crowdfunding amidst Financial Crisis," *Social Science & Medicine* 187 (August 2017): 233–242, https://doi.org/10.1016/j.socscimed.2017.02.008; Nora Kenworthy and Mark Igra, "Medical Crowdfunding and Disparities in Health Care Access in the United States, 2016–2020," *American Journal of Public Health* 112, no. 3 (March 2022): 491–498, https://doi.org/10.2105/AJPH.2021.306617.

6. Paul Belleflamme, Nessrine Omrani, and Martin Peitz, "The Economics of Crowdfunding Platforms," *Information Economics and Policy* 33 (December 2015): 11–28, https://doi.org/10.1016/j.infoecopol.2015.08.003.

7. Gaia Bassani, Nicoletta Marinelli, and Silvio Vismara, "Crowdfunding in Healthcare," *The Journal of Technology Transfer* 44, no. 4 (August 2019): 1290–1310, https://doi.org/10.1007/s10961-018-9663-7; Ralph Van Wingerden and Jessica Ryan, "Fighting for Funds: An Exploratory Study into the Field of Crowdfunding," Lund University School of Economics and Management, 2011.

8. Julia Sisler, "Crowdfunding for Medical Expenses," *Canadian Medical Association Journal* 184, no. 2 (February 2012): E123–E124, https://doi.org/10.1503/cmaj.109-4084; Anna Helhoski and Victoria Simons, "Seeking Medical Debt Relief? Crowdfunding Rarely Pays Off the Bills," NerdWallet, November 2, 2016, https://www.nerdwallet.com/blog/loans/medical-debt-crowdfunding-bankruptcy/; "Medical Fundraising," GoFundMe, 2020, https://www.gofundme.com/start/medical-fundraising.

9. Berliner and Kenworthy, "Producing a Worthy Illness."

10. Mary L. Gray and Siddharth Suri, *Ghost Work: How to Stop Silicon Valley from Building a New Global Underclass* (Boston, MA: Houghton Mifflin Harcourt, 2019); Lilly Irani, "Difference and Dependence among Digital Workers: The Case of Amazon Mechanical Turk," *South Atlantic Quarterly* 114, no. 1 (January 2015): 225–234, https://doi.org/10.1215/00382876-2831665; Veena Dubal, "A Brief History of the Gig," *Logic Magazine*, May 4, 2020, https://logicmag.io/security/a-brief-history-of-the-gig/.

11. Douglas MacMillan and Gillian Tan, "GoFundMe Founders to Reap a Fortune in Buyout," *Wall Street Journal*, June 24, 2015, sec. Digits, https://www.wsj.com/articles/BL-DGB-42425.

12. Susan Adams, "Free Market Philanthropy: GoFundMe Is Changing the Way People Give to Causes Big and Small," *Forbes*, November 7, 2016, sec. Education, https://www.forbes.com/sites/susanadams/2016/10/19/free-market-philanthropy-gofundme-is-changing-the-way-people-give-to-causes-big-and-small/.

13. Rob Solon, interviewed by Ronan Leonard, "Rob Solomon the CEO of GoFundMe," *Irish Tech News Podcast*, podcast audio, accessed October 31, 2021, https://anchor.fm/irish-tech-news/episodes/Rob-Solomon-the-CEO-of-GoFundMe-eok8st.

14. Seth Stevenson, "The Dark Side of GoFundMe," *Slate*, December 9, 2020, https://slate.com/business/2020/12/gofundme-dark-side-fraud-social-media-health-care.html.

15. "About GoFundMe," GoFundMe, accessed September 27, 2021, https://www.gofundme.com/c/about-us/.

16. "GoFundMe Press & Media," GoFundMe, accessed October 31, 2022, https://www.gofundme.com/c/press/.

17. Matt Wade, "'The Giving Layer of the Internet': A Critical History of GoFundMe's Reputation Management, Platform Governance, and Communication Strategies in Capturing Peer-to-Peer and Charitable Giving Markets," *Journal of Philanthropy and Marketing* (October 2022), https://doi.org/10.1002/nvsm.1777.

18. Startup Grind, "Rob Solomon (GoFundMe) and Ryan Sweeny (Accel Partners) at Startup Grind Global 2016," March 11, 2016, YouTube video, 22:27, https://www.youtube.com/watch?v=E0aElkhmgyE; Lucy Bernholz, *How We Give Now: A Philanthropic Guide for the Rest of Us* (Cambridge, MA: The MIT Press, 2021).

19. "GoFundMe CEO Rob Solomon on the Power of Social Fundraising," BrainStation, November 10, 2017, https://brainstation.io/magazine/vanguards-gofundme-rob-solomon.

20. "Rob Solomon (GoFundMe) and Ryan Sweeny (Accel Partners)."

21. "Rob Solomon (GoFundMe) and Ryan Sweeny (Accel Partners)." Solomon observed in an interview in 2016 that "the giving space is a 300 billion dollar a year market in North America."

22. Rachel Monroe, "When GoFundMe Gets Ugly," *The Atlantic*, November 2019, https://www.theatlantic.com/magazine/archive/2019/11/gofundme-nation/598369/.

23. Glenn O'Neill, "Saving Eliza," GoFundMe, accessed July 1, 2019, https://www.gofundme.com/ElizaONeill.

24. GoFundMe, "Thanks to a $2 Million GoFundMe Campaign, Eliza Begins Experimental Treatment," *Medium* (blog), May 18, 2016, https://medium.com/@gofundme/thanks-to-a-2-million-gofundme-campaign-eliza-begins-experimental-treatment-62dac12b2184.

25. Jackie Wattles and Amy Chillag, "Orlando GoFundMe Campaign Sets Record," CNNMoney, June 14, 2016, https://money.cnn.com/2016/06/14/technology/gofundme-orlando-pulse-shooting/index.html.

26. Brian Kolfage, "We the People Will Build the Wall," GoFundMe, December 16, 2018, https://www.gofundme.com/TheTrumpWall; Nora J. Kenworthy, "Crowdfunding and Global Health Disparities: An Exploratory Conceptual and Empirical Analysis," *Globalization and Health* 15, no. S1 (November 2019): 71, https://doi.org/10.1186/s12992-019-0519-1.

27. "Official George Floyd Memorial Fund, Organized by Philonise Floyd," GoFundMe, accessed November 4, 2022, https://www.gofundme.com/f/georgefloyd.

28. Arianne Cohen, "GoFundme's Biggest Campaigns in History Are a Chilling Window into Our Needs, Desires, and Broken Safety Nets," *Fast Company*, December 8, 2020, https://www.fastcompany.com/90583816/gofundmes-biggest-campaigns-in-history-are-a-chilling-window-into-our-needs-desires-and-broken-safety-nets.

29. Berliner and Kenworthy, "Producing a Worthy Illness."

30. Mark Igra et al., "Crowdfunding as a Response to COVID-19: Increasing Inequities at a Time of Crisis," *Social Science & Medicine* 282 (August 2021): 114105, https://doi.org/10.1016/j.socscimed.2021.114105. In this study, which looked at campaigns that mentioned COVID-19 or related terms, 43.2 percent had no donations.

31. Lauren V. Ghazal et al., "'Both a Life Saver and Totally Shameful': Young Adult Cancer Survivors' Perceptions of Medical Crowdfunding," *Journal of Cancer Survivorship* 17 (February 2022): 332–341, https://doi.org/10.1007/s11764-022-01188-x.

32. Ruha Benjamin, *Race after Technology: Abolitionist Tools for the New Jim Code* (Medford, MA: Polity, 2019); David Harvey, *A Brief History of Neoliberalism* (2007; repr., Oxford: Oxford University Press, 2011); Nancy Fraser, "Clintonism, Welfare, and the Antisocial Wage: The Emergence of a Neoliberal Political Imaginary," *Rethinking Marxism* 6, no. 1 (March 1993): 9–23, https://doi.org/10.1080/08935699308658040; Ruth Wilson Gilmore, "In the Shadow of the Shadow State," in *The Revolution Will Not Be Funded* (Durham, NC: Duke University Press, 2017), 41–52, https://doi.org/10.1215/9780822373001-003; David Graeber, "Neoliberalism, or the Bureaucratization of the World," in *The Insecure American*, ed. Hugh Gusterson and Catherine Besteman (Berkeley: University of California Press, 2019), 79–96, https://doi.org/10.1525/9780520945081-007; Elizabeth A. Povinelli, *Economies of Abandonment: Social Belonging and Endurance in Late Liberalism* (Durham, NC: Duke University Press, 2011).

33. Michael B. Katz, *The Undeserving Poor: America's Enduring Confrontation with Poverty*, 2nd ed. (Oxford: Oxford University Press, 2013).

34. Jeremy Snyder et al., "Appealing to the Crowd: Ethical Justifications in Canadian Medical Crowdfunding Campaigns," *Journal of Medical Ethics* 43, no. 6 (June 2017): 364–367, https://doi.org/10.1136/medethics-2016-103933.

35. Eric Young, "Millions of Americans Donate through Crowdfunding Sites to Help Others Pay for Medical Bills," NORC at the University of Chicago, February 19, 2020, https://www.norc.org/NewsEventsPublications/PressReleases/Pages/millions-of-americans-donate-through-crowdfunding-sites-to-help-others-pay-for-medical-bills aspx.

36. "NORC AmeriSpeak Omnibus Survey: Millions of Americans Donate through Crowdfunding Sites to Help Others Pay for Medical Bills," NORC at the University of Chicago, February 19, 2020, https://www.norc.org/PDFs/ASonHealth/AmeriSpeak%20Omnibus%20-%20Crowdfunding.pdf.

37. Carmen Reinicke, "56% of Americans Can't Cover a $1,000 Emergency Expense with Savings," CNBC, January 19, 2022, https://www.cnbc.com/2022/01/19/56 percent-of-americans-cant-cover-a-1000-emergency-expense-with-savings.html.

38. Susan L. Hayes, Sara R. Collins, and David C. Radley, "How Much US Households with Employer Insurance Spend on Premiums and Out-of-Pocket Costs: A State-by-State Look," The Commonwealth Brief, May 23, 2019, https://doi.org/10.26099/s50f-rs05.

39. Emily R. Adrion et al., "Out-of-Pocket Spending for Hospitalizations Among Nonelderly Adults," *JAMA Internal Medicine* 176, no. 9 (September 2016), https://doi.org/10.1001/jamainternmed.2016.3663.

40. Kenworthy and Igra, "Medical Crowdfunding and Disparities in Health Care Access."

41. Kenworthy and Igra, "Medical Crowdfunding and Disparities in Health Care Access."

42. Igra, Kenworthy, Luchsinger, and Jin-Kyu Jung, "Crowdfunding as a Response to COVID-19."

43. Massimo Airoldi, "Ethnography and the Digital Fields of Social Media," *International Journal of Social Research Methodology* 21, no. 6 (November 2018): 661–673, https://doi.org/10.1080/13645579.2018.1465622; E. Gabriella Coleman, "Ethnographic Approaches to Digital Media," *Annual Review of Anthropology* 39 (October 2010): 487–505, https://doi.org/10.1146/annurev.anthro.012809.104945; Tom Boellstorff, ed., *Ethnography and Virtual Worlds: A Handbook of Method* (Princeton, NJ: Princeton University Press, 2012); Janet Vertesi and David Ribes, eds., *DigitalSTS: A Field Guide for Science & Technology Studies* (Princeton, NJ: Princeton University Press, 2019).

44. GoFundMe, "Expanding the Giving Layer of the Internet—GoFundMe Charity Is Here!," Medium, November 7, 2019, https://medium.com/gofundme-stories/expanding-the-giving-layer-of-the-internet-gofundme-charity-is-here-3794532b8502.

CHAPTER 1

1. Rachel Garfield, Kendal Orgera, and Anthony Damico, *The Coverage Gap: Uninsured Poor Adults in States That Do Not Expand Medicaid* (Washington, DC: Kaiser Family Foundation, 2021), https://www.kff.org/medicaid/issue-brief/the-coverage-gap-uninsured-poor-adults-in-states-that-do-not-expand-medicaid/.

2. "Texas Performance Data," The Commonwealth Fund, accessed November 6, 2022, https://www.commonwealthfund.org/datacenter/texas.

3. "The Uninsured in Texas," Texas Mediacl Association, accessed November 6, 2022, https://www.texmed.org/uninsured_in_texas/.

4. Ricardo Nuila, "Poor and Uninsured in Texas," *The New Yorker*, August 18, 2016, https://www.newyorker.com/news/news-desk/poor-and-uninsured-in-texas; "2022 Scorecard on State Health System Performance," The Commonwealth Fund, June 16, 2022, https://doi.org/10.26099/3127-xy78.

5. Carolyn Schwarz, "Freed from Insurance: Health Care Sharing Ministries and the Moralization of Health Care," *Social Science & Medicine* 268 (January 2021): 113453, https://doi.org/10.1016/j.socscimed.2020.113453; Carolyn Schwarz, "Thrifting for More: Savings and Aspirations in Health Care Sharing Ministries after the Affordable Care Act," *Medical Anthropology Quarterly* 33, no. 2 (June 2019): 226–241, https://doi.org/10.1111/maq.12515.

6. Adam Gaffney, David U. Himmelstein, and Steffie Woolhandler, "Prevalence and Correlates of Patient Rationing of Insulin in the United States: A National Survey," *Annals of Internal Medicine* (October 2022): M22–2477, https://doi.org/10.7326/M22-2477. Researchers estimate that approximately 16.5 percent of insulin users in the United States are forced to ration insulin each year. Bartering, trading, and sharing insulin is also very common.

7. Raphael G. Warnock, "Affordable Insulin Now Act," Pub. L. No. S.3700 (2022), http://www.congress.gov/. In 2022 Congress passed the Affordable Insulin Now Act, which limits the cost of insulin to $35 a vial but only for Medicare patients. Jason likely would not have benefited from this bill.

8. William T. Cefalu et al., "Insulin Access and Affordability Working Group: Conclusions and Recommendations," *Diabetes Care* 41, no. 6 (June 2018): 1299–1311, https://doi.org/10.2337/dci18-0019.

9. Madeline Pesec et al., "Primary Health Care That Works: The Costa Rican Experience," *Health Affairs* 36, no. 3 (March 2017): 531–538, https://doi.org/10.1377/hlthaff.2016.1319; "Out-of-Pocket Expenditure per Capita, PPP (Current International $)," The World Bank, January 30, 2022, https://data.worldbank.org/indicator/SH.XPD.OOPC.PP.CD.

10. Luke O'Neil, "$50 Could Have Saved Him, but His GoFundMe Pitch Didn't Get the Clicks," *The Boston Globe*, March 7, 2019, https://www.bostonglobe.com/ideas/2019/03/07/could-have-saved-him-but-his-gofundme-pitch-didn-get-clicks/44416UyhI0XUfDRIxE5SlI/story.html.

11. Ted Closson, "A GoFundMe Campaign Is Not Health Insurance," *The Nib* (blog), May 25, 2017, https://thenib.com/a-gofundme-campaign-is-not-health-insurance/.

12. Elisabeth Rosenthal, *An American Sickness: How Healthcare Became Big Business and How You Can Take It Back* (New York: Penguin Books, 2018), 2.

13. Harvey, *A Brief History of Neoliberalism* (2007; repr., Oxford: Oxford University Press, 2011).

14. Harvey, *A Brief History of Neoliberalism*; Salmaan Keshavjee, *Blind Spot: How Neoliberalism Infiltrated Global Health*, California Series in Public Anthropology 30 (Oakland: University of California Press, 2014); Ellen E. Foley, *Your Pocket Is What Cures You: The Politics of Health in Senegal* (New Brunswick, NJ: Rutgers University Press, 2010); Vicente Navarro, "Neoliberalism as a Class Ideology; Or, the Political Causes of the Growth of Inequalities," *International Journal of Health Services* 37, no. 1 (2007): 47–62.

15. George Monbiot, "Neoliberalism—The Ideology at the Root of All Our Problems," *The Guardian*, April 15, 2016, sec. Books, https://www.theguardian.com/books/2016/apr/15/neoliberalism-ideology-problem-george-monbiot.

16. Rosenthal, *An American Sickness*; Abdul El-Sayed and Micah Johnson, *Medicare for All: A Citizen's Guide* (New York: Oxford University Press, 2021).

17. Gerard F. Anderson et al., "It's the Prices, Stupid: Why the United States Is So Different from Other Countries," *Health Affairs* 22, no. 3 (May 2003): 89–105,

https://doi.org/10.1377/hlthaff.22.3.89; Gerard F. Anderson et al., "It's Still the Prices, Stupid: Why the US Spends So Much on Health Care, and a Tribute to Uwe Reinhardt," *Health Affairs* 38, no. 1 (January 2019): 87–95, https://doi.org/10.1377/hlthaff.2018.05144. While the original article with this title was published in 2003, little has changed to alter the fundamental challenge of high prices in the US health-care system. In 2019 an update to the original article was published under the title "It's Still the Prices, Stupid."

18. Andrew W. Mulcahy, Daniel Schwam, and Nathaniel Edenfield, *Comparing Insulin Prices in the United States to Other Countries: Results from a Price Index Analysis* (Santa Monica, CA: RAND Corporation, October 2020), https://www.rand.org/pubs/research_reports/RRA788-1.html.

19. Schwarz, "Freed from Insurance."

20. Office of the Press Secretary, "Remarks by the President on Health Insurance Reform in Fairfax, Virginia," March 19, 2010, https://obamawhitehouse.archives.gov/the-press-office/remarks-president-health-insurance-reform-fairfax-virginia.

21. Rosenthal, *An American Sickness*, 6. As Rosenthal notes, "currently we buy and sell medical encounters and accoutrements like commodities, but how do participants in the marketplace make purchasing choices? Prices are often unknowable and unpredictable, there's little robust competition for our business, we have scant information on quality to guide our decisions; and very often we lack the power ourselves to even choose."

22. Rosenthal, *An American Sickness*, 2.

23. El-Sayed and Johnson, *Medicare for All*; David U. Himmelstein, Terry Campbell, and Steffie Woolhandler, "Health Care Administrative Costs in the United States and Canada, 2017," *Annals of Internal Medicine* 172, no. 2 (January 2020): 134, https://doi.org/10.7326/M19-2818.

24. "Current Health Expenditure per Capita (Current US$)," World Bank, January 30, 2022, https://data.worldbank.org/indicator/SH.XPD.CHEX.PC.CD?most_recent_value_desc=true.

25. "Current Health Expenditure per Capita (Current US$)."

26. Stephen Bezruchka, "Bezruchka's Blog: The Health Olympics," *Planetary Health Weekly* (blog), February 17, 2022, https://planetaryhealthweekly.com/2022/02/17/bezruchkas-blog-the-health-olympics/; see also Stephen Bezruchka, *Inequality Kills Us All: COVID-19's Health Lessons for the World* (New York: Routledge, 2022).

27. "Life Expectancy at Birth, Total (Years)," World Bank, accessed November 11, 2022, https://data.worldbank.org/indicator/SP.DYN.LE00.IN?most_recent_value_desc=true.

28. "Mortality Analyses," Johns Hopkins Coronavirus Resource Center, accessed August 24, 2022, https://coronavirus.jhu.edu/data/mortality; Bezruchka, *Inequality Kills Us All*.

29. "Mortality Analyses."

30. Jared Ortaliza et al., "How Does US Life Expectancy Compare to Other Countries?," *Peterson-KFF Health System Tracker* (blog), September 28, 2021, https://www.healthsystemtracker.org/chart-collection/u-s-life-expectancy-compare-countries/.

31. National Research Council and Institute of Medicine, *US Health in International Perspective: Shorter Lives, Poorer Health* (Washington, DC: National Academies Press, 2013), 4, https://doi.org/10.17226/13497.

32. National Research Council and Institute of Medicine, *US Health in International Perspective*.

33. National Research Council and Institute of Medicine, *US Health in International Perspective*.

34. Jonathan Metzl, *Dying of Whiteness* (New York: Basic Books, 2019); Alberto Alesina, Edward Glaeser, and Bruce Sacerdote, "Why Doesn't the US Have a European-Style Welfare System?" (working paper no. 8524, National Bureau of Economic Research, October 2001), https://doi.org/10.3386/w8524; Bryce Covert, "There's a Reason We Can't Have Nice Things: Guest Essay," *New York Times*, July 21, 2022, https://www.nytimes.com/2022/07/21/opinion/racism-paid-leave-child-care.html.

35. Ange-Marie Hancock, *The Politics of Disgust: The Public Identity of the Welfare Queen* (New York: New York University Press, 2004); Lisa S.-H. Park, "Criminalizing Immigrant Mothers: Public Charge, Health Care, and Welfare Reform," *International Journal of Sociology of the Family* 37, no. 1 (2011): 27–47; Amy L. Fairchild, *Science at the Borders: Immigrant Medical Inspection and the Shaping of the Modern Industrial Labor Force* (Baltimore, MD: Johns Hopkins University Press, 2003).

36. Metzl, *Dying of Whiteness*.

37. Metzl, *Dying of Whiteness*, 4.

38. Cedric J. Robinson, *Black Marxism: The Making of the Black Radical Tradition*, 3rd ed., revised and updated (Chapel Hill: University of North Carolina Press, 2020).

39. El-Sayed and Johnson, *Medicare for All*, 85.

40. El-Sayed and Johnson, *Medicare for All*, 91.

41. Daniel Crespin and Thomas DeLeire, "As Insurers Exit Affordable Care Act Marketplaces, So Do Consumers," *Health Affairs* 38, no. 11 (November 2019): 1893–1901, https://doi.org/10.1377/hlthaff.2018.05475.

42. Metzl, *Dying of Whiteness*, 124.

43. Metzl, *Dying of Whiteness*, 125.

44. Jessica M. Mulligan and Emily K. Brunson, "Structures of Resentment: On Feeling—and Being—Left Behind by Health Care Reform," *Cultural Anthropology* 35, no. 2 (May 2020): 319, 324, https://doi.org/10.14506/ca35.2.10.

45. Schwarz, "Thrifting for More."

46. Schwarz, "Freed from Insurance," 2.

47. Mulligan and Brunson, "Structures of Resentment," 319.

48. Jessica M. Mulligan and Heide Castañeda, eds., *Unequal Coverage: The Experience of Health Care Reform in the United States* (New York: New York University Press, 2018), 12.

49. Jennifer Tolbert, Kendal Orgera, and Anthony Damico, "Key Facts about the Uninsured Population," *KFF* (blog), November 6, 2020, https://www.kff.org/uninsured/issue-brief/key-facts-about-the-uninsured-population/.

50. Tolbert, Orgera, and Damico, "Key Facts about the Uninsured Population." The largest population of uninsured people in the United States in 2019 were nonelderly, poor adults, and cost remains the primary reason people remain uninsured. Undocumented mmigrants are also often ineligible for coverage and make up another significant group of the uninsured.

51. Joseph R. Antos and James C. Capretta, "The ACA: Trillions? Yes. A Revolution? No," Health Affairs Forefront, April 10, 2020, https://doi.org/10.1377/forefront.20200406.93812.

52. El-Sayed and Johnson, *Medicare for All*, 43.

53. Noam N. Levey, "100 Million People in America Are Saddled with Health Care Debt," *Kaiser Health News* (blog), June 16, 2022, https://khn.org/news/article/diagnosis-debt-investigation-100-million-americans-hidden-medical-debt/.

54. Mulligan and Castañeda, *Unequal Coverage*, 11.

55. Mulligan and Castañeda, *Unequal Coverage*, 18.

56. Mulligan and Castañeda, *Unequal Coverage*.

57. S. Yousuf Zafar and Amy P. Abernethy, "Financial Toxicity, Part I: A New Name for a Growing Problem," *Oncology* 27, no. 2 (February 2013): 80–81, 149.

58. Zafar and Abernethy, "Financial Toxicity, Part I."

59. Zafar and Abernethy, "Financial Toxicity, Part I"; Reginald D. Tucker-Seeley, and K. Robin Yabroff, "Minimizing the 'Financial Toxicity' Associated with Cancer Care: Advancing the Research Agenda," *Journal of the National Cancer Institute* 108, no. 5 (May 2016): djv410, https://doi.org/10.1093/jnci/djv410; Shankaran et al., "Risk Factors for Financial Hardship in Patients Receiving Adjuvant Chemotherapy for Colon Cancer."

60. Adrienne M. Gilligan et al., "Death or Debt? National Estimates of Financial Toxicity in Persons with Newly-Diagnosed Cancer," *The American Journal of Medicine* 131, no. 10 (October 2018): 1187–1199.e5, https://doi.org/10.1016/j.amjmed.2018.05.020.

61. Kathryn E. Weaver et al., "Forgoing Medical Care Because of Cost: Assessing Disparities in Healthcare Access among Cancer Survivors Living in the United States," *Cancer* 116, no. 14 (June 2010): 3493–3504, https://doi.org/10.1002/cncr.25209.

62. Libby Ellis et al., "Trends in Cancer Survival by Health Insurance Status in California from 1997 to 2014," *JAMA Oncology* 4, no. 3 (March 2018): 317, https://doi.org/10.1001/jamaoncol.2017.3846.

63. "How the Crowdsourcing Website GoFundMe Is Changing Charity," CBS News, December 22, 2019, https://www.cbsnews.com/news/gofundme-how-the-crowdsourcing-website-is-changing-charity/. At the time of their campaign, GoFundMe had a standardized fee structure for campaigns where 5 percent went to the platform and they charged 2.9 percent on top of that for transaction fees. In 2017 the platform switched to a tip-based model for collecting money from donations, offering users standard options of 10, 15, and 20 percent tips. In a 2019 interview, CEO Rob Solomon said "the majority of people" leave tips on donations.

64. Nicholas Freudenberg, *At What Cost: Modern Capitalism and the Future of Health* (New York: Oxford University Press, 2021).

65. Freudenberg, *At What Cost*, 151.

66. Nancy Fraser, "Contradictions of Capital and Care," *New Left Review* 100, no. Jul/Aug (August 2016): 99–117.

67. Fraser, "Contradictions of Capital and Care," 101.

68. Valerie (@ValeeGrrl), "Welcome to America your health insurance options are GoFundMe or the Ellen show lol good luck," Twitter, August 15, 2018.

69. Gordon Burtch and Jason Chan, "Reducing Medical Bankruptcy through Crowdfunding: Evidence from GiveForward," *Management Information Systems Quarterly* 43, no. 1 (2019): 237–262, https://doi.org/10.25300/MISQ/2019/14569.

70. Lauren S. Berliner and Nora J. Kenworthy, "Producing a Worthy Illness: Personal Crowdfunding amidst Financial Crisis," *Social Science & Medicine* 187 (August 2017): 233–242, https://doi.org/10.1016/j.socscimed.2017.02.008; Anna Helhoski and Victoria Simons, "Seeking Medical Debt Relief? Crowdfunding Rarely Pays Off the Bills," NerdWallet, November 2, 2016, https://www.nerdwallet.com/blog/loans/medical-debt-crowdfunding-bankruptcy/; Nora Kenworthy and Mark Igra, "Medical Crowdfunding and Disparities in Health Care Access in the United States, 2016–2020," *American Journal of Public Health* 112, no. 3 (March 2022): 491–498, https://doi.org/10.2105/AJPH.2021.306617"; Nora Kenworthy, "Like a Grinding Stone: How Crowdfunding Platforms Create, Perpetuate, and Value Health Inequities," *Medical Anthropology Quarterly* 35, no. 3 (2021): 327–345, https://doi.org/10.1111/maq.12639.

71. Kenworthy and Igra, "Medical Crowdfunding and Disparities in Health Care Access."

72. Kenworthy and Igra, "Medical Crowdfunding and Disparities in Health Care Access."

73. Kara Swisher, "If Government Did Its Job We Might Not Need GoFundMe," Sway, accessed November 11, 2022, https://www.nytimes.com/2021/03/01/opinion/sway-kara-swisher-tim-cadogan.html.

74. Swisher, "If Government Did Its Job We Might Not Need GoFundMe."

75. "Answers to Common Fundraising Questions," GoFundMe, accessed September 20, 2020, https://www.gofundme.com/c/questions; Kathryn Lundstrom, "GoFundMe's First Brand Campaign Tells Stories of Kindness," *Adweek*, May 11, 2021, https://

www.adweek.com/brand-marketing/gofundme-celebrates-nycs-generosity-and-establishes-its-brand-as-the-currency-of-kindness/.

76. Tim Cadogan, "GoFundMe CEO: Hello Congress, Americans Need Help and We Can't Do Your Job for You," USA Today, February 11, 2021, https://www.usatoday.com/story/opinion/voices/2021/02/11/gofundme-ceo-congress-pass-covid-relief-desperate-americans-column/4440425001/.

77. Cadogan, "GoFundMe CEO."

78. Berliner and Kenworthy, "Producing a Worthy Illness."

79. Lilly Irani, "Hackathons and the Making of Entrepreneurial Citizenship," *Science, Technology, & Human Values* 40, no. 5 (September 2015): 799–824, https://doi.org/10.1177/0162243915578486.

80. Dan Pfeiffer, "Empowering People to Help People: Why I Am Joining GoFundMe," *Medium* (blog), December 10, 2015, https://medium.com/@danpfeiffer/empowering-people-to-help-people-why-i-am-joining-gofundme-44d0867c987e.

81. Mark Igra et al., "Crowdfunding as a Response to COVID-19: Increasing Inequities at a Time of Crisis," *Social Science & Medicine* 282 (August 2021): 114105, https://doi.org/10.1016/j.socscimed.2021.114105.

82. GoFundMe, "The Mental Health Fund," 2020, https://www.gofundme.com/f/thementalhealthfund.

83. Swisher, "If Government Did Its Job We Might Not Need GoFundMe."

84. Nora J. Kenworthy, "Crowdfunding and Global Health Disparities: An Exploratory Conceptual and Empirical Analysis," *Globalization and Health* 15, no. S1 (November 2019): 71, https://doi.org/10.1186/s12992-019-0519-1.

85. Sibel B. Kusimba, *Reimagining Money: Kenya in the Digital Finance Revolution*, Culture and Economic Life (Stanford, CA: Stanford University Press, 2021); Verah Okeyo, "Kenyans Turn to the Internet to Raise Money for Their Medical Bills," *Nation*, April 24, 2017, https://nation.africa/kenya/healthy-nation/kenyans-turn-to-the-internet-to-raise-money-for-their-medical-bills-389438.

86. Arnaldo Espinoza, "GoFundMe: Venezuelans' Lifesaver against COVID-19," Caracas Chronicles, April 15, 2021, https://www.caracaschronicles.com/2021/04/15/gofundme-venezuelans-lifesaver-against-covid-19/; Francesca Ebel, "'The Ship Is Sinking': Citizen-Led Initiatives Rally to Bridge Gap in Tunisia's Covid-19 Response," Middle East News, https://www.middleeasteye.net/news/citizen-led-initiatives-rally-bridge-gap-tunisias-covid-19-response.

87. "Crowdfunding's Potential for the Developing World" (working paper, World Bank, 2013), 4.

88. Sanjay Basu, Megan A. Carney, and Nora J. Kenworthy, "Ten Years after the Financial Crisis: The Long Reach of Austerity and Its Global Impacts on Health," *Social Science & Medicine* 187 (August 2017): 203–207, https://doi.org/10.1016/j.socscimed.2017.06.026.

89. Keshavjee, *Blind Spot*; Foley, *Your Pocket Is What Cures You*; James Pfeiffer and Rachel Chapman, "Anthropological Perspectives on Structural Adjustment and

Public Health," *Annual Review of Anthropology* 39 (October 2010): 149–165, https://doi.org/10.1146/annurev.anthro.012809.105101; Howard Waitzkin, *Medicine and Public Health at the End of Empire* (Boulder, CO: Paradigm Publishers, 2011).

90. Pooja Bishnoi et al., "Medical Crowdfunding and COVID-19: Awareness and Perception of Healthcare Professionals and Role of Crowdfunding Platforms in India," *International Journal Of Community Medicine And Public Health* 9, no. 4 (March 2022): 1884, https://doi.org/10.18203/2394-6040.ijcmph20220869.

91. Keshi Ndirangu, "Comedian Akuku Danger Detained at Hospital, Pleads for Assistance," Nairobi News, January 26, 2022, https://nairobinews.nation.africa/comedian-akuku-danger-detained-at-hospital-pleads-for-assistance/.

92. Michael Otremba, Gretchen Berland, and Joseph J. Amon, "Hospitals as Debtor Prisons," *The Lancet Global Health* 3, no. 5 (May 2015): e253–e254, https://doi.org/10.1016/S2214-109X(15)70073-2; Krisna Handayani et al., "Global Problem of Hospital Detention Practices," *International Journal of Health Policy and Management* 9, no. 8 (August 2020): 319–326, https://doi.org/10.15171/ijhpm.2020.10.

93. Ellen Stewart, "Crowdfunding Healthcare in Shetland: Maakin the NHS," *The Polyphony* (blog), July 6, 2021, https://thepolyphony.org/2021/07/06/crowdfunding-healthcare-in-shetland-maakin-the-nhs/; Ellen Stewart et al., "Doing 'Our Bit': Solidarity, Inequality, and COVID-19 Crowdfunding for the UK National Health Service," *Social Science & Medicine* 308 (September 2022): 115214, https://doi.org/10.1016/j.socscimed.2022.115214.

94. Sameh N. Saleh et al., "A Comparison of Online Medical Crowdfunding in Canada, the UK, and the US," *JAMA Network Open* 3, no. 10 (October 2020): e2021684, https://doi.org/10.1001/jamanetworkopen.2020.21684; Gaia Bassani, Nicoletta Marinelli, and Silvio Vismara, "Crowdfunding in Healthcare," *The Journal of Technology Transfer* 44, no. 4 (August 2019): 1290–1310, https://doi.org/10.1007/s10961-018-9663-7; Sumin Lee and Vili Lehdonvirta, "New Digital Safety Net or Just More 'Friendfunding'? Institutional Analysis of Medical Crowdfunding in the United States," *Information, Communication & Society* 25, no. 8 (December 2020): 1151–1175, https://doi.org/10.1080/1369118X.2020.1850838; Jeremy Snyder and Leigh Turner, "Crowdfunding, Stem Cell Interventions and Autism Spectrum Disorder: Comparing Campaigns Related to an International 'Stem Cell Clinic' and US Academic Medical Center," *Cytotherapy* 23, no. 3 (October 2020): 198–202, https://doi.org/10.1016/j.jcyt.2020.09.002.

95. Jeremy Snyder et al., "What Medical Crowdfunding Campaigns Can Tell Us about Local Health System Gaps and Deficiencies: Exploratory Analysis of British Columbia, Canada," *Journal of Medical Internet Research* 22, no. 5 (May 2020): e16982, https://doi.org/10.2196/16982; Isabel P. Coutrot, Richard Smith, and Laura Cornelsen, "Is the Rise of Crowdfunding for Medical Expenses in the United Kingdom Symptomatic of Systemic Gaps in Health and Social Care?," *Journal of Health Services Research & Policy* 25, no. 3 (July 2020): 181–186, https://doi.org/10.1177/1355819619897949; Saleh et al., "A Comparison of Online Medical Crowdfunding in Canada, the UK, and the US."

96. Kenworthy and Igra, "Medical Crowdfunding and Disparities in Health Care Access."

97. Cadogan, "GoFundMe CEO."

98. Jeremy Snyder, "Implications of Inequities in Health-Related Crowdfunding for the Business of Crowdfunding," *American Journal of Public Health* 112, no. 3 (March 2022): 357–359, https://doi.org/10.2105/AJPH.2021.306679. This point is also made by Matt Wade, "'The Giving Layer of the Internet': A Critical History of GoFundMe's Reputation Management, Platform Governance, and Communication Strategies in Capturing Peer-to-Peer and Charitable Giving Markets," *Journal of Philanthropy and Marketing* (October 2022), https://doi.org/10.1002/nvsm.1777.

99. GoFundMe, "New Report: Giving Goes Viral, Donations on GoFundMe Exceed $1 Billion in the Last Year," *GoFundMe Stories* (blog), December 1, 2015, https://medium.com/gofundme-stories/new-report-giving-goes-viral-donations-on-gofundme-exceed-1-billion-in-the-last-year-e2a422196019.

100. GoFundMe, "New Report."

101. Luis Lang, "Need Help to Save My Eye Sight," GoFundMe, April 18, 2015, https://www.gofundme.com/s78e9w.

102. Ann D. Helms, "Who Should Save Sight of SC Man Who Can't Afford Surgery?," *Charlotte Observer,* May 12, 2015, http://www.charlotteobserver.com/news/business/health-care/health-care-challenge-blog/article20696283.html.

103. Charles Gaba, "See Man Hate Obamacare. See Man Refuse to Get Obamacare. See Man Whine That He Can't Get Obamacare When He Needs It," *ACA Signups* (blog), May 12, 2015, https://acasignups.net/15/05/12/updated-x3-see-man-hate-obamacare-see-man-refuse-get-obamacare-see-man-whine-he-cant-get.

104. Lang, "Need Help to Save My Eye Sight."

105. Charles Gaba, "UPDATE: The Luis Lang Saga, Part VI: The Interview," *ACA Signups* (blog), May 28, 2015, https://acasignups.net/15/05/28/luis-lang-saga-part-vi-interview.

106. Gaba, "UPDATE"; Harold Pollack, "A Conversation with Crowdfunder Luis Lang," *Healthinsurance.Org* (blog), May 16, 2015, https://www.healthinsurance.org/blog/a-conversation-with-crowdfunder-luis-lang/.

107. Helms, "Who Should Save Sight of SC Man Who Can't Afford Surgery?"

108. Ruth W. Gilmore, *Golden Gulag: Prisons, Surplus, Crisis, and Opposition in Globalizing California*, American Crossroads 21 (Berkeley: University of California Press, 2007).

CHAPTER 2

1. Michael Young, *The Rise of the Meritocracy*, 1st ed. (Oxfordshire: Routledge, 2017), https://doi.org/10.4324/9781315134642.

2. Michael Young, "Down with Meritocracy," *The Guardian*, June 29, 2001, sec. Politics, https://www.theguardian.com/politics/2001/jun/29/comment.

3. Daniel Markovits, *The Meritocracy Trap: How America's Foundational Myth Feeds Inequality, Dismantles the Middle Class, and Devours the Elite* (New York: Penguin Press, 2019).

4. Young, "Down with Meritocracy."

5. Tressie M. Cottom, *Thick: And Other Essays* (New York: The New Press, 2019), 207.

6. Elizabeth Anderson, "What Is the Point of Equality?," *Ethics* 109 (1999): 287–337.

7. Steve Hindle, "Dependency, Shame and Belonging: Badging the Deserving Poor, 1550–1750," *Cultural and Social History* 1, no. 1 (January 2004): 6–35, https://doi.org/10.1191/1478003804cs0003oa.

8. Anderson, "What Is the Point of Equality?," 311.

9. Gay Becker, "The Uninsured and the Politics of Containment in US Health Care," *Medical Anthropology* 26 (2007): 299–321; Carolyn Sargent, "Special Issue Part I: 'Deservingness' and the Politics of Health Care," *Social Science & Medicine* 74, no. 6 (March 2012): 855–857, https://doi.org/10.1016/j.socscimed.2011.10.044; Theda Skocpol, *Protecting Soldiers and Mothers: The Political Origins of Social Policy in the United States* (Cambridge, MA: Harvard University Press, 1992); Sandra J. Tanenbaum, "Medicaid Eligibility Policy in the 1980s: Medical Utilitarianism and the 'Deserving' Poor," *Journal of Health Politics, Policy and Law* 20, no. 4 (1995): 933–954, https://doi.org/10.1215/03616878-20-4-933.

10. Nancy Fraser, "Clintonism, Welfare, and the Antisocial Wage: The Emergence of a Neoliberal Political Imaginary," *Rethinking Marxism* 6, no. 1 (March 1993): 9, https://doi.org/10.1080/08935699308658040.

11. Sargent, "Special Issue Part I," 855; see also Hancock, *The Politics of Disgust*.

12. Becker, "The Uninsured and the Politics of Containment in US Health Care," 258.

13. Herbert J. Gans, "Positive Functions of the Undeserving Poor: Uses of the Underclass in America," *Politics & Society* 22, no. 3 (1994): 269–283, https://doi.org/10.1177/0032329294022003002; Ampson Hagan, "How Medicare for All Challenges Our Ideas of Black Deservingness," *Somatosphere* (blog), May 27, 2019, http://somatosphere.net/2019/how-medicare-for-all-challenges-our-ideas-of-black-deservingness.html/?fbclid=IwAR3Z0v2okbRDS3UmkQ6lydkvtrHt02iNB-X82TAKwCdA4hmll7cYMO5oXrU; Anderson, "What Is the Point of Equality?"; Theda Skocpol and Vanessa Williamson, *The Tea Party and the Remaking of Republican Conservatism* (Oxford: Oxford University Press, 2012).

14. Anderson, "What Is the Point of Equality?," 308.

15. Hagan, "How Medicare for All Challenges Our Ideas of Black Deservingness."

16. Celeste Watkins-Hayes and Elyse Kovalsky, "The Discourse of Deservingness: Morality and the Dilemmas of Poverty Relief in Debate and Practice," in *The Discourse of Deservingness*, ed. David Brady and Linda M. Burton, vol. 1 (Oxford: Oxford University Press, 2017), https://doi.org/10.1093/oxfordhb/9780199914050.013.10.

17. Lauren S. Berliner and Nora J. Kenworthy, "Producing a Worthy Illness: Personal Crowdfunding amidst Financial Crisis," *Social Science & Medicine* 187 (August

2017): 233–242, https://doi.org/10.1016/j.socscimed.2017.02.008; Trena M. Paulus and Katherine R. Roberts, "Crowdfunding a 'Real-Life Superhero': The Construction of Worthy Bodies in Medical Campaign Narratives," *Discourse, Context & Media* 21 (March 2018): 64–72, https://doi.org/10.1016/j.dcm.2017.09.008.

18. Paulus and Roberts, "Crowdfunding a 'Real-Life Superhero.'"

19. "The GoFundMe Heroes Celebration," GoFundMe, accessed October 21, 2021, https://charity.gofundme.com/o/en/campaign/gofundme-heroes-an-event-to-celebrate-changemakers.

20. "Heroes Archive," GoFundMe, accessed October 21, 2021, https://www.gofundme.com/c/heroes.

21. "Answers to Common Fundraising Questions," GoFundMe, accessed September 20, 2020, https://www.gofundme.com/c/questions.

22. "An Infant Orphan Election at the London Tavern, 'Polling' by George Elgar Hicks," Art Fund, accessed October 21, 2021, https://www.artfund.org/supporting-museums/art-weve-helped-buy/artwork/5574/an-infant-orphan-election-at-the-london-tavern-.

23. Shusaku Kanazawa, "'To Vote or Not to Vote': Charity Voting and the Other Side of Subscriber Democracy in Victorian England," *The English Historical Review* 131, no. 549 (April 2016): 353–383, https://doi.org/10.1093/ehr/cew077.

24. Kanazawa, "'To Vote or Not to Vote.'"

25. Kanazawa, "'To Vote or Not to Vote.'"

26. Amber Watts, "Queen for a Day: Remaking Consumer Culture, One Woman at a Time," in *The Great American Makeover*, ed. Dana Heller (New York: Palgrave Macmillan, 2006), 141–157, https://doi.org/10.1057/9780312376178_9.

27. Erin Blakemore, "This Midcentury Show Turned Unhappy Housewives into TV Royalty," History, July 19, 2017, https://www.history.com/news/this-midcentury-show-turned-unhappy-housewives-into-tv-royalty.

28. Erica Bornstein, "Child Sponsorship, Evangelism, and Belonging in the Work of World Vision Zimbabwe," *American Ethnologist* 28 (2001): 595–622.

29. Nora J. Kenworthy, *Mistreated: The Political Consequences of the Fight against AIDS in Lesotho* (Nashville, TN: Vanderbilt University Press, 2017).

30. Bornstein, "Child Sponsorship, Evangelism, and Belonging in the Work of World Vision Zimbabwe."

31. Karen McVeigh, "'Sponsor a Child' Schemes Attacked for Perpetuating Racist Attitudes," *The Guardian*, May 31, 2021, sec. Global Development, https://www.theguardian.com/global-development/2021/may/31/sponsor-a-child-schemes-attacked-for-perpetuating-racist-attitudes.

32. Liisa H. Malkki, *The Need to Help: The Domestic Arts of International Humanitarianism* (Durham, NC: Duke University Press, 2015).

33. Bornstein, "Child Sponsorship, Evangelism, and Belonging in the Work of World Vision Zimbabwe."

34. "Kiva—Loans That Change Lives," Kiva, accessed October 21, 2021, https://www.kiva.org/.

35. Megan Moodie, "Microfinance and the Gender of Risk: The Case of Kiva.Org," *Signs: Journal of Women in Culture and Society* 38, no. 2 (January 2013): 279–302, https://doi.org/10.1086/667448.

36. Moodie, "Microfinance and the Gender of Risk"; Naila Kabeer, "Conflicts Over Credit: Re-Evaluating the Empowerment Potential of Loans to Women in Rural Bangladesh," *World Development* 29, no. 1 (2001): 63–84.

37. Lamia Karim, "Demystifying Micro-Credit: The Grameen Bank, NGOs, and Neoliberalism in Bangladesh," *Cultural Dynamics* 20, no. 1 (March 2008): 7, https://doi.org/10.1177/0921374007088053; see also Aminur Rahman, *Women and Microcredit in Rural Bangladesh: Anthropological Study of the Rhetoric and Realities of Grameen Bank Lending* (Boulder, CO: Westview Press, 1999).

38. Moodie, "Microfinance and the Gender of Risk," 281.

39. David Roodman, "Kiva Is Not Quite What It Seems," *Center for Global Development* (blog), October 2, 2009, https://www.cgdev.org/blog/kiva-not-quite-what-it-seems.

40. Roodman, "Kiva Is Not Quite What It Seems."

41. Vincanne Adams, ed., *Metrics: What Counts in Global Health*, Critical Global Health—Evidence, Efficacy, Ethnography (Durham, NC: Duke University Press, 2016), 48.

42. Friedemann Polzin, Helen Toxopeus, and Erik Stam, "The Wisdom of the Crowd in Funding: Information Heterogeneity and Social Networks of Crowdfunders," *Small Business Economics* 50, no. 2 (February 2018): 251–273, https://doi.org/10.1007/s11187-016-9829-3.

43. Washington Department of Health, "Yakima County Chronic Disease Profile," accessed September 20, 2020, https://www.doh.wa.gov/portals/1/Documents/Pubs/345-271-ChronicDiseaseProfileYakima.pdf.

44. Nancy K. Baym, "Connect with Your Audience! The Relational Labor of Connection," *The Communication Review* 18, no. 1 (January 2015): 14–22, https://doi.org/10.1080/10714421.2015.996401; Brooke E. Duffy, "Gendering the Labor of Social Media Production," *Feminist Media Studies* 15, no. 4 (July 2015): 710–714, https://doi.org/10.1080/14680777.2015.1053715.

45. Sargent, "Special Issue Part I."

46. Baym, "Connect with Your Audience! The Relational Labor of Connection."

47. Ralph Nader, "From Charity to Justice," *The Register Citizen*, May 9, 2011, sec. News, https://www.registercitizen.com/news/article/RALPH-NADER-From-charity-to-justice-12052462.php.

CHAPTER 3

1. "Rob Solomon the CEO of GoFundMe," *Irish Tech News Podcast*, accessed October 31, 2021, https://anchor.fm/irish-tech-news/episodes/Rob-Solomon-the-CEO-of-GoFundMe-eok8st.

2. Rob Solomon, "Giving Gone Wild," *@Accel* (blog), June 20, 2016, https://medium.com/accel-insights/giving-gone-wild-54ab55ad653e.

3. "Creating a GoFundMe from Start to Finish," GoFundMe, accessed September 20, 2020, https://support.gofundme.com/hc/en-us/articles/360001992627-Creating-a-GoFundMe-From-Start-to-Finish.

4. "Personal Fundraising: How Individuals Can Raise Money Online," *Fundly* (blog), accessed August 18, 2022, https://blog.fundly.com/personal-fundraising/.

5. "Creating a GoFundMe from Start to Finish"; "Personal Fundraising."

6. GoFundMe, "GoFundMe Guide: Creating a Fundraiser," August 15, 2022, YouTube video, 2:44, https://www.youtube.com/watch?v=_byBCmiV6dM.

7. "GoFundMe Guide."

8. "Creating a GoFundMe from Start to Finish."

9. "Mobile Fact Sheet," Pew Research Center, April 7, 2021, https://www.pewresearch.org/internet/fact-sheet/mobile/; "Social Media Fact Sheet," Pew Research Center, April 7, 2021, https://www.pewresearch.org/internet/fact-sheet/social-media/.

10. Colleen McClain et al., "The Internet and the Pandemic," Pew Research Center, September 1, 2021, https://www.pewresearch.org/internet/2021/09/01/the-internet-and-the-pandemic/.

11. US Government Accountability Office, *Banking Services: Regulators Have Taken Actions to Increase Access, but Measurement of Actions' Effectiveness Could Be Improved* (Washington, DC: US Government Accountability Office, 2022), https://www.gao.gov/products/gao-22-104468.

12. See also Lauren S. Berliner and Nora J. Kenworthy, "Producing a Worthy Illness: Personal Crowdfunding amidst Financial Crisis," *Social Science & Medicine* 187 (August 2017): 233–242, https://doi.org/10.1016/j.socscimed.2017.02.008.

13. Shanyang Zhao, "Parental Education and Children's Online Health Information Seeking: Beyond the Digital Divide Debate," *Social Science & Medicine* 69, no. 10 (November 2009): 1501–1505, https://doi.org/10.1016/j.socscimed.2009.08.039; Jan van Dijk and Kenneth Hacker, "The Digital Divide as a Complex and Dynamic Phenomenon," *The Information Society* 19, no. 4 (September 2003): 315–326, https://doi.org/10.1080/01972240309487; Daniel Greene, *The Promise of Access: Technology, Inequality, and the Political Economy of Hope* (Cambridge, MA: The MIT Press, 2021).

14. Safiya U. Noble and Brendesha M. Tynes, eds., *The Intersectional Internet: Race, Sex, Class and Culture Online*, Digital Formations, vol. 105 (New York: Peter Lang Publishing, 2015), 2 emphasis original.

15. Safiya U. Noble, *Algorithms of Oppression: How Search Engines Reinforce Racism* (New York: New York University Press, 2018); Benjamin, *Race after Technology*; Philip E. Bickler, John R. Feiner, and John W. Severinghaus, "Effects of Skin Pigmentation on Pulse Oximeter Accuracy at Low Saturation," *Anesthesiology* 102, no. 4 (April 2005): 715–719, https://doi.org/10.1097/00000542-200504000-00004.

16. Benjamin, *Race after Technology*, x.

17. Bruce G. Link and Jo C. Phelan, "Social Conditions as Fundamental Causes of Disease," *Journal of Health and Social Behavior* 35, no. s1 (1995): 80–94; Stefan Timmermans and Rebecca Kaufman, "Technologies and Health Inequities," *Annual Review of Sociology* 46, no. 1 (July 2020): 583–602, https://doi.org/10.1146/annurev-soc-121919-054802.

18. Benjamin, *Race after Technology*; Virginia Eubanks, *Automating Inequality: How High-Tech Tools Profile, Police, and Punish the Poor*, 1st ed. (New York: St. Martin's Press, 2017); Tawana Petty et al., "Our Data Bodies: Reclaiming Our Data," ODB Project, June 15, 2018, https://www.odbproject.org/wp-content/uploads/2016/12/ODB.InterimReport.FINAL_.7.16.2018.pdf.

19. Noble, *Algorithms of Oppression*; Jessie Daniels, "Race and Racism in Internet Studies: A Review and Critique," *New Media & Society* 15, no. 5 (August 2013): 695–719, https://doi.org/10.1177/1461444812462849; Zeynep Tufekci, "Algorithmic Harms beyond Facebook and Google: Emergent Challenges of Computational Agency," *Colorado Technology Law Journal*, 13, no. 2 (2015): 203–217; Safiya U. Noble, "Teaching Trayvon: Race, Media, and the Politics of Spectacle," *The Black Scholar* 44, no. 1 (March 2014): 12–29, https://doi.org/10.1080/00064246.2014.11641209.

20. Benjamin, *Race after Technology*; Petty et al., "Our Data Bodies: Reclaiming Our Data"; Eubanks, *Automating Inequality*.

21. André Brock, *Distributed Blackness: African American Cybercultures*, Critical Cultural Communication (New York: New York University Press, 2020), https://books.google.com/books?id=pfLRDwAAQBAJ; Benjamin, *Captivating Technology: Race, Carceral Technoscience, and Liberatory Imagination in Everyday Life* (Durham, NC: Duke University Press, 2019); Amy L. Gonzales, "Disadvantaged Minorities' Use of the Internet to Expand Their Social Networks," *Communication Research* 44, no. 4 (June 2017): 467–486, https://doi.org/10.1177/0093650214565925.

22. Wesley M. Durand et al., "Medical Crowdfunding for Patients Undergoing Orthopedic Surgery," *Orthopedics* 41, no. 1 (January 2018): e58–e63, https://doi.org/10.3928/01477447-20171114-04; Deserina Sulaeman and Mei Lin, "Reducing Uncertainty in Charitable Crowdfunding," in *PACIS 2018 Proceedings* (Yokohama, Japan: PACIS 2018), https://aisel.aisnet.org/pacis2018/134; Elisabeth R. Silver et al., "Association of Neighborhood Deprivation Index with Success in Cancer Care Crowdfunding," *JAMA Network Open* 3, no. 12 (December 3, 2020): e2026946, https://doi.org/10.1001/jamanetworkopen.2020.26946.

23. Berliner and Kenworthy, "Producing a Worthy Illness," 240.

24. Mark Igra et al., "Crowdfunding as a Response to COVID-19: Increasing Inequities at a Time of Crisis," *Social Science & Medicine* 282 (August 2021): 114105, https://doi.org/10.1016/j.socscimed.2021.114105.

25. Alysha van Duynhoven et al., "Spatially Exploring the Intersection of Socioeconomic Status and Canadian Cancer-Related Medical Crowdfunding Campaigns," *BMJ Open* 9, no. 6 (June 2019): e026365, https://doi.org/10.1136/bmjopen-2018-026365.

26. Chris A. Barcelos, "Go Fund Inequality: The Politics of Crowdfunding Transgender Medical Care," *Critical Public Health* 30, no. 3 (May 2020): 330–339, https://doi.org/10.1080/09581596.2019.1575947.

27. Nora Kenworthy et al., "A Cross-Sectional Study of Social Inequities in Medical Crowdfunding Campaigns in the United States," *PLOS ONE* 15, no. 3 (March 2020): e0229760, https://doi.org/10.1371/journal.pone.0229760.

28. Kenworthy et al., "Cross-Sectional Study of Social Inequities."

29. Robin A. Cohen, Emily P. Terlizzi, and Michael E. Martinez, "Health Insurance Coverage: Early Release of Estimates from the National Health Interview Survey, 2018," National Center for Health Statistics, May 2019, https://www.cdc.gov/nchs/data/nhis/earlyrelease/insur201905.pdf; Jacqueline C. Wiltshire et al., "Medical Debt and Related Financial Consequences among Older African American and White Adults," *American Journal of Public Health* 106, no. 6 (2016): 1086–1091, https://doi.org/10.2105/AJPH.2016.303137; National Academies of Sciences, Engineering, and Medicine, *Communities in Action: Pathways to Health Equity* (Washington, DC: National Academies Press, 2017), https://www.ncbi.nlm.nih.gov/books/NBK425844/.

30. Kenworthy et al., "A Cross-Sectional Study of Social Inequities."

31. Jeremy Snyder, Valorie A. Crooks, and Tyler Cole, "Impacts of News Media Coverage on Canadian Medical Crowdfunding Campaigns," *Journal of Philanthropy and Marketing* 28, no. 1 (February 2023), https://doi.org/10.1002/nvsm.1778.

32. NORC Amerispeak Omnibus Survey, "Millions of Americans Continue to Donate to Crowdfunding Sites to Help Others Pay Medical Bills Despite Economic Hardships of the Pandemic," NORC at the University of Chicago, April 1, 2021, https://www.norc.org/NewsEventsPublications/PressReleases/Pages/millions-of-americans-continue-to-donate-to-crowdfunding-sites-to-help-others-pay-medical-bills-despite-economic-hardships.aspx.

33. Miller McPherson, Lynn Smith-Lovin, and James M. Cook, "Birds of a Feather: Homophily in Social Networks," *Annual Review of Sociology* 27, no. 1 (August 2001): 415–444, https://doi.org/10.1146/annurev.soc.27.1.415.

34. McPherson, Smith-Lovin, and Cook, "Birds of a Feather"; see also Jason Greenberg and Ethan Mollick, "Leaning In or Leaning On? Gender, Homophily, and Activism in Crowdfunding," *Academy of Management Proceedings* 2015, no. 1 (January 2015): 18365, https://doi.org/10.5465/ambpp.2015.18365abstract.

35. Pierre Bourdieu, "The Forms of Capital," in *Handbook of Theory and Research for the Sociology of Education*, ed. John G. Richardson (New York: Greenwood Press, 1981), 248.

36. Paul DiMaggio and Filiz Garip, "Network Effects and Social Inequality," *Annual Review of Sociology* 38, no. 1 (August 2012): 93–118, https://doi.org/10.1146/annurev.soc.012809.102545.

37. Sumin Lee and Vili Lehdonvirta, "New Digital Safety Net or Just More 'Friendfunding'? Institutional Analysis of Medical Crowdfunding in the United States,"

Information, Communication & Society 25, no. 8 (December 2020): 19, https://doi.org/10.1080/1369118X.2020.1850838.

38. Guy Raz, "Study: Poor Are More Charitable than the Wealthy," *NPR*, August 8, 2010, sec. Research News, https://www.npr.org/templates/story/story.php?storyId=129068241.

39. Paul K. Piff et al., "Having Less, Giving More: The Influence of Social Class on Prosocial Behavior," *Journal of Personality and Social Psychology* 99, no. 5 (2010): 771–784, https://doi.org/10.1037/a0020092.

40. Tyler Davis, Drew Lindsay, and Brian O'Leary, "How America Gives Data: Leaders and Laggards, Giving Opportunities, and More," The Chronicle of Philanthropy, October 2, 2017, https://www.philanthropy.com/article/how-america-gives-data-leaders-and-laggards-giving-opportunities-and-more/.

41. NORC Amerispeak Omnibus Survey, "Millions of Americans Continue to Donate to Crowdfunding Sites."

42. Lana Swartz, *New Money: How Payment Became Social Media* (New Haven, CT: Yale University Press, 2020); Arun Sundararajan, *The Sharing Economy: The End of Employment and the Rise of Crowd-Based Capitalism*, 1st ed. (Cambridge, MA: The MIT Press, 2017).

43. Larry Z. Xu, "Will a Digital Camera Cure Your Sick Puppy? Modality and Category Effects in Donation-Based Crowdfunding," *Telematics and Informatics* 35, no. 7 (October 2018): 1914–1924, https://doi.org/10.1016/j.tele.2018.06.004; Sulaeman and Lin, "Reducing Uncertainty in Charitable Crowdfunding"; Romina Alicia Ortiz et al., "Engaging a Community for Rare Genetic Disease: Best Practices and Education from Individual Crowdfunding Campaigns," *Interactive Journal of Medical Research* 7, no. 1 (2018): e3, https://doi.org/10.2196/ijmr.7176.

44. Kenworthy et al., "A Cross-Sectional Study of Social Inequities"; van Duynhoven et al., "Spatially Exploring the Intersection of Socioeconomic Status and Canadian Cancer-Related Medical Crowdfunding Campaigns"; Igra et al., "Crowdfunding as a Response to COVID-19"; Barcelos, "Go Fund Inequality"; Erica Mark et al., "Crowdsourcing Medical Costs in Dermatology: Cross-Sectional Study Analyzing Dermatologic GoFundMe Campaigns," *JMIR Dermatology* 5, no. 2 (April 2022): e34111, https://doi.org/10.2196/34111.

45. Benjamin Edelman and Michael Luca, "Digital Discrimination: The Case of Airbnb.Com" (working paper no. 14–054, Harvard Business School, January 2014; Venoo Kakar et al., "The Visible Host: Does Race Guide Airbnb Rental Rates in San Francisco?," *Journal of Housing Economics* 40 (June 2018): 25–40, https://doi.org/10.1016/j.jhe.2017.08.001.

46. Peter Younkin and Venkat Kuppuswamy, "The Colorblind Crowd? Founder Race and Performance in Crowdfunding," *Management Science* 64, no. 7 (July 2018): 3269–3287, https://doi.org/10.1287/mnsc.2017.2774.

47. Peter Younkin and Venkat Kuppuswamy, "Discounted: The Effect of Founder Race on the Price of New Products," *Journal of Business Venturing* 34, no. 2 (March 2019): 389–412, https://doi.org/10.1016/j.jbusvent.2018.02.004.

48. Lauren Rhue and Jessica Clark, "Who Gets Started on Kickstarter? Racial Disparities in Crowdfunding Success," SSRN Electronic Journal, 2016, https://doi.org/10.2139/ssrn.2837042.

49. Greenberg and Mollick, "Leaning In or Leaning On?"

50. Greenberg and Mollick, "Leaning In or Leaning On?"

51. Martin Lukk, Erik Schneiderhan, and Joanne Soares, "Worthy? Crowdfunding the Canadian Health Care and Education Sectors: Health Care and Education Crowdfunding," *Canadian Review of Sociology/Revue Canadienne de Sociologie* 55, no. 3 (August 2018): 404–424, https://doi.org/10.1111/cars.12210.

52. Barcelos, "Go Fund Inequality."

53. Varsha Palad and Jeremy Snyder, "'We Don't Want Him Worrying about How He Will Pay to Save His Life': Using Medical Crowdfunding to Explore Lived Experiences with Addiction Services in Canada," *International Journal of Drug Policy* 65 (March 2019): 73–77, https://doi.org/10.1016/j.drugpo.2018.12.016.

54. Kenworthy et al., "A Cross-Sectional Study of Social Inequities."

55. Mark Igra, "Donor Financial Capacity Drives Racial Inequality in Medical Crowdsourced Funding," *Social Forces* 100, no. 4 (July 2022): 1856–1883, https://doi.org/10.1093/sf/soab076.

56. Igra, "Donor Financial Capacity Drives Racial Inequality," 2.

57. Aaron Davis, Shauna Carlisle, and Nora Kenworthy, "Racial and Gender Disparities in High-Earning Medical Crowdfunding Campaigns," *Social Science & Medicine* 324, no. May (2023): 115852, https://doi.org/10.1016/j.socscimed.2023.115852.

58. Davis, Carlisle, and Kenworthy, "Racial and Gender Disparities."

59. While I do not get into the lengthy and multifaceted literatures on the science of crowd-based "wisdom" here, it is worth mentioning that crowdfunding platforms don't harness a crowd as much as they play host to a popularity contest waged across multiple social media spaces. Algorithmic choices and cross-platform integrations disrupt any true crowd effect occuring here. Instead, platforms amplify social hierarchies that have been shown to undermine the accuracy of crowd-based decisions and increase biases. See Ricardo Baeza-Yates and Diego Saez-Trumper. "Wisdom of the Crowd or Wisdom of a Few?: An Analysis of Users' Content Generation," in *Proceedings of the 26th ACM Conference on Hypertext & Social Media—HT '15* (Guzelyurt, Northern Cyprus: ACM Press, 2015), 69–74, https://doi.org/10.1145/2700171.2791056; Jan Lorenz et al., "How Social Influence Can Undermine the Wisdom of Crowd Effect," *Proceedings of the National Academy of Sciences* 108, no. 22 (May 2011): 9020–9025, https://doi.org/10.1073/pnas.1008636108; Friedemann Polzin, Helen Toxopeus, and Erik Stam, "The Wisdom of the Crowd in Funding: Information Heterogeneity and Social Networks of Crowdfunders," *Small Business Economics* 50, no. 2 (February 2018): 251–273, https://doi.org/10.1007/s11187-016-9829-3; Dandan Zhao and Zhen Zhou, "Biased Wisdom from the Crowd," PBCSF-NIFR Research Paper, 2023, https://doi.org/10.2139/ssrn.4360736.

60. Gordan Burtch and Jason Chan, "Investigating the Relationship between Medical Crowdfunding and Personal Bankruptcy in the United States: Evidence of a Digital Divide," *MIS Quarterly* 43, no. 1 (January 2019): 237–262, https://doi.org/10.25300/MISQ/2019/14569.

61. Silver et al., "Association of Neighborhood Deprivation Index," 7.

62. Silver et al., "Association of Neighborhood Deprivation Index," 8.

63. Lee and Lehdonvirta, "New Digital Safety Net or Just More 'Friendfunding'?," 20.

64. Nora Kenworthy and Mark Igra, "Medical Crowdfunding and Disparities in Health Care Access in the United States, 2016–2020," *American Journal of Public Health* 112, no. 3 (March 2022): 491–498, https://doi.org/10.2105/AJPH.2021.306617.

65. Naomi Klein, *The Shock Doctrine: The Rise of Disaster Capitalism* (New York: Metropolitan Books, 2007).

66. Igra et al., "Crowdfunding as a Response to COVID-19"; Nora Kenworthy, Jin-Kyu Jung, and Emily Hops, "Struggling, Helping and Adapting: Crowdfunding Motivations and Outcomes during the Early US COVID-19 Pandemic," *Sociology of Health & Illness* 45, no. 2 (February 2023): 298–316, https://doi.org/10.1111/1467-9566.13568.

67. Igra et al., "Crowdfunding as a Response to COVID-19."

68. Kenworthy, Jung, and Hops, "Struggling, Helping and Adapting."

69. Bonnie Goldstein, "Crowdfunding: The Kindness of Strangers," *Washington Post*, July 7, 2012, sec. Politics, https://www.washingtonpost.com/blogs/she-the-people/post/crowdfunding-and-the-kindness-of-strangers/2012/07/07/gJQAzSUvTW_blog.html.

70. See, for example, Burtch and Chan, "Investigating the Relationship between Medical Crowdfunding and Personal Bankruptcy in the United States."

71. Kenworthy and Igra, "Medical Crowdfunding and Disparities in Health Care Access."

72. Berliner and Kenworthy, "Producing a Worthy Illness"; Kenworthy and Igra, "Medical Crowdfunding and Disparities in Health Care Access"; Nora Kenworthy, "Like a Grinding Stone: How Crowdfunding Platforms Create, Perpetuate, and Value Health Inequities," *Medical Anthropology Quarterly* 35, no. 3 (September 2021): 327–345, https://doi.org/10.1111/maq.12639; Anna Helhoski and Victoria Simons, "Seeking Medical Debt Relief? Crowdfunding Rarely Pays Off the Bills," NerdWallet, November 2, 2016, https://www.nerdwallet.com/blog/loans/medical-debt-crowdfunding-bankruptcy/.

73. Kenworthy and Igra, "Medical Crowdfunding and Disparities in Health Care Access."

74. Kenworthy and Igra, "Medical Crowdfunding and Disparities in Health Care Access"; Davis, Carlisle, and Kenworthy, "Racial and Gender Disparities."

75. Kenworthy, Jung, and Hops, "Struggling, Helping and Adapting."

76. Kenworthy and Igra, "Medical Crowdfunding and Disparities in Health Care Access."

77. Mean scores of estimates offered by focus group participants; n = 25.

CHAPTER 4

1. Arthur Frank, "The Cost of Appearances," in *The Social Medicine Reader, Volume I, Third Edition*, ed. Jonathan Oberlander et al. (Durham, NC: Duke University Press, 2019), 20–24, https://doi.org/10.1215/9781478004356-005.

2. Alondra Nelson, *Body and Soul: The Black Panther Party and the Fight against Medical Discrimination* (Minneapolis: University of Minnesota Press, 2013); Audre Lorde, *The Cancer Journals* (London: Penguin Books, 2020).

3. Lauren G. Berlant, *Cruel Optimism* (Durham, NC: Duke University Press, 2011); Tamara Kneese and Beza Merid, "Illness Narratives, Networked Subjects, and Intimate Publics," *Catalyst: Feminism, Theory, Technoscience* 4, no. 1 (May 2018): 1–6, https://doi.org/10.28968/cftt.v4i1.29627.

4. Kneese and Merid, "Illness Narratives, Networked Subjects, and Intimate Publics," 3; Nicholas Carah, Amy Shields Dobson, and Brady Robards, eds., *Digital Intimate Publics and Social Media*, 1st ed., Palgrave Studies in Communication for Social Change (Cham, Switzerland: Springer International Publishing, 2018), https://doi.org/10.1007/978-3-319-97607-5.

5. Carsten Stage, Karen Hvidtfeldt, and Lisbeth Klastrup, "Vital Media: The Affective and Temporal Dynamics of Young Cancer Patients' Social Media Practices," *Social Media + Society* 6, no. 2 (April 2020): 205630512092476, https://doi.org/10.1177/2056305120924760.

6. Paul Rabinow, "Artificiality and Enlightenment: From Sociobiology to Biosociality," in *Essays on the Anthropology of Reason* (Princeton, NJ: Princeton University Press, 1996), 91–111.

7. Anika Vassell, Valorie A. Crooks, and Jeremy Snyder, "What Was Lost, Missing, Sought and Hoped For: Qualitatively Exploring Medical Crowdfunding Campaign Narratives for Lyme Disease," *Health: An Interdisciplinary Journal for the Social Study of Health, Illness and Medicine* 25, no. 6 (March 2020, https://doi.org/10.1177/1363459320912808.

8. Amy L Gonzales et al., "'Better Everyone Should Know Our Business than We Lose Our House': Costs and Benefits of Medical Crowdfunding for Support, Privacy, and Identity," *New Media & Society* 20, no. 2 (February 2018): 641–658, https://doi.org/10.1177/1461444816667723.

9. It's worth pointing out here that other, more formal ways of finding social support can also involve significant disclosures, privacy infringements, and vulnerability. This includes, perhaps most acutely, applying for public benefits programs in the United States. Digital technology use in these programs has increased both the amount that people must disclose to qualify and the extent to which they are

subjected to surveillance and privacy infringements if and once they qualify. See Eubanks, *Automating Inequality*.

10. Ghazal et al., "'Both a Life Saver and Totally Shameful.'"

11. Berlant, *Cruel Optimism*, 2.

12. "About GoFundMe," GoFundMe, accessed September 27, 2021, https://www.gofundme.com/c/about-us/.

13. Gofundme, "A Universal Desire to Help: How GoFundMe Reached 40 Million Donors," Medium, June 9, 2019, https://medium.com/gofundme-stories/a-universal-desire-to-help-how-gofundme-reached-40-million-donors-fe1c32b04dcc.

14. "Start a Fundraiser on GoFundMe," accessed August 18, 2022, https://www.gofundme.com/start.

15. GoFundMe, "Here to Help: GoFundMe Happiness Agents Share Tricks of the Trade," *GoFundMe Stories* (blog), February 18, 2019, https://medium.com/gofundme-stories/here-to-help-gofundme-happiness-agents-share-tricks-of-the-trade-d6489b6724a8.

16. Lauren Rhue and Lionel P. Robert, "Emotional Delivery in Pro-Social Crowdfunding Success," in *Extended Abstracts of the 2018 CHI Conference on Human Factors in Computing Systems* (Montreal, Quebec: Association for Computing Machinery, 2018), 1–6, https://doi.org/10.1145/3170427.3188534.

17. Lauren S. Berliner and Nora J. Kenworthy, "Producing a Worthy Illness: Personal Crowdfunding amidst Financial Crisis," *Social Science & Medicine* 187 (August 2017): 233–242, https://doi.org/10.1016/j.socscimed.2017.02.008.

18. Berlant, *Cruel Optimism*, 81.

19. Berlant, *Cruel Optimism*, 116–117.

20. Robin G. Nelson, "How a Virus Exposed the Myth of Rugged Individualism," *Scientific American*, March 1, 2022, https://doi.org/10.1038/scientificamerican0322-32.

21. Nora Kenworthy, Jin-Kyu Jung, and Emily Hops, "Struggling, Helping and Adapting: Crowdfunding Motivations and Outcomes during the Early US COVID-19 Pandemic," *Sociology of Health & Illness* 45, no. 2 (February 2023): 298–316, https://doi.org/10.1111/1467-9566.13568.

22. Nelson, "How a Virus Exposed the Myth of Rugged Individualism."

23. Susan Wardell, "To Wish You Well: The Biopolitical Subjectivities of Medical Crowdfunders during and after Aotearoa New Zealand's COVID-19 Lockdown," *BioSocieties* 18 (September 2021): 52–78, https://doi.org/10.1057/s41292-021-00251-7.

24. Mark Duffield, "The Resilience of the Ruins: Towards a Critique of Digital Humanitarianism," *Resilience* 4, no. 3 (September 2016): 147–165, https://doi.org/10.1080/21693293.2016.1153772.

25. To maintain the anonymity of those involved, I am keeping details of this story especially vague since it received a lot of unwanted public attention,.

26. Safiya U. Noble and Brendesha M. Tynes, eds., *The Intersectional Internet: Race, Sex, Class and Culture Online*, Digital Formations, vol. 105 (New York: Peter Lang Publishing, 2015).

27. Brooke E. Duffy, "The Romance of Work: Gender and Aspirational Labour in the Digital Culture Industries," *International Journal of Cultural Studies* 19, no. 4 (July 2016): 441–457, https://doi.org/10.1177/1367877915572186; Brooke E. Duffy, "Gendering the Labor of Social Media Production," *Feminist Media Studies* 15, no. 4 (July 2015): 710–714, https://doi.org/10.1080/14680777.2015.1053715; Noble and Tynes, *The Intersectional Internet*.

28. Noble and Tynes, *The Intersectional Internet*; Eubanks, *Automating Inequality*; Benjamin, *Captivating Technology*.

29. Nancy Fraser, "Contradictions of Capital and Care," *New Left Review* 100, no. Jul/Aug (August 2016): 99–117.

30. Fraser, "Contradictions of Capital and Care"; Karl Marx, *Capital: A Critique of Political Economy, Volume 1* (Hamburg, Germany: Otto Meissner Verlag, 1867); Lise Vogel, *Marxism and the Oppression of Women: Toward a Unitary Theory*, Historical Materialism Book Series 45 (Leiden: Brill, 2013).

31. Bruce G. Link and Jo C. Phelan, "Social Conditions as Fundamental Causes of Disease," *Journal of Health and Social Behavior* 35, no. s1 (1995): 80–94.

32. I am certainly not the first scholar to use the term "precarious care," though in the crowdfunding environment, care is precarious for different reasons. For a particularly strong example of the term's other uses and theorization, see Tomas Antero Matza, *Shock Therapy: Psychology, Precarity, and Well-Being in Postsocialist Russia* (Durham, NC: Duke University Press, 2018).

33. Lana Swartz, *New Money: How Payment Became Social Media* (New Haven, CT: Yale University Press, 2020).

34. Swartz, *New Money*, 2.

35. Swartz, *New Money*, 2.

36. Hannah Zeavin, "A New AI Lexicon: CARE," Medium, June 22, 2021, https://medium.com/a-new-ai-lexicon/a-new-ai-lexicon-care-a1243f0e2bad.

37. Berlant, *Cruel Optimism*.

38. "Creating a GoFundMe from Start to Finish," GoFundMe, accessed September 20, 2020, https://support.gofundme.com/hc/en-us/articles/360001992627-Creating-a-GoFundMe-From-Start-to-Finish.

CHAPTER 5

1. This parable is originally attributed to Irving Zola in John B. McKinlay, "A Case for Refocusing Upstream—The Political Economy of Sickness," in *Applying Behavioral Science to Cardiovascular Risk* (Dallas, TX: American Heart Association, 1975), 9–25.

2. CDC, "What Is Type 1 Diabetes?," March 11, 2022, https://www.cdc.gov/diabetes/basics/what-is-type-1-diabetes.html.

3. César Caraballo et al., "Burden and Consequences of Financial Hardship from Medical Bills among Nonelderly Adults with Diabetes Mellitus in the United States," *Circulation: Cardiovascular Quality and Outcomes* 13, no. 2 (February 2020), https://doi.org/10.1161/CIRCOUTCOMES.119.006139.

4. Beza Merid, "Fight for Our Health: Activism in the Face of Health Insurance Precarity," *BioSocieties* 15, no. 2 (June 2020): 159–181, https://doi.org/10.1057/s41292-019-00145-9.

5. Julia E. Blanchette et al., "GoFundMe as a Medical Plan: Ecological Study of Crowdfunding Insulin Success," *JMIR Diabetes* 7, no. 2 (April 2022): e33205, https://doi.org/10.2196/33205.

6. Bruce G. Link and Jo C. Phelan, "Social Conditions as Fundamental Causes of Disease," *Journal of Health and Social Behavior* 35, no. s1 (1995): 80–94; Stefan Timmermans and Rebecca Kaufman, "Technologies and Health Inequities," *Annual Review of Sociology* 46, no. 1 (July 2020): 583–602, https://doi.org/10.1146/annurev-soc-121919-054802.

7. Andrew Pulrang, "A Simple Fix for One of Disabled People's Most Persistent, Pointless Injustices," *Forbes*, August 31, 2020, sec. Diversity, Equity, and Inclusion, https://www.forbes.com/sites/andrewpulrang/2020/08/31/a-simple-fix-for-one-of-disabled-peoples-most-persistent-pointless-injustices/.

8. Nora Kenworthy and Mark Igra, "Medical Crowdfunding and Disparities in Health Care Access in the United States, 2016–2020," *American Journal of Public Health* 112, no. 3 (March 2022): 491–498, https://doi.org/10.2105/AJPH.2021.306617.

9. "GoFundMe 2022 Year in Help," GoFundMe (blog), accessed December 12, 2022, https://www.gofundme.com/c/gofundme-2022-year-in-help.

10. Katerini Storeng and Nora Kenworthy, "Global Health 2.0? Digital Technologies, Disruption, and Power," in *Global Health Watch 6: In the Shadow of the Pandemic* (New York: Bloomsbury Publishing, 2022).

11. Ruha Benjamin, *Race after Technology: Abolitionist Tools for the New Jim Code* (Medford, MA: Polity, 2019); Timmermans and Kaufman, "Technologies and Health Inequities"; Katerini Storeng and Nora Kenworthy, "Global Health 2.0?"; Katerini Storeng et al., "Digital Technology and the Political Determinants of Health Inequities: Special Issue Introduction," *Global Policy* 12, no. S6 (2021): 5–11, https://doi.org/10.1111/1758-5899.13001; Nick Couldry and Ulises Mejias, *The Costs of Connection: How Data Is Colonizing Human Life and Appropriating It for Capitalism*, Culture and Economic Life (Stanford, CA: Stanford University Press, 2019), http://www.sup.org/books/title/?id=28816; Marco Zenone, Nora Kenworthy, and Nason Maani, "The Social Media Industry as a Commercial Determinant of Health," *International Journal of Health Policy and Management* 12, no. 1 (2023): 1–4, https://doi.org/10.34172/ijhpm.2022.6840; Ilona Kickbusch, "Advancing the Global Health Agenda," *UN Chronicle* 48 no. 4 (December 2011), https://unchronicle.un.org/article/advancing-global-health-agenda.

12. David Sessions, "The Rise of the Thought Leader," *The New Republic*, June 28, 2017, https://newrepublic.com/article/143004/rise-thought-leader-how-superrich

-funded-new-class-intellectual; Y Combinator, "Chase Adam at Startup School NY 2014," June 19, 2014, YouTube video, 24:41, https://www.youtube.com/watch?v=Z8_8jNLsZms.

13. "Medical Crowdfunding Attracts Top Silicon Valley Investors," *Here and Now*, August 8, 2013, http://hereandnow.legacy.wbur.org/2013/08/08/medical-crowd-funding; Erica Bornstein, "Child Sponsorship, Evangelism, and Belonging in the Work of World Vision Zimbabwe," *American Ethnologist* 28 (2001): 595–622.

14. This is a common turn of phrase in the philanthrocapitalist and social responsibility realms but one that is more frequently expressed as "doing good by doing well." For a critique of this concept, see Dinah Rajak, *In Good Company: An Anatomy of Corporate Social Responsibility* (Redwood City, CA: Stanford University Press, 2011).

15. Yesh Yendamuri, "Chase Adam (Watsi)," *Startup School (2013)* (blog), 2014, http://notebook.readthedocs.io/en/latest/startup_school/chase_adam.html.

16. "FAQ," Watsi, accessed January 22, 2019, https://watsi.org/faq.

17. "FAQ."

18. "FAQ."

19. Jennifer C. Rubenstein, "The Lessons of Effective Altruism," *Ethics & International Affairs* 30, no. 4 (2016): 511–526, https://doi.org/10.1017/S0892679416000484.

20. Nora Kenworthy, "Drone Philanthropy? Global Health Crowdfunding and the Anxious Futures of Partnership," *Medicine Anthropology Theory* 5, no. 2 (May 2018), https://doi.org/10.17157/mat.5.2.532.

21. Prof Mthuli Ncube (@MthuliNcube), "Together with my colleagues at Min of Health, we have set up an auditable emergency crowdfund to further efforts to fight cholera to date. Together we can win! Min of Finance Cholera Crowd Fund: EcoCash Biller Code 140286; CBZ Treasury, ACC 21537300017, Selous REF: FIGHT CHOLERA," Twitter, September 13, 2018, https://twitter.com/MthuliNcube/status/1040306748408713218.

22. Ellen Stewart, "Crowdfunding Healthcare in Shetland: Maakin the NHS," *The Polyphony* (blog), July 6, 2021, https://thepolyphony.org/2021/07/06/crowdfunding-healthcare-in-shetland-maakin-the-nhs/.

23. Michaelanne Dye, "Un Grano de Arena: Infrastructural Care, Social Media Platforms, and the Venezuelan Humanitarian Crisis," *Proceedings of the ACM on Human-Computer Interaction* 4, no. CSCW3 (January 2021): 1–28, https://doi.org/10.1145/3432946.

24. "Department of State Partners with GoFundMe.Org," *United States Department of State* (blog), accessed March 25, 2022, https://www.state.gov/department-of-state-partners-with-gofundme-org/.

25. Koen P. Grietens et al., "Misdirection in Global Health: Creating the Illusion of (Im)Possible Alternatives in Global Health Research and Practice," *Science & Technology Studies* 35, no. 2 (May 2022): 2–12, https://doi.org/10.23987/sts.115410.

26. Andrew D. Selbst et al., "Fairness and Abstraction in Sociotechnical Systems," in *Proceedings of the Conference on Fairness, Accountability, and Transparency* (Atlanta, GA: Association for Computing Machinery, 2019), 59–68, https://doi.org/10.1145/3287560.3287598.

27. Melissa Mialon, "An Overview of the Commercial Determinants of Health," *Globalization and Health* 16, no. 1 (August 2020): 74, https://doi.org/10.1186/s12992-020-00607-x; Ilona Kickbusch, Luke Allen, and Christian Franz, "The Commercial Determinants of Health," *The Lancet Global Health* 4, no. 12 (December 2016): e895–896, https://doi.org/10.1016/S2214-109X(16)30217-0; Nason Maani, Mark Petticrew, and Sandro Galea, eds., *The Commercial Determinants of Health* (New York: Oxford University Press, 2023).

28. Zenone, Kenworthy, and Maani, "The Social Media Industry as a Commercial Determinant of Health"; Storeng and Kenworthy, "Global Health 2.0?"; Nora J. Kenworthy, "Crowdfunding and Global Health Disparities: An Exploratory Conceptual and Empirical Analysis," *Globalization and Health* 15, no. S1 (November 2019): 71, https://doi.org/10.1186/s12992-019-0519-1.

29. James Chauvin and Laetitia Rispel, "Digital Technology, Population Health, and Health Equity," *Journal of Public Health Policy* 37, no. S2 (November 2016): 145–153, https://doi.org/10.1057/s41271-016-0041-0; World Health Organization, *Global Strategy on Digital Health, 2020–2025* (Geneva: World Health Organization, 2021), https://www.google.com/url?sa=t&rct=j&q=&esrc=s&source=web&cd=&cad=rja&uact=8&ved=2ahUKEwiZ7MmUp4P7AhUBJ30KHT-fCIoQFnoECBgQAQ&url=https%3A%2F%2Fwww.who.int%2Fdocs%2Fdefault-source%2Fdocuments%2Fgs4dhdaa2a9f352b0445bafbc79ca799dce4d.pdf&usg=AOvVaw2f3QnjV9DJnxlDOrbOl2M1.

30. Michael N. Cantor and Lorna Thorpe, "Integrating Data on Social Determinants of Health into Electronic Health Records," *Health Affairs* 37, no. 4 (April 2018): 585–490, https://doi.org/10.1377/hlthaff.2017.1252.

31. Jeff Byers, "Social Determinants Tech Field Wide Open for Health Industry," Healthcare Dive, June 7, 2018, https://www.healthcaredive.com/news/sdoh-social-determinants-health-tech-adoption/525122/.

32. Kelly J. T. Craig et al., "Leveraging Data and Digital Health Technologies to Assess and Impact Social Determinants of Health (SDoH)," *Online Journal of Public Health Informatics* 13, no. 3 (December 2021), https://doi.org/10.5210/ojphi.v13i3.11081; Cantor and Thorpe, "Integrating Data."

33. There are, of course, important exceptions: notably, the Anti-Eviction Mapping Project has been instrumental in tackling upstream causes of evictions and tracking their downstream effects in rapidly gentrifying places like San Francisco's Bay Area. "About the Anti-Eviction Mapping Project (AEMP)" Anti-Eviction Mapping Project, Accessed July 31 2023, https://antievictionmap.com/about-the-aemp.

34. Interviews by Emmanuel Dzotsi, "The Least You Could Do," *Reply All* (Gimlet Media), June 18, 2020, https://gimletmedia.com:443/shows/reply-all/z3h94o.

35. "The Least You Could Do."

36. Hannah Zeavin, "A New AI Lexicon: CARE," Medium, June 22, 2021, https://medium.com/a-new-ai-lexicon/a-new-ai-lexicon-care-a1243f0e2bad.

37. Lana Swartz, *New Money: How Payment Became Social Media* (New Haven, CT: Yale University Press, 2020); Lucy Bernholz, *How We Give Now: A Philanthropic Guide for the Rest of Us* (Cambridge, MA: The MIT Press, 2021).

38. "The Least You Could Do."

39. Jeremy Snyder, "Is GoFundMe Violating Its Own Terms of Service on the 'Freedom Convoy?,'" The Conversation, February 2, 2022, http://theconversation.com/is-gofundme-violating-its-own-terms-of-service-on-the-freedom-convoy-176147.

40. Erin Carson, "Here's Where Nazi Sympathizers Go to Raise Money," CNET, December 4, 2017, https://www.cnet.com/culture/neo-nazi-sympathizers-crowdfunding/.

41. GoFundMe, "GoFundMe Policy on Fundraisers for the Legal Defense of Violent Crimes," *GoFundMe Stories* (blog), November 19, 2021, https://medium.com/gofundme-stories/gofundme-policy-on-fundraisers-for-the-legal-defense-of-violent-crimes-975aff8ba5f6; Michael Tarm and Amy Forliti, "Acquitted and in Demand, Rittenhouse Ponders What's Next," AP NEWS, November 29, 2021, https://apnews.com/article/kyle-rittenhouse-donald-trump-entertainment-tucker-carlson-mar-a-lago-a852da724d4e06438da0cef6d02fc8f3. GoFundMe prohibits fundraising for what it calls the "legal defense of violent crimes." When Rittenhouse was later acquitted, his fundraisers were once again allowed on GoFundMe.

42. Vera Bergengruen and Chris Wilson, "Crowdfunding Site For Right-Wing Causes Generates Windfall," *Time*, March 3, 2022, https://time.com/6150317/givesendgo-trucker-convoy-canada-profits/; Talia Lavin, "Crowdfunding Hate in the Name of Christ," The Nation, April 5, 2021, https://www.thenation.com/article/society/givesendgo-crowdfunding-extremism/.

43. Benjamin, *Race after Technology*.

44. Marco A. Zenone and Jeremy Snyder, "Crowdfunding Abortion: An Exploratory Thematic Analysis of Fundraising for a Stigmatized Medical Procedure," *BMC Women's Health* 20, no. 1 (December 2020): 90, https://doi.org/10.1186/s12905-020-00938-2; Snyder, "Is GoFundMe Violating Its Own Terms of Service on the 'Freedom Convoy'?"; Kenworthy et al., "A Cross-Sectional Study of Social Inequities"; Christopher Zara, "GoFundMe Critics Raise Billboard in San Diego, Launch #DontFundHate over Officer Darren Wilson Campaign," *International Business Times*, October 9, 2014, https://www.ibtimes.com/gofundme-critics-raise-billboard-san-diego-launch-dontfundhate-over-officer-darren-1702134.

45. Peter Nagy and Gina Neff, "Imagined Affordance: Reconstructing a Keyword for Communication Theory," *Social Media + Society* 1, no. 2 (July 2015): 205630511560338, https://doi.org/10.1177/2056305115603385; Daniel Halpern and Jennifer Gibbs, "Social Media as a Catalyst for Online Deliberation? Exploring the Affordances of Facebook and YouTube for Political Expression," *Computers in Human Behavior* 29, no. 3 (May 2013): 1159–1168, https://doi.org/10.1016/j.chb.2012.10.008; Sandra K. Evans et al., "Explicating Affordances: A Conceptual Framework for Understanding Affordances in Communication Research," *Journal of Computer-*

Mediated Communication 22, no. 1 (January 2017): 35–52, https://doi.org/10.1111/jcc4.12180.

46. Megan Cerullo, "Their Twins' Medical Costs Total $750,000—Each. They and Thousands of Others Are Counting on GoFundMe," CBS News, January 28, 2019, https://www.cbsnews.com/news/crushed-by-medical-bills-many-americans-go-online-to-beg-for-help/?ftag=CNM-00-10aag7e.

47. Tamara Kneese, "Mourning the Commons: Circulating Affect in Crowdfunded Funeral Campaigns," *Social Media + Society* 4, no. 1 (January 2018): 8, https://doi.org/10.1177/2056305117743350.

48. Lauren Berlant, "The Subject of True Feeling: Pain, Privacy, and Politics," in *Left Legalism/Left Critique*, ed. Janet Halley and Wendy Brown (Durham, NC: Duke University Press, 2002), 109, https://doi.org/10.1215/9780822383871-004.

49. Berlant, "The Subject of True Feeling," 112.

50. Cerullo, "Their Twins' Medical Costs Total $750,000."

CHAPTER 6

1. Annie Correal and Andrew Jacobs, "'A Tragedy Is Unfolding': Inside New York's Virus Epicenter," *The New York Times*, April 9, 2020, sec. New York, https://www.nytimes.com/2020/04/09/nyregion/coronavirus-queens-corona-jackson-heights-elmhurst.html.

2. Nora Kenworthy, Jin-Kyu Jung, and Emily Hops, "Struggling, Helping and Adapting: Crowdfunding Motivations and Outcomes during the Early US COVID-19 Pandemic," *Sociology of Health & Illness* 45, no. 2 (February 2023): 298–316, https://doi.org/10.1111/1467-9566.13568.

3. Doug Oman, Carl E. Thoresen, and Kay Mcmahon, "Volunteerism and Mortality among the Community-Dwelling Elderly," *Journal of Health Psychology* 4, no. 3 (May 1999): 301–316, https://doi.org/10.1177/135910539900400301; Sae H. Han, Kyungmin Kim, and Jeffrey A. Burr, "Stress-Buffering Effects of Volunteering on Salivary Cortisol: Results from a Daily Diary Study," *Innovation in Aging* 2, no. suppl_1 (November 2018): 75, https://doi.org/10.1093/geroni/igy023.283; Elizabeth W. Dunn, Lara B. Aknin, and Michael I. Norton, "Spending Money on Others Promotes Happiness," *Science* 319, no. 5870 (March 2008): 1687–1688, https://doi.org/10.1126/science.1150952; Ashley V. Whillans et al., "Is Spending Money on Others Good for Your Heart?," *Health Psychology* 35, no. 6 (June 2016): 574–583, https://doi.org/10.1037/hea0000332.

4. Liisa H. Malkki, *The Need to Help: The Domestic Arts of International Humanitarianism* (Durham, NC: Duke University Press, 2015); Ivan Illich, "To Hell with Good Intentions" (Conference on InterAmerican Student Projects, Cuernavaca, Mexico, 1968); Ruth J. Prince and Hannah Brown, eds., *Volunteer Economies: The Politics & Ethics of Voluntary Labour in Africa*, African Issues (Woodbridge, Suffolk: James Currey, 2016).

5. Ruha Benjamin, *Race after Technology: Abolitionist Tools for the New Jim Code* (Medford, MA: Polity, 2019).

6. Ruha Benjamin, *Viral Justice: How We Grow the World We Want*, 1st ed. (Princeton, NJ: Princeton University Press, 2022).

7. Mark Igra et al., "Crowdfunding as a Response to COVID-19: Increasing Inequities at a Time of Crisis," *Social Science & Medicine* 282 (August 2021): 114105, https://doi.org/10.1016/j.socscimed.2021.114105; Kenworthy, Jung, and Hops, "Struggling, Helping and Adapting."

8. Kenworthy, Jung, and Hops, "Struggling, Helping and Adapting."

9. Eric Klinenberg, "We Need Social Solidarity, Not Just Social Distancing," *The New York Times*, March 14, 2020, sec. Opinion, https://www.nytimes.com/2020/03/14/opinion/coronavirus-social-distancing.html.

10. Alexandra Samuel, "How to Make Health-Care Crowdfunding Work for Everyone," *Wall Street Journal*, September 15, 2019, https://www.wsj.com/articles/how-to-make-health-care-crowdfunding-work-for-everyone-11568599500.

11. Samuel, "How to Make Health-Care Crowdfunding Work for Everyone."

12. Samuel, "How to Make Health-Care Crowdfunding Work for Everyone"; Igra et al., "Crowdfunding as a Response to COVID-19."

13. NORC Amerispeak Omnibus Survey, "Millions of Americans Continue to Donate to Crowdfunding Sites."

14. Benjamin, *Race after Technology*.

15. Benjamin, *Race after Technology*, 105.

16. Hollie Silverman et al., "Navajo Nation Surpasses New York State for Highest Covid-19 Infection Rate in the US," CNN, May 18, 2020, https://www.cnn.com/2020/05/18/us/navajo-nation-infection-rate-trnd/index.html.

17. Marc A. Emerson and Teresa Montoya, "Confronting Legacies of Structural Racism and Settler Colonialism to Understand COVID-19 Impacts on the Navajo Nation," *American Journal of Public Health* 111, no. 8 (August 2021): 1465–1469, https://doi.org/10.2105/AJPH.2021.306398.

18. Austin Fisher, "'We've Always Been Surplus': Individual Tragedy and Collective Trauma from COVID," *Source New Mexico*, December 23, 2022, https://sourcenm.com/2022/12/23/weve-always-been-surplus-individual-tragedy-and-collective-trauma-from-covid/; Ruth W. Gilmore, *Golden Gulag: Prisons, Surplus, Crisis, and Opposition in Globalizing California*, American Crossroads 21 (Berkeley: University of California Press, 2007).

19. "Crowdfunding Creates a de Facto Food Bank for the Navajo Nation," *Mountain West News Bureau*, March 26, 2020), https://www.wyomingpublicmedia.org/tribal-news/2020-03-26/crowdfunding-creates-a-de-facto-food-bank-for-the-navajo-nation.

20. Madeleine Ptacin, "This Native Crowdfunding Campaign Is Providing Hundreds of Elders with Basic Supplies," NowThis News, April 9, 2020, https://nowthisnews.com/news/navajo-nation-tribe-works-to-crowdfund-for-elders-basic-supplies.

21. Erik Ortiz, "A Native Health Center Asked for COVID-19 Medical Supplies. It Got Body Bags Instead," NBC News, May 5, 2020, https://www.nbcnews.com/news/us-news/native-american-health-center-asked-covid-19-supplies-they-got-n1200246.

22. Ortiz, "A Native Health Center Asked for COVID-19 Medical Supplies."

23. Ed O'Loughlin and Mihir Zaveri, "Irish Return an Old Favor, Helping Native Americans Battling the Virus," *The New York Times*, May 5, 2020, sec. World, https://www.nytimes.com/2020/05/05/world/coronavirus-ireland-native-american-tribes.html.

24. Naomi O'Leary (@NaomiOhReally), "Native Americans raised a huge amount in famine relief for Ireland at a time when they had very little. It's time for is to come through for them now," Twitter, May 2, 2020, https://twitter.com/NaomiOhReally/status/1256674443029614594.

25. Ronan McGreevy, "Irish People Donate €2.5m to Native American Tribe Devastated by Coronavirus," *The Irish Times*, November 20, 2020, https://www.irishtimes.com/news/ireland/irish-news/irish-people-donate-2-5m-to-native-american-tribe-devastated-by-coronavirus-1.4414963.

26. Sriram Shamasunder and Priti Krishtel, "What Native Americans Can Teach Rich Nations about Generosity in a Pandemic," *NPR*, May 10, 2021, https://www.npr.org/sections/goatsandsoda/2021/05/10/994254810/opinion-what-native-americans-can-teach-us-about-generosity-in-a-pandemic.

27. Shamasunder and Krishtel, "What Native Americans Can Teach Rich Nations."

28. "Crowdfunding Creates a de Facto Food Bank for the Navajo Nation."

29. J. Kēhaulani Kauanui, "The Politics of Indigeneity, Anarchist Praxis, and Decolonization," *Anarchist Developments in Cultural Studies* 2021, no. 1 (2021): 9–42.

30. Kauanui, "The Politics of Indigeneity, Anarchist Praxis, and Decolonization"; Emerson and Montoya, "Confronting Legacies of Structural Racism and Settler Colonialism."

31. Rachel Treisman, "Outpacing the US, Hard-Hit Navajo Nation Has Vaccinated More than Half of Adults," *NPR*, April 26, 2021, sec. Coronavirus Crisis, https://www.npr.org/sections/coronavirus-live-updates/2021/04/26/990884991/outpacing-the-u-s-hard-hit-navajo-nation-has-vaccinated-more-than-half-of-adults.

32. Amelia Nierenberg, "For the Navajo Nation, a Fight for Better Food Gains New Urgency," *The New York Times*, August 3, 2020, sec. Food, https://www.nytimes.com/2020/08/03/dining/navajo-nation-food-coronavirus.html.

33. Nierenberg, "For the Navajo Nation, a Fight for Better Food Gains New Urgency."

34. Mary Shinn, "Tipping Point: Colorado River Tribes Fight for Their Water Rights," *Colorado Springs Gazette*, August 19, 2022, https://gazette.com/premium/ignored-for-decades-colorado-river-tribes-fight-for-their-water-rights/article_f57f89fa-19df-11ed-bc84-03490e3bbe0c.html.

35. Shinn, "Tipping Point."

36. Savannah Maher, "Native American Advocates Welcome Advance Funding for Indian Health Service," Marketplace, December 27, 2022, https://www.marketplace.org/2022/12/27/native-american-advocates-welcome-advance-funding-for-indian-health-service/; CDC, "Risk for COVID-19 Infection, Hospitalization, and Death By Race/Ethnicity," February 28, 2022, https://www.cdc.gov/coronavirus/2019-ncov/covid-data/investigations-discovery/hospitalization-death-by-race-ethnicity.html.

37. Fisher, "'We've Always Been Surplus.'"

38. Steven J. Jackson, "Rethinking Repair," in *Media Technologies: Essays on Communication, Materiality, and Society* (Cambridge, MA: The MIT Press, 2014), 221–239.

39. Jackson, "Rethinking Repair," 231.

40. Tedros A. Ghebreyesus, "Health Is a Fundamental Human Right," *World Health Organization* (blog), December 10, 2017, https://www.who.int/news-room/commentaries/detail/health-is-a-fundamental-human-right.

41. Tim Cadogan, "GoFundMe CEO: Hello Congress, Americans Need Help and We Can't Do Your Job for You," USA Today, February 11, 2021, https://www.usatoday.com/story/opinion/voices/2021/02/11/gofundme-ceo-congress-pass-covid-relief-desperate-americans-column/4440425001/.

42. Swisher, "If Government Did Its Job We Might Not Need GoFundMe"; Cadogan, "GoFundMe CEO."

43. Angela Y. Davis, *The Meaning of Freedom*, Open Media Series (San Francisco, CA: City Lights Books, 2012), 30.

44. "Margaret Thatcher: A Life in Quotes," *The Guardian*, April 8, 2013, sec. Politics, https://www.theguardian.com/politics/2013/apr/08/margaret-thatcher-quotes. Thatcher also famously said of British citizens that "they are casting their problems at society. And, you know, there's no such thing as society. There are individual men and women and there are families. And no government can do anything except through people, and people must look after themselves first. It is our duty to look after ourselves and then, also, to look after our neighbours."

45. Paul Farmer, "Forward," in *Blind Spot: How Neoliberalism Infiltrated Global Health*, California Series in Public Anthropology 30 (Oakland: University of California Press, 2014), xxviii.

46. Lauren G. Berlant, *Cruel Optimism* (Durham, NC: Duke University Press, 2011), 3; Tamara Kneese and Beza Merid, "Illness Narratives, Networked Subjects, and Intimate Publics," *Catalyst: Feminism, Theory, Technoscience* 4, no. 1 (May 2018): 1–6, https://doi.org/10.28968/cftt.v4i1.29627.

47. Benjamin, *Viral Justice*, 18.

48. "Homepage," RIP Medical Debt, accessed May 5, 2023, https://ripmedicaldebt.org/.

49. Dean Spade, *Mutual Aid: Building Solidarity during This Crisis (and the Next One)* (New York: Verso Books, 2020); Alexandria Ocasio-Cortez and Mariame Kaba, "Rep.

Alexandria Ocasio-Cortez and Organizer Mariame Kaba: Mutual Aid during COVID-19," accessed December 31, 2022, https://www.ocasiocortez.com/mutual-aid.

50. Spade, *Mutual Aid*; Nora Kenworthy, Emily Hops, and Amy Hagopian, "Mutual Aid Praxis Aligns Principles and Practice in Grassroots COVID-19 Responses across the US," *Kennedy Institute of Ethics Journal* (under review); Maya Adereth, "The United States Has a Long History of Mutual Aid Organizing," *Jacobin*, June 2020, https://www.jacobinmag.com/2020/06/mutual-aid-united-states-unions.

51. Adereth, "The United States Has a Long History of Mutual Aid Organizing."

52. Kenworthy, Hops, and Hagopian, "Mutual Aid Praxis."

53. Kenworthy, Hops, and Hagopian, "Mutual Aid Praxis."

54. David Boarder Giles, *A Mass Conspiracy to Feed People: Food Not Bombs and the World-Class Waste of Global Cities* (Durham, NC: Duke University Press, 2021); Mariame Kaba, *We Do This 'til We Free Us: Abolitionist Organizing and Transforming Justice*, Abolitionist Papers (Chicago, IL: Haymarket Books, 2021); Dean Spade, "Solidarity Not Charity," *Social Text* 38, no. 1 (March 2020): 131–151, https://doi.org/10.1215/01642472-7971139.

55. Spade, *Mutual Aid*.

56. Kenworthy, Hops, and Hagopian, "Mutual Aid Praxis."

57. This quotation was initially published in Kenworthy, Hops, and Hagopian, "Mutual Aid Praxis."

58. See also Tamara Kneese, "Pay It Forward: Crowdfunding Is Not Mutual Aid," June 22, 2020, https://reallifemag.com/pay-it-forward/.

59. Spade, *Mutual Aid*, 148.

APPENDIX

1. Mark Igra, "Donor Financial Capacity Drives Racial Inequality in Medical Crowdsourced Funding," *Social Forces* 100, no. 4 (July 2022): 1856–1883, https://doi.org/10.1093/sf/soab076; Jin-Kyu Jung and Nora Kenworthy, "(Un)Mapping Digital Social Inequality of Health: COVID-19 and Medical Crowdfunding," American Association of Geographers, virtual, 2021); Lauren S. Berliner, "Towards a Methodology of Unwatched Digital Media," *Feminist Media Histories* 8, no. 2 (April 2022): 219–230, https://doi.org/10.1525/fmh.2022.8.2.219.

2. Julia Sisler, "Crowdfunding for Medical Expenses," *Canadian Medical Association Journal* 184, no. 2 (February 2012): E123–E124, https://doi.org/10.1503/cmaj.109-4084.

3. Lauren S. Berliner and Nora J. Kenworthy, "Producing a Worthy Illness: Personal Crowdfunding amidst Financial Crisis," *Social Science & Medicine* 187 (August 2017): 233–242, https://doi.org/10.1016/j.socscimed.2017.02.008.

4. Nora Kenworthy et al., "A Cross-Sectional Study of Social Inequities in Medical Crowdfunding Campaigns in the United States," *PLOS ONE* 15, no. 3 (March 2020): e0229760, https://doi.org/10.1371/journal.pone.0229760.

5. Nora Kenworthy, "Drone Philanthropy? Global Health Crowdfunding and the Anxious Futures of Partnership," *Medicine Anthropology Theory* 5, no. 2 (May 2018), https://doi.org/10.17157/mat.5.2.532.

6. For an example of this work, see Nora J. Kenworthy, "Crowdfunding and Global Health Disparities: An Exploratory Conceptual and Empirical Analysis," *Globalization and Health* 15, no. S1 (November 2019): 71, https://doi.org/10.1186/s12992-019-0519-1.

7. Monique Hennink and Bonnie N. Kaiser, "Sample Sizes for Saturation in Qualitative Research: A Systematic Review of Empirical Tests," *Social Science & Medicine* 292 (January 2022): 114523, https://doi.org/10.1016/j.socscimed.2021.114523.

8. Mark Igra et al., "Crowdfunding as a Response to COVID-19: Increasing Inequities at a Time of Crisis," *Social Science & Medicine* 282 (August 2021): 114105, https://doi.org/10.1016/j.socscimed.2021.114105.

9. Nora Kenworthy, Jin-Kyu Jung, and Emily Hops, "Struggling, Helping and Adapting: Crowdfunding Motivations and Outcomes during the Early US COVID-19 Pandemic," *Sociology of Health & Illness* 45, no. 2 (February 2023): 298–316, https://doi.org/10.1111/1467-9566.13568.

10. Nora Kenworthy and Mark Igra, "Medical Crowdfunding and Disparities in Health Care Access in the United States, 2016–2020," *American Journal of Public Health* 112, no. 3 (March 2022): 491–498, https://doi.org/10.2105/AJPH.2021.306617

11. Aaron Davis, Shauna Carlisle, and Nora Kenworthy, "Racial and Gender Disparities in High-Earning Medical Crowdfunding Campaigns," *Social Science & Medicine* 324, no. May (2023): 115852, https://doi.org/10.1016/j.socscimed.2023.115852.

12. Nora Kenworthy, Emily Hops, and Amy Hagopian, "Mutual Aid Praxis Aligns Principles and Practice in Grassroots COVID-19 Responses across the US," *Kennedy Institute of Ethics Journal* (under review).

13. "Exploring Digital Inequities in American Crowdfunding," Go Fund US, November 11, 2022, https://experience.arcgis.com/experience/a866a9088fb94dbda2dc79d0b9ff13e0/page/Welcome/.

INDEX